THE CONTENT OF PSYCH[illegible]

The Content of Psychological Distress

Addressing Complex Personal Experience

Jack Chalkley
Chartered Clinical Psychologist

palgrave

First published 2015 by
PALGRAVE

Palgrave in the UK is an imprint of Macmillan Publishers Limited, registered in England, company number 785998, of 4 Crinan Street, London N1 9XW.

Palgrave Macmillan in the US is a division of St Martin's Press LLC, 175 Fifth Avenue, New York, NY 10010.

Palgrave is a global imprint of the above companies and is represented throughout the world.

Palgrave® and Macmillan® are registered trademarks in the United States, the United Kingdom, Europe and other countries.

ISBN 978–1–137–34974–3

This book is printed on paper suitable for recycling and made from fully managed and sustained forest sources. Logging, pulping and manufacturing processes are expected to conform to the environmental regulations of the country of origin.

A catalogue record for this book is available from the British Library.

A catalog record for this book is available from the Library of Congress.

To my teachers at the Hill School Westerham, Lancing College and the Institute of Psychiatry: R.C.M. Wright ("Basher"), Robin Reeve and Monte Shapiro

Contents

Boxes and Tables

Boxes

Tables

Preface

This is a short book and, as one reviewer rather interestingly put it, written at times in a "declamatory" style. The style belies the reality that, despite appearances to the contrary, the journey behind this narrative has been a stumbling, faltering one. Had I traced its ups and downs more closely and reflected more fully on them, the book would have become immensely long and perhaps exhausted the reading appetites of busy practitioners and trainee practitioners, even very thoughtful ones.

Much of the material was only really worked through to any significant degree after I left the National Health Service (NHS). Leaving the NHS gave me the opportunity at last to read more and think more about the work I had been doing for the previous thirty years. The pressure and intensity of working in the field of mental health do not readily allow time for reflection. Finally, I was in a position to think about what people, patients as well as colleagues, had been trying to teach me. This important period of digestion has allowed me to reflect on my working life and understand better where I should have been heading but often wasn't.

The settings of most of the work described are outpatient clinics in psychiatric hospitals, community mental health centres and GP surgeries. When I started working in these places, I was already converted to personalized assessment, but without quite knowing why. In hindsight, I think it was more than anything else the sense that the type of personalized assessment that I had been so inspiringly taught at the Maudsley by Monte Shapiro seemed immediately to touch people's concerns; also, it offered me structure as I moved into the comparative unknown of my first health service job. Personal questionnaires, to which frequent reference is made in what follows, although not the subject of the book, provided a procedure, an anchor, a discipline and a creative *form*. However, I really didn't understand very well the broader rationale for working in this personalized way. This rationale and the consequences of adopting it are the central subject that I explore in this book.

I think of the way I have worked as theoretically orthodox but not mainstream. At least, it hasn't *seemed* mainstream, because while I suspect that many of my colleagues, in practice, work in the largely bottom-up way that Monte Shapiro favoured, this is not the way the psychological literature is typically written. Those practitioners who contribute most to it tend to have university responsibilities and academic interests, which may help explain a little further why that literature is so much more construct driven than content driven. There is, therefore, little illustration of a content-oriented kind to cite from it. Consequently, this book contains illustrative material that for the most part originates from either close colleagues or myself.

I have had to think carefully about the presentation of this illustrative material. The dilemma posed was how to keep it authentic while protecting confidentiality. Making cases up didn't seem to be the answer. "Making cases up from what?" one might ask. Patients may well justifiably feel themselves to have been present, hovering ghostlike in the writer's head, even when there was no conscious intention for them to be there as pen was put to paper.

The challenge is less to protect patients from being identified by third parties than from being identified by the patients themselves ("the first-party"). This is especially a problem in a book on this particular subject, where so much depends on descriptions of personal experience laid out in lists of concerns and sets of questionnaire items. The problem is not so much in the individual statements. Few, if any, among the three hundred or so expressions of concern and distress spread across the chapters that follow are unique to anyone. Many of them are very common indeed. What is personal and telltale is someone's precise combination of expressions, that is, the composite picture of what concerns and distresses him or her.

The solution I finally adopted, after much discussion of what was right and for the best, was to develop an *explicit* process for *fictionalizing* the illustrations. The steps taken have been as follows:

(1) Start with a real person.
(2) Change all information that might make it possible for third parties to identify the person (a selection from such variables as age, sex, location, occupation and position in family).
(3) Change as many of the person's concerns as is necessary to make them into someone "different" and unrecognizable to themselves: adding some, removing some, altering some, while still retaining a coherent, meaningful set of them.

(4) Set out the "before" and "after" third-party and first-party information, patient by patient.
(5) Present this to a professional colleague and ask for the colleague's judgement on whether fictionalizing has been achieved.
(6) Make further changes as required until, in the colleague's judgement, fictionalizing *has* been achieved.

In most cases, it has not been possible to contact patients. Where patients gave consent, third-party information was changed, but only such first-party information as might be recognized by third parties.

While many of the ideas I write about come from psychology, it would have been altogether wrong to write just for counselling and clinical *psychologists*. I have addressed myself to "counsellors and clinicians" regularly throughout, although more often I have referred to them as "practitioners". I have stuck to speaking about "patients", rather than "clients", and in one way or another there can be little doubt who my paymaster has been all these years. While I am sure that my identity as a clinical psychologist and my debt to my profession will be obvious to everybody, so will be my National Health Service affiliation. Most of my time in the first half of my NHS career was spent working in psychiatric rehabilitation ("recovery") during the period of resettlement that preceded the closure of the old psychiatric hospitals, more of my time than I was then spending in adult mental health outpatient clinics. The experience of working mostly with people with long-term mental health difficulties affected the way I came in time to see my work in those outpatient clinics. This is perhaps why I was later to become so impressed by the ideas of Alvan Feinstein and his insistence on people's experience of illness as being not just about the illness itself but also about its consequences and complications.

Long live the NHS and publicly funded health services everywhere!

Acknowledgements

To my teachers at Birkbeck College University of London and the Institute of Psychiatry and all my colleagues in general practice, in adult mental health and in recovery in Frenchay, Torbay and Bath.

To David Childs for inviting me to share an office with him for fifteen years and then meals for another seven, up and down the Whiteladies Road and beyond, over which we clarified for each other many of what were to become the book's philosophical underpinnings.

To Monte Shapiro and Chris Bilsbury for their profound knowledge and thinking about personalized assessment.

To Bushy Bennun, Jennie Boland, Caroline Dancyger, Matthew Faull, Mary Rudolf, Sam Saunders and Hanna van der Woude for providing significant parts of the clinical material and the ideas that came with it.

To Mark Barrington, Nathalie Chalkley, Chris Gielgud and Ann Lawrie for their readiness to read large portions of the book at various stages of its composition, perceptively, constructively and – often – quickly and at short notice.

For all kinds of advice, encouragement, support and help (those people not already acknowledged): Gloria Babiker, Nick Behrens, Michael Berg, Linda Blair, James Brennan, Tom Chalkley, Katharine Christie, Diane Cole, Lauren Colgan, Madeleine Dangeon-Duhamel, Olivia Donnelly, Phil Evans, Stephen Frosh, Philippa Garety, John Greenaway, Alan Hayward, Minty Hull, Derek Indoe, Lucy Johnstone, Alysun Jones, Sandy Koun, Fiona MacCarthy, Mary Massey, David and Sarah Mulhall, Luke Mulhall, Bernadette Mulley, Kanan Pandaya, Gordon Purdy, Anthony Rudolf, Glen Saunders, Elsa Schmidt, Helen Schur, Herb and Anne Tandrée, Damian Taylor, David Torpy, Richard Velleman, Meg Wilkinson-Tough, Claire Williamson and Nick Wood.

To the eighteen people who provided thoughts about, and suggestions for, the cover.

To the Louisiana Chalkley cousins for their friendship and help in making my financial position sufficiently sound over the years to allow me the luxury of writing this book quite comfortably on a pension.

To everyone at Palgrave Macmillan for their friendliness, forbearance and professionalism.

Finally, acknowledgement for contributions difficult to categorize, in fact too large to categorize, owed to three people:

- Raymond Chadwick, who, over the last year, has read everything, supplied clinical material and suggested a way of re-organizing the chapters, which has made them much more interesting.
- Ruth Williams, who, over five years, month by month, has read every word, advised me on anything I have asked her and seen me through the various trials and tribulations of writing.
- Annie Saunders, my wife, who did all that too (pretty much daily), in her special steadfast, penetrating and thoroughgoing way.

Introduction

This book is written for practitioners and would-be practitioners, working (or intending to work) psychologically in mental health and with those in emotional distress. Central to the book is the importance of *content*, which is used here to refer to the concerns a patient brings to a practitioner expressed in the patient's own words. Through content, the book identifies the need for and explores the consequences of exploiting the richness of surfaces and the nuances of ordinary language in describing a patient's personal, problematic experience and in laying foundations for individual pieces of psychological work.

Such a focus on the content of psychological distress frequently goes by the board. Even where a psychological initiative advances a strong claim to be person-centred and therefore to be critical of reliance on a superstructure of general categories of disorder or set types of therapy, no basis in underlying phenomenology is established; no foundation in content is laid.

The times have not made it easy to prioritize content and the complexity associated with it.

- Considerable pressure exists now on practitioners to keep work short and highly structured.
- The wish to spread therapies among a wider public, but simultaneously cut costs, has meant that services have come under greater managerial directive.
- More questioning of professional ways and means prevails in society, and it is sometimes argued that comparable results could be achieved with a great deal less training.
- The growth of standard protocols and packages is also noticeable, not just in the United Kingdom but in the United States too, giving rise to concern that cookbook diagnoses and treatments may become the norm.
- The continuing dominance of the prevailing construct paradigm remains. This fosters an over-reliance on diagnostic classification

and, more generally, on the categorizing of disorders and things "wrong" with people as the basis for understanding their emotional difficulties; and while such a basis for understanding is unpopular in many circles, it prospers not just in psychiatry, where it might reasonably be expected to do well, but in much of mainstream clinical psychological practice and research too.
- The present economic situation aggravates these trends towards order, simplicity and control and makes a coherent response both more necessary and more difficult.

At the same time, patients' expectations are rising, as their knowledge of the subject matters of mental health, physical health, counselling and therapy increases, and as they look for practitioners who will construct the work around them and their needs, rather than squeeze them and their needs into preconceived categories and standard interventions. If the patient is to be absolutely central to proceedings, the understanding and addressing of people's concerns need to be something truly personal and faithful to the experience of each individual.

This requires that, however discouraging the trends of the times, the importance of content is re-stated and re-affirmed. We practitioners need the confidence to show how the content of patients' distressing personal experience can be systematically and constructively embraced. This involves more than just attention to the therapeutic relationship and to interpersonal *process*; it requires that *content* is identified, acknowledged, explicated in some way and, beyond that, worked with or on or through. These tasks require a *concept* of content.

This position is not to be confused with the notion of an *approach* to patients. As an approach, much of what follows will have a degree of familiarity. It is very likely that people reading it will see similarities between this as an approach and someone else's, or be reminded of things they actually themselves do, at least sometimes.

Reduced to its simplest, no doubt the book *can* be viewed as an approach. Seen this way, it is most readily viewed as an approach to assessment. It describes taking the distressing concerns that patients bring, retaining them in the patients' own words and creating a unique set of potentially rich material to be held in consciousness by the reflective practitioner. In following this progression step by step, the book seeks to demonstrate the possibility of practical application and to provide illustration of what colleagues and I have found useful.

However, to view this book as an approach misses the broad thrust of the argument on show here. The argument asserts that a concept of content is *fundamental* in face-to-face, one-to-one work with patients.

It seeks to present the kind of foundation in ordinary language and personal experience on which approaches of *various* kinds can rest.

- Chapter 1 introduces the argument by reference to the neglect of phenomenology, the need to embrace a greater degree of complexity through capturing the content of people's concerns in their own language and the importance of the distinction between content and construct.
- Chapter 2 places the case for content in a historical context starting with Monte Shapiro's attempts to improve the quality of psychological assessment. It describes how these attempts gradually led Shapiro to conclude that individual assessment needed to be rooted in procedures that were personal to each patient. It goes on to argue that, apart from Shapiro, attempts to improve assessment tended for many years to prioritize the better measurement of constructs and ignore the sampling of content.
- In Chapter 3, the argument is at its most pragmatic and approach-like. It describes the set of personalized procedures used in generating most of the book's illustrative data. The procedures consist of a form of personal interview (or purposeful conversation), and the construction of a personal questionnaire from the concerns that are described during the interview. Sampling the concerns takes priority over measuring them. Later in the chapter, space is given to how practitioners can reflect on and review the material they generate.
- Chapter 4 is the first of four chapters that consider how attention to content supports and sustains psychological work. The focus in this one is on the use made of the sets of psychological concerns generated by the procedures described in the previous chapter.
- Chapter 5 distinguishes *general work* from *special work*. The chapter goes on to outline nine illustrations of general work, naming each and showing how content personalizes each piece.
- In Chapter 6, attention switches to special work, in particular to established forms of psychological therapy: psychodynamic, systemic, Eye Movement Desensitization and Reprocessing (EMDR) and cognitive behavioural. Here, the illustrations show how content aids either referral for, or the course of, such therapies. This chapter ends with some discussion of the importance of the distinction between general and special work, and the confusion that results when special work is treated as general.
- In Chapter 7, the focus shifts to the application of content in fields beyond the home territory of mental health and recovery services. Five areas are looked at: pain, intensive care, cancer and palliative

care, poor weight gain in the very young and forensic learning difficulties. Some thought is given to how far it has been possible to make use of content assessment in each of these.
- Chapter 8 changes course. It seeks to situate the place of content as argued here in relation to four other person-centred and humanizing psychologies and philosophies. These psychologies and philosophies are Rogerian and post-Rogerian, Personal Construct Theory and Therapy, writings around the concept of *clinimetrics* and ideas coming from the Critical Psychiatry movement.
- In Chapter 9, the argument of the book is recapitulated and broken down into sections that reflect upon the significance of content: for assessment, for counsellors and clinicians, for evaluation and accountability, and for psychology. With the section on psychology comes a final opportunity to draw out the ramifications of the distinction between constructs and content.

In this book, I have not considered the application of the argument to research. Missing from these pages therefore is any consideration of how the present propositions fit with single-case qualitative research methods like Interpretative Phenomenological Analysis (IPA), Thematic Analysis, Q Methodology or Grounded Theory. The consequence is that there is more here about how practitioners might draw on research and the literature than there is about how researchers and academics might assimilate and adapt the various practices described.

It has seemed crucial though to write in a way to appeal both to more data-driven and more ideas-driven practitioners. At the heart of the book is the notion that practitioners need both recourse to data and recourse to ideas to see them through. Admittedly, they differ from one another regarding which of these courses of action they instinctively turn to when the going gets tough. The majority of practitioners nonetheless look to each at different times and are concerned both that their data are meaningful and that their ideas rest on a sound footing. Therefore, there needs to be a more empirical element of the argument which relates to the nature of the evidence necessary to support claims that a piece of work is truly specific and personal, and a more rationalist one which seeks out the links the argument has with better-established practices and more influential ideas, particularly those with claims to be patient-centred.

As an approach to assessment, the book lies somewhere between the quantitative and the qualitative, inclining towards the qualitative, but I hope not too far; its position might be summed up as “qualitative with numbers”.

There is a more significant divide than that between data and ideas, and it is the one that runs through the whole book, both where the text is at its more practical and where it is at its more philosophical. On this side of the divide, content can be found aligned with involvement, directness, sampling, surfaces, human contexts and ontology, while on the far side are those more familiar stalwarts: constructs, detachment, indirectness, measurement, depth, philosophical and psychological categories and epistemology. To my mind, most of us spend proportionately too little thinking time on this side and too much time on the far side. We belong to begin with on this side, immersed in content, perhaps overwhelmed by it. We tend to cross over as soon as we seek to systematize our thoughts; but it seems, especially when we encounter the new and unfamiliar in our day-to-day psychological work, that we are at risk of turning tail and legging it across too soon.

CHAPTER 1

Capturing Content

> We suspect that perhaps one reason why... patients feel misunderstood is that the complexity of their experience isn't adequately represented in contemporary explanatory and descriptive schemas...While outsiders may conceptualize it under a generic category, suffering remains a uniquely personal affair.
>
> Vicky Rippere and Ruth Williams, *Wounded Healers*, 1985

Perhaps one of the greatest tensions in psychological work is the struggle to reconcile the complexity of someone's distress with the need to bring constructive order to it, drawing on the "explanatory and descriptive schemas" that are available at the time (p.2). In the first few contacts between patient and practitioner, this dilemma is particularly apparent in decisions about the way issues and difficulties are to be defined. While practitioners are usually well aware of their patients' wish for understanding and their fear that they will be misunderstood (perhaps *completely* misunderstood), practitioners need the reassurance of a framework that enables them to work without being forever lost in the forest of their patients' expressions of concern.

Psychological concerns and their definition

A definition of "concern" close to a dictionary one is "a distressing feeling that something is not right, that it matters, and that something should be done about it". We are dealing here with concerns in the sense of the content of what patients bring and view as problematic (and not, for example, in the sense of concerns about the nature of the work to be undertaken, or its significance, duration, confidentiality and so on). The word "content" itself requires more precise examination, but for now its meaning will be left a little vague and returned to when it crops up again in the context of assessment theory.

Here are some examples of sets of concerns, each condensed from assessment interviews at a first or second meeting in an English Community Mental Health Centre:

> A man in his fifties: "I find it difficult to open up. I find it difficult to decide what *is* a problem. I am aware I have pervasive low self-esteem, but should I see this as actually a problem? So much of my life is trivial. I am concerned about my feelings of detachment. My relationships all seem pointless. I mull over the past. I try and put it all right again in my head. I fear that soon I am going to be overwhelmed by sadness."

> A teenage mother: "I keep washing my face. I just have to clean away anything that seems not right with it. I do it a lot, especially if there is time to fill... Sometimes I feel I just exist, and nothing more. I find it difficult to stop washing once I start, and I am ashamed of myself after I have done it. I also snap at my mum and dad and my daughter when I've done it. Life seems confusing and out of control. I feel I am dirty when I wait to collect my daughter from nursery and know that the other parents can see I'm not holding it together at all."

> A woman in her late forties: "I feel desperate. I feel people are staring at me. I'm nervous about the way I walk. I am cut off from my feelings and have a strange feeling in my head. I am frightened I am going to have to go back to the mental hospital. It's an effort to talk. I have a confusion of thoughts. They are out of control. The thoughts aren't really me. They control me... Then I'll not have any thoughts at all. I'll feel total fatigue and lack of energy. But I am unable to get to sleep. I can't tell people about things I have done. I lie there knowing there are things I can't be forgiven for."

> A woman in her mid-twenties: "I am frightened I am not going to be able to sleep. I panic that I might be sick. I'm scared at how strongly my moods affect me. But I am unable to say to anyone how bad I feel. People won't understand if I tell them. I am alone with this. I feel I have so much to deal with and there is no one supporting me with it. I feel I have to keep distracting myself so I don't lose it. I am in a distressing muddle about it all. I am concerned that my sense of self-pity won't go away. I sometimes freak myself out that I might be putting it all on just for attention."

The tenor varies from person to person. Sometimes the concerns are vague, sometimes focused; sometimes they are urgent and pressing, sometimes hesitant. Some are more familiar, some less. Some have a strong smack of psychiatric illness about them; others hover in much less definable territory.

The subject of concerns has been curiously ignored. Writing forty years ago within the framework of Personal Construct Theory, Landfield (1975) looked at the concept of "The Complaint", subtitling his chapter "A Confrontation of Personal Urgency and Professional Construction". He looked at the subject from various angles: the complexity and variety of complaints; problems in defining, elaborating and working with them; options for categorizing them; and their status as a criterion of improvement. These matters crop up in the pages that follow.

One could ask how important it is it to take full measure of the language of the presentation and the direct expression of the person's distress. One could argue that the consequence of doing so could simply be that the psychologist is just left at best confused and at worst overwhelmed. And one might fear that in terms of the tension in psychological work between respecting complexity of content and establishing constructive order, there is a risk that the balance will shift precariously towards complexity and away from order.

But patients' concerns *are* complex. Indeed, one might put it another way and say that the complexity of cases arises in large measure from the nature of concerns. However, the argument that follows presents a case for saying that if one loosens the reins and gives complexity of content its head in the form of a personalized type of assessment, order can still be maintained and indeed a claim made that the order achieved is better.

What is the nature of the complexity? What causes the discomfort? When meeting a patient for the first time, we seem to be entering something similar to the maelstrom facing historians seeking to understand the past. Somewhere in a short book entitled *A Concussed History of Scotland*, the following sentence appears: "History is a surface so complicated it looks like infinite depth" (Kuppner, 1990, p.170). Yet, a surface is all history offers us. It looks like depth, but actually it is just surface. It has a roughness and irregularity that defy organization and systematization. From this, it is not clear where profundity lies and whether it is attainable. The historian is required to look beyond superficialities, but perhaps it is actually the rawness and uniqueness of historical events that are the defining qualities of the subject. Maybe, as the monk and historian of the Benedictine order, Father Jacobus suggests in Hermann Hesse's novel *The Glass Bead Game*, the historian's task is simultaneously necessary and impossible. How he arrives at his view that to study history means submitting to chaos and nevertheless retaining faith in order and meaning is shown in Box A.

Box A: *The Glass Bead Game*

In Hermann Hesse's novel of 1943, set some two hundred years in the future, there has been a revival of high culture after the painful trivialities of "the age of feuilleton" (magazine feature writing, glossy Sunday supplements, soaps and worse), a time now passed of untrammelled individualism, a period perhaps a little like our own. This high culture, however, is set apart in the "elite schools" of the tranquil and serene province of Castalia in an unnamed mountainous Central European country. At the heart of this culture are the highly abstract disciplines of philosophy, music and mathematics. More abstract and systematic than any of these, however, is the practice of the Glass Bead Game. The future of the province is under threat as the climate of the times worsens, its values now barely tolerated; and its survival may depend on links being formed with other powerful institutions, notably the Benedictine foundation. One of the most able and dedicated of the younger members of the Castalian order of elite schools, ultimately to rise to the highest rank and to become Magister Ludi (Master of the Glass Bead Game), is Joseph Knecht. In mid-career, he is given the mission of building bridges with the Benedictines and ultimately with the papacy, an institution experienced in surviving difficult times. The success of his mission appears to rest on the understanding he manages to establish with the elderly historian of the Benedictine foundation. Joseph debates with Father Jacobus over many months the case for the detached, unearthly Castalia as against that for the Church, firmly rooted in history and the world.

" 'Of course one should bring order into history', Jacobus thundered. 'Every science is, among other things, a method of ordering, simplifying, making the indigestible digestible for the mind.... I have no quarrel with the student of history who brings to his work a touchingly childish, innocent faith in the power of our minds and our methods to order reality; but first and foremost he must respect the incomprehensible truth, reality, and uniqueness of events. Studying history, my friend, is no joke and no irresponsible game. To study history one must know in advance that one is attempting something fundamentally impossible, yet necessary and highly important. To study history means submitting to chaos and nevertheless retaining faith in order and meaning' " (Hesse, *The Glass Bead Game*, pp.158–159).

Phenomenology and scientific method

The surface alluded to seems similar to what is known to phenomenology as the *Lebenswelt* ("Lifeworld"). In his book on sexual desire, Roger Scruton (1986) outlines how phenomenologists have used this term of Edmund Husserl's to identify a world not necessarily separate from the world of science, but a world described in such a way as to make it alive to our experience and purposes. Scruton describes it as "the surface on which we live and act" (p.12).

He goes on to say that, while not altogether separate from the world of science, the *Lebenswelt* sometimes lives in uncomfortable relation to it. "The scientific attempt to penetrate to 'the depths' of human beings is accompanied almost universally by a loss of response to 'the surface'... Science estranges us from the world by causing us to mistrust the concepts through which we respond to it."

Sexual desire especially, Scruton continues, may be an area where scientific scrutiny into the depth of things may render the surface unintelligible. We need to think about it as "active and contemplative human beings", not as scientists, and employ a language suitable for that purpose. The philosopher, particularly, must attend "to the things themselves". "What things?" one may ask. Scruton suggests rather more than a traditional "scientific" psychology of sexuality usually does. He wishes to include beauty, caresses, chastity, *Don Juanism* (this perhaps edging a little towards the "scientific"), glances, kisses, love and friendship, love and indolence, modesty, shame, tensions in love and *Tristanism* (this too sounding somewhat technical). Scruton argues that both sociobiology and Freudian psychology fail, either by not explaining such phenomena rigorously or not explaining them at all.

Mental health may be another such area where over-rapid scientific penetration renders the surface unintelligible. To the extent that the task is descriptive, at first at any rate, matters need to remain on the surface, and science only enters the picture to the extent that it equates with the task of observing things well. "Observing things well", for present purposes, means accurately and systematically paying attention to the rich expression of people's experience, once ordinary language has been allowed to reveal it.

One's relation to this "surface", as a practitioner listening to someone else's account of what troubles them, depends in part on how one views the sheer complexity of it, its highly charged, personal, idiosyncratic, particularized, even disorganized nature, and especially on whether despite all this one feels one can in some way bring "constructive order" to it.

Playing into the practitioner's deliberations is perhaps the worry that surfaces are just precisely that: superficial. One of the worries is that attention to the contents of experience does not offer enough. As a practitioner, one is expected to penetrate "deeper", beyond mere verbalization, and find what lies below the surface. Worse still, and perhaps particular to psychological work, is the notion that to attend too closely to the content of what people say betrays a certain naivety.

With experience, it appears, must come the willingness to see past the mystifying fog of content. Fraser Watts contrasted strategies in clinical interviewing. There were, he said, low-risk, content-based strategies available (Watts, 1980). He described as the most straightforward approach the one recommended by Monte Shapiro in his 1979 paper on the assessment interview. This approach involved the recording of a set of statements about the patient's experiences and observations in the patient's own words. For his part, Watts felt that clinicians probably underestimated the difficulty of achieving even this most modest goal of eliciting clear statements and recording them accurately:

> They may become sceptical of the validity of patients' statements about themselves and pay more attention to what topics are raised, to the sequence in which they occur and to the non-verbal and paralinguistic behaviour with which they are associated than to the actual content of what the patients say. (Watts, 1980, p.97)

Watts went on to suggest that training actually encouraged increased risk taking. He cited a study where the authors had found that with more highly trained interviewers there were relatively larger discrepancies between people's own reports of their attitudes and the estimates of those attitudes made by interviewers. He went on to cite a second study that had found that medical students given training in doctor–patient relationships showed larger discrepancies between their estimates of patients' personality characteristics and patients' views of themselves. The finding had suggested to the author that after training the students would be less likely to accept patients' statements about themselves at face value.

In mental health work, there has stood over and in opposition to content at one moment "form", at another "process" and at a third "constructs". Traditionally, following Jaspers, psychiatrists have seen the *form* of symptoms as more fundamental to descriptive psychopathology than their content, while in psychoanalysis interpersonal *process* is usually viewed as more important than symptom content. Here, in this book, the drama revolves most insistently around the third of these, *constructs*, and their relationship with content, particularly as the drama plays out in psychological assessment. Constructs, or "some postulated attribute of people", as a paper by Cronbach and Meehl (1955, p.283) defined them, and which include traits, drives, defence mechanisms, motives, needs and many other psychological concepts, have buttressed work of both psychiatric and psychotherapeutic kinds and evolved into fundamental categories in scientific research as well as diagnostic classification.

All three, form, process and constructs, feature further in this or later chapters. All three have at times lauded it over content, much like three sisters from an earlier marriage over a young and immature stepbrother. There is though nothing inherently unscientific in seeking to pay close attention to the content of patients' subjective experiences. However, the temptation is to think of such subjective experiences as merely indicative of the presence of something else, something more *real*; in different hands "real" here variously means something more observable, more objective or more profound. The physicist Arthur Zajonc, writing about experiences of meditation, suggests that "rather than thinking of... experiences as merely subjective impressions thrown up by the 'real world', we set aside all notions of a real world beyond experience and stay with experience itself" (Zajonc, 2009, p.145). He emphasizes that all experiences count. "All phenomena occupy the same space" (p.146), whether we are dealing with reported sense impressions, dreams, memories, thoughts or feelings. Zajonc stresses that we need to "resist the tendency to explain them away as merely brain oscillations, or to imagine them as the visitation of angelic presences" (p.147).

One could add at this point that as practitioners working with the concerns of patients we should similarly resist the temptation to rush to subsume their experiences within categories and classifications, whether psychological dimensions or psychiatric illnesses, or commonly encountered but less formal terms like "adjustment difficulty", "stress" and "psychological vulnerability". Don't such concepts rather explain things away? David Smail talks of their "magical seductiveness" and their "attractive pseudo-authority" (Smail, 2001, p.59). There is then the risk of losing the ordinary language of the *Lebenswelt* and straying too far into expert territory too soon.

However, to stick to the resolve and stay with subjective experience, and not immediately seek overarching physical, social, mental or spiritual explanations for it, requires both determination and resilience when faced by colleagues who insist we have not grasped *enough*. What helps keep the resolve? In part, luck. While there are ways to permit an ordering of complex subjective experience, not a great deal of use has been made of them in routine psychological work; and it is something of a chance matter whether one stumbles upon them or not.

In my case, some years before I began clinical training, I was helped by a fortunate encounter with the writings of the French philosopher, Maurice Merleau-Ponty, through Mme Souche, whose classes at Montpellier University I rather casually decided to attend after I discovered that I was insufficiently qualified to be enrolled for a *maîtrise* in late nineteenth-century French history. She introduced me to French phenomenology. It was possibly this perspective that allowed someone like myself, whose instincts otherwise were somewhat positivist and reductionist, to view speech as something more than mere *self-report*, and not just something to be viewed as one rather fallible and cloudy indicator of what might be the matter, to be subdued, tamed and ultimately broken down by "objective" procedures of one kind or another; rather, allow myself to see it as *personal experience*, the richness and importance of which lay precisely in its idiosyncrasies, ambiguities and untidiness. Passages like the following helped me to stop seeking to pare everything down to some simpler, notionally less equivocal essence, constituent part or "mental chemistry":

> The physicist's atoms will always appear more real than the historical and qualitative face of the world, the physico-chemical processes more real than the organic forms, the psychological atoms of empiricism more real than perceived phenomena, the intellectual atoms represented by the "significations" of the Vienna Circle more real than consciousness, as long as the attempt is made to build up the shape of the world (life, perception, mind) instead of recognizing, as the source that stares us in the face and as the ultimate court of appeal in our knowledge of these things, our *experience* of them. (Merleau-Ponty, 1945, pp.26–7)

Along with the idea that experience cannot be broken into little pieces comes the further proposition that experience must not be swallowed whole, neither by some overweening causal scientific explanation nor by an arrogant piece of psychological theorizing. "I cannot shut myself up within the realm of science. All my knowledge of the world, even my scientific knowledge is gained from my own particular point of view, or from some experience of the world without which the symbols of science would be meaningless" (Merleau-Ponty, 1945, p.ix). One must conjure with the notion that with phenomenology experience comes first and science and psychology limp along afterwards, they being just one way of dealing with it. Experience, as what lives consist of, should be understood as something personally contextualized and meaningful and on the whole easier and more appropriate to describe than to explain.

The practical issue left unaddressed, and which now begins to need consideration, is how a practitioner, who refuses to marginalize a patient's experience and wants to do justice to an important part of it in a direct way, is to do so systematically.

Embracing patients' personal experience

With this issue, I was greatly helped by Monte Shapiro, my teacher on the Maudsley clinical psychology training course at the Institute of Psychiatry. (See below: Box B this chapter, page 17.) Shapiro had founded the course some thirty years before my arrival there. He offered his trainees, if not a phenomenological approach to clinical work, at least one which, among much else, emphasized the importance of the *direct* observation of phenomena, including the patient's own reporting of their subjective experiences. The prevailing lack of such direct observation sometimes seemed to him suggestive of a lack of true curiosity among clinical psychologists about their patients, while an over-reliance on *indirect* measures risked taking them either too far from the phenomena of concern or too quickly into contentious explanatory theorizing (Shapiro and Ravenette, 1959). In his view:

> The phenomena which are chosen for investigations appear, at first sight, to have little relationship to the disorders which bring psychiatric patients into hospital. Psychiatric patients suffer from a variety of disorders of affect, cognition, and volition. A large number, if not the majority, of papers published by psychologists do not deal with these phenomena. Instead they report upon the performance, by psychiatric patients, of a variety of tasks which might be described, without much loss of accuracy, as puzzles and indoor games. (p.296)

And still on the subject of publications by psychologists, he felt:

> Their work is directed mainly at proving or disproving certain theories rather than at explaining and controlling certain phenomena which have excited their interest. In fact it sometimes seems that some psychologists look upon experimental method merely as the most convincing method of persuading people to accept their ideas. It thus ceases to become a method of determining the actual state of affairs, independent of a priori conceptions. (p.297)

Tables 1.1 and 1.2 illustrate the difference between indirect and direct data in the form of questionnaire results. Table 1.1 lists in summary form the items from an ordinary "standard" (prefabricated) questionnaire. In this particular example, the data consist of two

Table 1.1 Parts of a definition

Two men, both in their early forties, one a security guard and the other a Baptist lay preacher, both married and without children: their scores on the original version of the Beck Depression Inventory on a scale where items are rated from 0 to 3.

The security guard	BDI item	The Baptist lay preacher
1	Sadness	0
1	Discouragement about the future	0
2	Feeling of failure	1
1	Feeling of dissatisfaction	1
2	Feeling of guilt	1
0	Feeling of being punished	1
1	Hatred of myself	2
2	Blaming myself	2
1	Thoughts of killing myself	0
0	Crying	0
1	Feeling irritated	1
1	Loss of interest	1
1	Difficulty making decisions	2
0	Feeling I look ugly	0
2	Inability to work	2
1	Not sleeping	3
1	Tiredness	2
1	Loss of appetite	0
0	Loss of weight	0
0	Worries about my health	0
1	Loss of interest in sex	1
20	Total scores	20

people's scores on a four-point scale. The table shows the results for each of them. The questionnaire is the earlier version of the Beck Depression Inventory (Beck, Ward, Mendelson, Mock and Erbaugh, 1961). This instrument, when the separate scores on each item are added together, provides a total, which – if high enough – suggests the presence of psychiatric depression. It was in order to supply a score on this measure, rather than for the separate scores on its constituent items, that the test was principally devised. What is shown here is a procedure that measures something by selecting a set of items seen as indicative of that something. Here lies the indirectness: the score the practitioner is after first requires a lot of other scores to be added together.

Table 1.2 Lines of a description

Two men, both in their early forties, one a security guard and one a Baptist lay preacher, both married and without children: ten personal questionnaire items for each.

The security guard	The Baptist lay preacher
Sense of an inner panic when crises occur	Sense of too much pressure within
Feeling concerned about my changes of mood	Concern about tendency to isolate myself
Fear of what may come up at work	Feeling of overwhelming tiredness
Difficulty understanding what is causing the feelings	Feeling of frustration with myself
Sense of dragging my wife down	Concern I can't stop doing too much
Sense of not liking myself very much	Sense I don't cope well with my feelings
Worry I may go overboard	Concern that I get in a frenzy
Constant feeling of nausea or indigestion	A core, almost physical feeling of pain
Feeling there is nothing to look forward to	Fear that life will pass me by
Sense of being stuck with the job I do	Guilt about not doing more

Table 1.2 shows data in the form of personal questionnaires, the way of working that Shapiro eventually adopted in tackling initial problem definition and outcome assessment. The patients are the same, but the items this time are much closer to what the two men actually said than those in Table 1.1. Where Table 1.1 might be viewed as consisting of *parts of a definition* (of psychiatric depression in this particular example), Table 1.2 might be seen as supplying the *lines of a description* of altogether rather looser material: the person's concerns in his or her own words (Chalkley, 2004).

The items of Table 1.1 will be familiar to practitioners. What there is in Table 1.2 is fresher even if rather ad hoc. The practitioner has apparently held back and resisted the framework of a pre-set procedure and indeed early recourse to the use of a familiar psychological concept ("psychiatric depression") in exchange for the richness of ordinary language and for evidence that while the two men were notionally the same in respect of the severity of their depression, they were not the same with respect to the nature of their concerns.

Box B: Monte Shapiro (1912–2000)

Monte Shapiro was born in the Transvaal in 1912, grew up in Zimbabwe (then Southern Rhodesia), was educated at Rhodes University South Africa, where he studied psychology and later pursued further psychology studies at Cambridge after emigrating to the United Kingdom. He joined the Communist Party during the 1930s and, when war broke out, volunteered for aircrew duties. He was shot down over the Netherlands in 1943, severely injuring an arm, and spent a year in a prisoner-of-war (POW) camp.

After being demobbed, he met Hans Eysenck who found Shapiro part-time work in the children's department of the Maudsley Hospital. Shapiro soon moved to adult services and in 1947 assumed responsibility both for the nation's first postgraduate course in clinical psychology and for providing psychology services to the Maudsley and Bethlem hospitals.

Shapiro left the Communist Party in 1956 after Khrushchev's denunciation of Stalin and the Soviet Union's invasion of Hungary. These events changed him profoundly, notably as a professional colleague. Science may have filled the vacuum left by his disillusionment with politics; but with science came philosophical doubt: *La conclusion de notre raisonnement doit toujours rester dubitative* ("What our reasoning has led us to conclude must always be viewed as open to question") (Claude Bernard, 1865, p.83). Michael Berger (2000), writing Shapiro's obituary in *The Independent*, described his sense of openness, a willingness to accept that his ideas could be wrong and an "ever-present enthusiasm to discuss and debate, accompanied by an infectious excitement about new ideas and new personal discoveries".

Stephen Morley (2000), writing Shapiro's obituary for *The Guardian*, described how as a clinician he was infinitely patient, tolerant, empathic and non-judgemental. This is how his many trainees would remember him. In 1979, having at last relinquished responsibility for the department a few years earlier, he moved to University College where he had been offered facilities as an honorary research fellow in the School of Medicine.

He left London in 1989 and moved with his wife Jean to a house at 20, Morley Square, Bristol. At his funeral, two Duke Ellington tracks were played: *Isfahan* from the Far East Suite and *Warm Valley* from the Blanton Webster Band.

Personal questionnaires arrived suddenly in the literature two years after the publication of Shapiro and Ravenette (1959). They are as sweet and simple an idea as ever came out of clinical psychology. The claim in the pages that follow is that they provide a way of ordering complexity of content. They allow the practitioner to capture something of a person's experience at a particular moment and to hold that experience in mind over a period of time. They can be shaped to accommodate all kinds of presentation. In this book, they are treated rather as "the" preferred procedure, when procedure is sought. Nonetheless, they are really just one among a number of direct approaches to identifying and beginning to tackle the complexity of concerns. In relation to the overall argument, it is the significance and properties of this procedure that matter, rather than the procedure itself.

The following is an example of a single personal questionnaire item and how it can be formed from something quite complicated: "How", Landfield asked, "does one conceptualize the verbalizations of Ann?" He continued:

> She states she has a problem, is unsure of its nature, feels that she does *not* have a problem, and definitely needs help.... Ann may be construed as confused. However, Ann does not complain of feeling confused. Can we say her problem of confusion is so profound that she is unable to state it? In other words, is she so confused that she does not have a stable base from which to judge her confusion?... Certainly, Ann's therapist experienced confusion as he listened to the unfolding of her life history. (Landfield, 1975, p.15)

What might Shapiro have done with these "verbalizations of Ann"? According to Landfield, after further discussion, Ann disclosed that people had been criticizing her for being different. While she had been comfortable with herself, she felt she had to take account of the opinions of others. Ann's therapist concluded that her complaint was a question: "Am I really that different from others and should I be concerned about it?" As a single personal questionnaire statement, she seems to be saying something like:

> I feel uncertain whether to be worried that other people have criticized me for being different.

An experienced practitioner may well feel that no classifying, explaining or understanding of any kind is much good if what has to be classified, explained or understood is unclear. He or she may wonder how without a surface one is to achieve a measure of depth. Nonetheless, it is hard as a professional person to take on the content of patients' concerns. One may recognize the value of approaching matters this way and see the opportunities it offers. But it does appear to risk obscuring the wood for the trees, and it is small wonder that the relative abstraction and formal precision of constructs have usually seemed preferable to the mire of content.

Then, how methodologically sound are personal questionnaires, anyway? These phrases and sentences of ordinary language, strung together, dressed in the finery of assessment instruments (particularly when their use is described as applying "*the* PQ", rather than just as using "*a* personal questionnaire"), may still at this stage seem rather shocking. Is such an approach really allowed? And, besides that, one might ask if such an approach is really necessary.

This chapter has looked at the argument for addressing the content of patients' concerns from the perspective of the counsellor or clinician, curious by nature, intent somehow to get to the heart of things. It is suggested here that counsellors and clinicians won't pursue curiosity heedless of price. There is an overriding need to preserve some kind of order. It is further suggested that, to embrace this content, practitioners need to feel able to act scientifically, in the best sense of the word, be keenly attentive to phenomena and achieve some kind of "direct" access to them. While the phenomena come first, and scientific method follows some way behind, there is a need to recognize the importance of both. A sentence from a psychology journal comes to mind: "The position taken in this paper is that personal meaning must not be sacrificed to scientific method; neither, however, must scientific method be abandoned in the pursuit of personal meaning..." (Wright, 1970, p.221). The chapter has ended by making reference to Monte Shapiro and the system of personal questionnaires he developed as a means of achieving such directness. In the next chapter, his work is placed in some sort of historical and theoretical context as the account turns to how he and others sought to improve the quality of psychological assessment.

CHAPTER 2

Better Assessment

I went to see Monte Shapiro the day after he gave a lecture to my group of clinical psychology trainees towards the end of my first term on the Maudsley course. At that lecture, we had been given the two typewritten parts of his revised *Assessment of Psychological Dysfunctions* (Shapiro, 1975a). Unsure quite why, but definitely reminded by it of Merleau-Ponty and Mme Souche and keen to think about phenomenology, I asked him if he would take me on for supervision. He agreed, and some months later, I began a year's placement with him, which subsequently was to turn into something different after both he and I left the Institute the following summer.

This chapter covers the following:

- It begins by looking at Shapiro's search for better quality in psychological assessment. This search ended by his arguing for the use of personal questionnaires as a means of making assessments more relevant to the needs of patients and practitioners.
- It goes on to consider other efforts, particularly in the 1980s, to make assessments more "realistic", highlighting the conceptual obstacles to shifting from standardized measures of personality to samplings of people's personal experience.
- The chapter also seeks to show how the obstacles to personalizing assessment have not in any very thoroughgoing way been overcome. But while personalized assessment cannot claim to be mainstream in relation to practice, it can at least claim to be orthodox in relation to assessment theory. The chapter examines this orthodoxy, proposing a distinction be drawn between work based on the assessment of content and work based on the assessment of constructs.
- Finally, it returns to Shapiro, who, having devised the method of personal questionnaires, gave much of his time in the later part of

his career to thinking and writing about the nature of the content he had begun to liberate.

Shapiro's search for precision, accuracy and relevance

Most of Shapiro's early clinical papers in one way or another tackled psychological "testing" as it was understood at the Maudsley in the early days of the training course. This was a time when psychologists' power and autonomy within the psychiatric team were very limited, and administering tests largely defined their professional role. Shapiro wanted a stronger, more influential profession and one which was more firmly rooted in scientific method. Clinical psychologists were, in his view, breaking rules, either in order to get more work done or simply to find more to say about it.

> There is considerable pressure from psychiatrists and social workers for quick and understandable results [that] serve as a short cut in the solution of difficult problems. There is a standing temptation for the psychologist to answer a query with "Yes, certainly. I'll give him the such-and-such and the so-and-so tests". (Shapiro, 1951, p.762)

He viewed precision, accuracy and relevance as essential to establishing the profession on a sounder scientific footing. Weaknesses, not only about the way tests were constructed, their standardization, validation and calibration but also about the way they were administered and interpreted, were a major preoccupation for him (Shapiro, 1957).

In talking to his trainees about science, he liked to define it as "any procedure that clarifies one's ideas about phenomena", and he believed that a scientific approach to clinical work was beneficial. He accepted that at this point the belief was of the order of an untested hypothesis. He might also have explained that the clarity he sought was more a certain care with words than the dogged pursuit of numerical exactitude. Nonetheless, his argument is at heart a technical one.

Around 1960, Shapiro turned his attention to psychiatric depression, having established from the records department that this was then the most frequently diagnosed disorder at the Maudsley. Hoping to develop psychological treatments for depression, he found himself instead confronted by problems with its psychological assessment. These, essentially, were of the same kind as before: precision, accuracy and – especially – relevance. Up until that moment, he had been prepared to consider diagnosis as a quicker, less time-consuming route towards treatment. But it was necessary to get the foundations right,

Box C: Relative specificity

Shapiro's argument seems technical because it presented itself as a critique of a particular kind of assessment *instrument*. It involved an analysis of standard questionnaire data. Standard questionnaires were in Shapiro's parlance "indirect" in nature (see Chapter 1). The value of indirect measures in assessing concerns or individual statements of "psychological dysfunction" (the term Shapiro had adopted at this time) was viewed as depending on how close the relationship was between the constituent items of such questionnaires and their totals when the constituent items were added together. If the correlations were high, then that would be evidence that the individual items were in a sense redundant and attention could be focused on the common factor that the questionnaire set out to measure.

The way he answered the question was by studying the statistical variance of a small number of particular tests. He looked at the results of the relatively few studies where someone had taken a multi-item questionnaire, administered to a largish number of subjects, purporting to measure something, and looked to see how far a general or "common" factor emerged. A common factor would be suggested if scores on each item correlated with the total. For example, to take an extreme case, supposing a questionnaire of say twenty-one items (like the Beck) always produced the same score on every item: for one person a "three" on item 1 ("sadness"), item 2 ("the future") and so on; for another a "four" on the same item 1, item 2 and so on. In such a situation, it would look very much as if each item measured the same thing, which is the common factor the test was designed to measure. This is the ideal, where what Shapiro called "the psychological ambiguity" (Shapiro, 1989, p.292) of interpretation is reduced to the absolute minimum. In reality, tests never behave quite like this. They contain statistical "error", hopefully error of a random kind, such that slightly lower scores on, for example, items 5 and 13 are compensated for by slightly higher scores on items 8 and 17.

The problem is the existence of *specific* factors, factors that in terms of the purpose of the test again represent "error", but error of a systematic, non-random kind that does not cancel itself out. First of all, such error undermines the notion of a single

Box C: (Continued)

common factor. The test is now also to be regarded as measuring specific factors (without so intending); and secondly, one simply does not know a priori from person to person what these specific factors are. They may routinely be associated with a particular subset of items (for example, the somatic items of the depression inventory), or worse – in a way – they may just be one particular patient's personal response to the test as a whole: an idiosyncratic but consistent response to some of the questions. One just doesn't know in any given instance how much of the result is the common factor and how much the specific ones. One can gain a sense of how much potential ambiguity there is in the system by trying to calculate how many different ways a score of say 25 on the Beck can be obtained.

Studies by Mosier (1937) and McNair and Lorr (1964) estimated these specific factors as high in relation to the common ones in terms of how much of the statistical variance they explained. There is some generality. The factors are not *just* specific, but they are *relatively* so.

and it was somewhat frustrating that the successes of psychiatry did not extend to the apparently rather humdrum business of the systematic identification of patients' psychological problems (or psychological *dysfunctions*).

The argument he came up with was based on analyses of the structure of standardized questionnaires, then as now in common use. In a nutshell, these analyses suggested to him that rather than measure the single "general" thing the questionnaires were supposed to measure (psychiatric depression, for example), groups of items from among the set of questionnaire items would cluster together and create "specific" factors in unpredictable, unintended and unwanted ways. These specific factors, although unpredictable, unintended and unwanted, rather better reflected what the questionnaire actually measured than did the general one. The argument is set out a little more fully in Box C. It led him to view psychological dysfunctions as "relatively specific" (Shapiro, 1966).

He liked, in presenting the argument, to refer to Charles Spearman (1927) on the subject of these general factors. Spearman attacked what he called "faculty error", or the "oligarchic doctrine". This is the idea of there being human *faculties*, a few "great powers" governing the organization of human attributes, people's strengths and weaknesses, into which everything could somehow be fitted. "Take, for instance, judgement", Spearman wrote. There is no single attribute called "judgement". Instead, "this . . . seems to break up into several kinds. Judgement for politics would be one thing; that for sports another; that for telepathy, yet a third; and so forth. Is not then . . . a separate measurement needed for each kind?" (p.35).

Shapiro took up this theme in Spearmanesque style. Generalizations will often be inaccurate: "A patient's apparent timidity in the consulting room may co-exist with considerable boldness on the football field." A person may be both fearful and brave, both selfish and generous. At the same time, Shapiro recognized that there might be more generality in a psychiatric population than in the general one (Shapiro, 1985, p.3). Members of a psychiatric population would be vulnerable to more pervasive negative traits. This greater generality of negative traits might actually in some sense define the psychiatric population. One could perhaps also argue that the more severe the state of affairs, the more similar constellations of symptoms will appear from case to case and the more syndrome-like presentations will be.

Overall, however, the attempt to squeeze a patient's experience within a number of bold, single, general factors seemed to him at risk of degenerating into vague abstraction. Once this train of thought is set in motion, how far does it run? How specific is specificity? If great powers fall before smaller ones, might not smaller powers give way before still smaller ones, the hosts of idiosyncratic experiences and vocabularies of individual people, before the *personally* specific?

This seems a serious consideration since there appears to be nothing left to measure of a general trait or personality or diagnostic type that can pass muster as trustworthy. However, before abandoning multi-item questionnaires as a means of making accurate descriptions, couldn't one settle for a looser kind of instrument? Perhaps, it might be something as simple as a problem checklist. Surely, all one really needs is a very rough idea of the type of material one is after and then to set about creating an assemblage of items in sufficient number. Length, therefore, is the answer. Could not this still win the day, if one burrowed for long enough in the *Shorter Oxford English Dictionary*, or *Roget's Thesaurus*, and mined thoroughly the huge lexicon of English trait words, or deployed a sufficient number of situational qualifiers (. . . "next to the cooker", . . . "at Tesco's", . . . "under the eaves", . . . "between the goalposts", . . . "during Lent")?

Table 2.1 The last twelve items of the Mooney Problem Checklist

277	Having unusual sex desires
278	Bothered by sexual thoughts or dreams
279	Worried about the effects of masturbation
280	Sexual needs unsatisfied
281	Sexually attracted to someone of my own sex
282	Sexual desires differ from husband's or wife's
283	Being bothered or interfered with in my work
284	Not liking some of the people I work with
285	Family disapproves of my present job
286	Dissatisfied with my present job
287	Poor prospects of advancement in my present job
288	Afraid of losing my job

Just how many items actually are required though? The last twelve items of the Mooney Problem Checklist (Gordon and Mooney, 1950) laid out in Table 2.1 illustrate the shortcomings of length as a solution. What about lack of any interest in sex? What about never having had any job? Without the boundaries provided by a defined trait or illness, the number of possible items falling under the vague heading "problem" is limitless. However sensitive and thorough the selection made, the author is vulnerable to Bilsbury and Richman's (2002) charge of *overgeneralization and irrelevance* (see below: this chapter); on the one hand, the selection will include large numbers of items that are irrelevant to the particular patient, while, on the other, contrive notwithstanding to omit items that may be of major concern.

Having rejected the problem checklist, the only way to avoid overgeneralization and irrelevance, it seemed, was to create a questionnaire de novo for each patient. Shapiro brought off this feat at the second attempt (Shapiro, 1961). At the first, the paper by Shapiro and Ravenette (1959), a fifty-item questionnaire had been specially constructed for a thirty-eight-year-old farm labourer diagnosed as paranoid schizophrenic. Twenty of the items were based on the patient's own material and thirty taken from a standard questionnaire devised by Sandler (1954). The authors afterwards, in painstakingly going through the ratings one by one with the patient, discovered that he had rejected thirteen of Sandler's items on the grounds that the wording was "inappropriate". With number 8 ("I feel now life is not worth living"), for example, Shapiro and Ravenette discovered that had they substituted "existence" for "life", the patient would have scored the item "definitely the case". One wonders if it was the experience with this patient that persuaded Shapiro to go the rest of the way and just use personalized items.

What has been the response among practitioners to Shapiro's line of argument? A few years after personal questionnaires first appeared, a debate was organized under the auspices of the *Journal of Psychosomatic Research* on the merits of personal questionnaires, specifically in research, although the topics touched on included practical clinical matters. Shapiro's best-known colleague in the discussion was the clinical psychologist, Graham Foulds, author of two highly acclaimed and original books critical of conventional accounts of mental illness (Foulds with Caine, 1965; Foulds, 1976).

Foulds is affable. He is appreciative of Shapiro's "careful and detailed work on the single case" but feels that "a good clinical psychologist is doing this, though possibly less systematically", anyway. And he cannot resist a hint that all this detail might be just a trifle nerdish:

> Is it not that, when a large number of cases have been studied, certain symptoms have been found to be associated together?... If we operate at the idiosyncratic level, we may find that X complains of panic attacks in the Tube between Victoria and Sloane Square, Y between Sloane Square and South Kensington, and Z between South Kensington and Gloucester Road. It seems for Shapiro's purposes claustrophobia would do quite well. (Foulds, 1964, p.274)

Yes, continues Foulds, "for the alleviation of the condition the more specific information might be invaluable" (p.274), but a "standard questionnaire" (that is, a prefabricated one) "is unlikely to miss anything of significance if the questions be sufficiently generalized" (p.275). (Foulds was the creator of more than one such standard questionnaire himself.)

To this Shapiro replied (in part) as follows:

> *A priori*, it is equally conceivable that questions that are generalised miss a great deal. There would of course be great saving in time if one could use a standard questionnaire instead of a personal questionnaire... We are only entitled to do so when we know that the two types of questionnaire give the same results. One wonders how many treatments have been found to be ineffective because patients were not asked questions relevant to their own disorders, and were put questions they did not understand, and which merely evoked irrelevant sets such as the tendency to say "Yes" or "No", or to say a lot or a little. (Shapiro, 1964, p.283)

This exchange doesn't quite manage to achieve the heat of the last two months of the Freud-Jung correspondence, but it does hint that Shapiro's opinions were not in for an effortless ride.

Looking back over half a century, it seems reasonable to say that while never *quite* out of the practitioner's repertoire, personal questionnaires have at no time been altogether securely in it. Local difficulties may at one time have played their part. It may be that Shapiro's view of clinical psychology as "the application of science" and the psychologist as "applied scientist" drew on a language that exposed fissures within the profession. While Shapiro's approach to psychological work was immensely broad and he had much that was favourable to say about many approaches, the Maudsley's association with behavioural and later cognitive behavioural approaches may have adversely affected the impact of other ideas emerging from that institution.

The published literature exploring or employing personal questionnaires is really rather small. In the years following Shapiro's original publication (Shapiro, 1961), there appeared a sequence of technical papers written by Patrick Phillips on the scaling of personal questionnaire data and the implications of this for administration and scoring. The series was later brought together in a single paper (Phillips, 1986). The MRC psychotherapy research project based on Sheffield made extensive use of personal questionnaires over several years, employing them usually as one among a number of outcome measures in extensive group designs (for example, Barkham, Shapiro and Firth-Cozens, 1989), but at least once to illustrate their clinical application in an intensive single case study (Parry, Shapiro and Firth, 1986). During the 1980s, there arose interest in the use of personal questionnaires in psychosis, beginning with Garety's papers on the feasibility of measuring delusional experiences (Brett-Jones, Garety and Hemsley, 1987; Garety, 1985) and continuing into the 1990s with Paul Chadwick's work on modifying delusional beliefs (Chadwick and Lowe, 1990). Later, refinements of administrative procedure were suggested for use with certain psychotic patients (Cliffe, Possamai and Mulhall, 1995).

Beyond these studies though, the published literature consists of little more than isolated papers backed by case illustration. The reported studies include Shapiro, Marks and Fox (1963) attempting a therapeutic experiment; McPherson and Le Gassicke (1965) testing a new drug; Shapiro (1969) looking at short-term improvements in affective disorder; Mitchell (1969) exploring process and meaning in counselling settings; (D.A.) Shapiro, Caplan, Rohde and Watson (1975) examining correlates of changes in personal questionnaire scores over the course of a psychotherapeutic group; Bennun, Chalkley and Donnelly (1985) proposing avenues of research in marital work; and Chalkley (1994a and 1994b) reviewing ways of helping people with concerns related to their experience of sexual variation.

What about the use of personal questionnaires in day-to-day work? Some dozen years ago, the results of a postal questionnaire study returned by 158 clinical psychologists working in England actually indicated that no use at all was being made of either personal questionnaires or indeed of any other procedure with comparable intention (Bekhit, Thomas, Lalonde and Jolley, 2002; Bekhit, 2003 [personal communication]). But Bekhit et al.'s paper suggests too that little use was being made of *any* type of formal, structured assessment by clinical psychologists, particularly in adult mental health, thus leaving the profession heavily reliant on unstructured clinical interviews.

What was described in the paper by Bekhit et al. was perceived shortcomings in routine psychological assessment in England around the turn of the century. Such a situation was a surprise, given the profession in question and given that these observations came ten years after the end of a very active period of research on psychological assessment. It is to this subject that the chapter now turns.

"Realistic dependent variables"

Chris Bilsbury has suggested to me that clinical psychology at the Maudsley in the thirty or thirty-five years that followed the opening of the course in 1947, the period that covers the time of its first two heads of department, contained two strands: the dependent variable strand and the independent variable strand.

The first strand, the dependent variable strand, is closely associated with Shapiro's name. He was head of department up to 1976 and remained thereafter a reader in clinical psychology for another three years. The strand represents a psychology of the dependent variable: its concern is with the nature and status of different kinds of outcome measure, with how change is to be assessed clinically and statistically and with many basic aspects of single case design. This line of work, of course, includes work on or with personal questionnaires.

The other strand is strongly associated with the name of Jack Rachman who was head of department from 1976 to 1982. It is a clinical psychology of the independent variable. The focus of much of the clinical research in, or in some way associated with, the department was on the impact of behavioural treatments and components of treatment (such as anxiety management, breathing retraining, contingent reinforcement, covert positive reinforcement, desensitization, exposure, flooding, mass practice, orgasmic reconditioning, overlearning, overt rehearsal, response prevention and self-monitoring) and the effect of these on an enormous range of disorders, habits and proclivities (such as blood phobia, bulimia, compulsive avoidance, dental anxiety, heart phobia, insomnia, pain sensitivity, panic disorder, rumination, school refusal, smoking, social phobia and tinnitus).

Writing in Jack Rachman's *Festschrift*, Terence Wilson and David Clark speak of how in those years behaviour therapy catapulted onto the international scene and of the Maudsley's prominence in this development (Wilson and Clark, 1999). Rachman, with Hans Eysenck, launched the journal *Behaviour Research and Therapy* ("BRAT") in 1963 and maintained a thriving research programme over the course of the time that followed. The Maudsley was a magnet "unsurpassed in influence and importance as arguably the leading centre of [behaviour therapy] in the world" (Wilson and Clark, 1999, p.S1). But, quite rightly, among Rachman's many accomplishments, Wilson and Clark remember his book on wine (Durac, 1979).

The Maudsley was, of course, also influenced by developments elsewhere, particularly in the United States. Looking back now, the 1980s seem a particularly crucial decade for innovations of a behavioural and cognitive behavioural kind. On the independent variable side came the advancement of cognitive behavioural therapy and the publication of influential texts on the treatment of psychiatric disorders, notably the books by Beck and his colleagues on depression, anxiety disorders and phobias, and the various hypothesized personality disorders. There were also journal articles, including journal articles in the new American journal *Cognitive Therapy and Research*, whose title plays a kind of homage to the older British one: *Behaviour Research and Therapy*.

On the dependent variable side, there was the movement called "behavioural assessment". This shared with Shapiro his concern with the shortcomings of standardized questionnaire construction and trait measurement. In an influential article, Goldfried and Kent (1972) analysed the deficiencies of what they called *traditional assessment*. They viewed it as haunted by a psychic determinism, which saw behaviour as the product of underlying needs, drives and defences, along with personality traits and types. They felt the measurement of constructs was far too dominated by this kind of thinking, which forced attention away from other sorts of explanation of people's behaviour, particularly situational ones. The result was tests, which, seen from the wider perspective, were badly constructed and wrongly interpreted.

Behavioural assessment sought instead "realistic dependent variables for clinical use", requiring the use of different types of measure, specific with regard to situation and behaviour, and conceived in sufficiently precise terms, to enable "systematic quantifications of clients' problems before, during and after treatment" (Nelson, 1981, p.168). The priorities were not just accuracy but functional utility (Cone, 1992). "Functional utility" implied a shift of emphasis away from personality description towards the measurement of change.

The pioneers of behavioural assessment insisted that diagnosis without clear behavioural referents did not provide a firm basis on which to build. But their position on constructs in general and diagnostic constructs in particular was more complicated. The final edition of the journal *Behavioral Assessment* included a ninety-two-page mini-series on behavioural assessment in the DSM era. Various views are expressed there. But perhaps the most telltale is the view expressed in the paper by First, Frances, Widiger, Pincus and Wakefield Davis (1992), whose view was that treatment recommendations depend on differential diagnosis and that therefore DSM-IV must be more construct driven and less specific than if the diagnostic system were only serving the purposes of behavioural assessment. Weighing things up, Follette and Hayes write: "Perhaps... on intellectual grounds the behavioural movement has evolved in such a way that the DSM system really does represent what we have to offer. If not, we need to consider how to proceed in the DSM era" (Follette and Hayes, 1992, p.295).

What behavioural assessment never seems to have set out to achieve was to move, or extend, from standardized forms of assessment to personal ones. Its achievement might be best summarized as the better measurement of psychological constructs. Improving the content *validity* of constructs (in other words, making sure the items included in a measure of a construct adequately represent all that should be seen as making up, or contributing to, that construct) is a necessary activity in strengthening the robustness of the construct and getting away from the traditional approach. But it doesn't challenge the status of constructs in general, or promote content's cause. Such success as there has been in developing personalized assessment lies elsewhere.

It is tempting to surmise that during the 1980s the successes of behavioural treatment were secured at the expense of behavioural assessment. So useful in supporting a rigorous empirical approach to the examination of descriptive and experimental psychopathology, the sophisticated array of behavioural measures became eternally tied to researching psychological and more particularly psychiatric disorders.

In their monograph, Bilsbury and Richman (2002) summarize the shortcomings of construct measures as an approach to defining problems and measuring outcomes. These weaknesses are listed in Box D.

Box D: Bilsbury and Richman's criticisms of constructs

- *Orientation towards classification*: construct measures seek to distinguish groups rather than individuals, and therefore the items chosen to define the construct are reduced to those that are the most common among the group.
- *Arbitrariness of scale selection*: the names of scales sometimes suggest they measure the same variable, when in fact they do not, while measures of purportedly different things overlap.
- *Overgeneralization and irrelevance*: they omit items that are the focal concern of the particular patient and include items that are irrelevant to him or her.
- *Proneness to obsolescence*: "standard" measures may be out of date as a construct shifts, spreads or narrows over time.
- *Tendency to obfuscation and misunderstanding*: the practice of relying on global scores may obscure the underlying phenomena as particular variables are conflated, data agglomerated and already impure, and compound measures further combined into "batteries".
- *Allure of rapid generation and processing*: the speed at which questionnaires can be administered and scored is allowed to commend their use, irrespective of the quality of the data they assemble.
- *Insensitivity to treatment*: scales designed to measure relatively stable dispositions and traits will tend to have items sensitive to change bred out of them.
- *Lack of context*: constructs are designed to be context free and so fail to take heed of people's natural surroundings.
- *Obliviousness to the stage of the disorder*: symptom counts and measures of severity are preferred to notions of a natural history, or process developing over time with attendant complexities and consequences.

Some of them will come to mind again if one looks back at the depression questionnaire in Table 1.1. For example, the two people there are measured on the same items: those being judged the most telltale in diagnosing psychiatric depression (*orientation towards classification*). These items fail to show how their problems are individually distinctive. The questionnaire doesn't pick out focal concerns, but instead rates various potential problems, some of which are not relevant to the two individuals. The price of this is reflected in the number of low scores of "0" and "1" (*overgeneralization and irrelevance*). The contents of the table may also trigger thoughts about the way the data have been collected and how the results might be explained to the person. In summarizing scores, important information may be lost. Notionally, on the chosen measure the two people are the "same" (both totalling 20). How else, or how better, might the data be understood than "slightly psychiatrically depressed"? In writing further about the risk of *obfuscation and misunderstanding*, Bilsbury and Richman quote Feinstein and Horwitz (1997):

> For example, in a clinical enquiry, we may ask the patient the following: "How are you? What would you like done?"
>
> Instead, with a multi-item instrument, we may say in effect: "Please complete these 43 questions, and then I'll tell you how you are and what we're going to do."

The counsellor or clinician has perhaps also fallen foul of the *allure of rapid generation and processing*, the temptation to turn to procedures which can be quickly administered and scored, irrespective of their appropriateness for the task.

Bilsbury and Richman refer to the sterility of the clinical landscape when patients are constrained by constructs, and lopped and stretched to fit them. They contrast this with the "colourful cornucopia of manifestations" when practitioners begin to take systematic account of the perceptions and understandings of their individual patients. "Let us emphasize our belief that clinical material comes from patients, not from constructs" (Bilsbury and Richman, 2002, p.33). Although some patients are psychologically comfortable with simply being told they are suffering from psychiatric illnesses such as anxiety and depression, most report their difficulties in ordinary language, granted that language sometimes includes ordinary words like "anxious" and "depressed".

Bilsbury and Richman next look at the various initiatives and technologies available for such systematic individual evaluation, avoiding much of the technical vocabulary that comes with constructs. The monograph has sections covering the measurement of target complaints; the theory and application of *Goal Attainment Scaling* (GAS); the use of self-anchoring scales; the development of configurational analysis for psychodynamic psychotherapy; Shapiro's work on personal questionnaires; and at some greater length their own work, developed from Singh and Bilbury's (1989) discretized analogue procedure ("Discan") for the assessment of subjective states. These initiatives seem increasingly to have been proposed less on the grounds of their being more accurate and more on the grounds of their being more ethical. At the heart of the argument lies the concept of *person-centredness.*

The heyday of behavioural assessment was the 1980s. It is poignant that the journal of the realistic dependent variables movement, *Behavioral Assessment*, ended by being incorporated into BRAT; its last bow being a bulky issue with a modest but dignified editorial valedictory summation in the closing months of 1992. With this the independent variable seems to have gracefully swallowed the dependent one. And with that necessarily died any attempt that might have been made to shift assessment from the standardized to the personal on the grounds of *that* being more "realistic".

Content, constructs and the "wedge"

To make the step from standardized to personalized assessment requires an understanding of how content and constructs are to be disentangled. This section seeks to sharpen the distinction between the two by looking at their respective places in assessment theory. It proposes that each is separated from the other by a theoretical "wedge". It then suggests that this wedge between these different types of assessment helps establish another distinction taken up later in the book (in chapters 5 and 6) between general and special work.

In an introduction to assessment theory written for trainee psychiatrists, Rowland (1985) suggested that to assess is "nothing more nor less than to ask a question" (p.223). Questions are asked about matters the practitioner is interested in, sometimes referred to as "criteria", and answers to those questions produced from "procedures" of greater or lesser formality. In theory, criteria are numerous and limited only by the range of matters practitioners profess to be interested in; in practice, the choice of criteria is more restricted and governed by the purpose of the assessment. For example: How depressed is this person? Are they safe to be treated psychodynamically? What problems have they got? The procedure can be a structured interview, or a psychometric test, or a self-report questionnaire, or an unstructured clinical interview, or data produced with some rationale designed expressly to answer the particular question.

Why talk of a *wedge* though? Rowland suggests that criteria fall into two categories in respect of the type of question put: "those which permit immediate and anticipated decisions to be made, and those which enable one to provide a description of an individual, descriptions which may have implications with respect to decisions which may have to be made in the future" (p.223).

This distinction ties in with that between constructs and content to the extent that questions which involve constructs are concerned with their presence or absence, *whether or not* they are present in some critical amount or to some critical degree, whereas questions relating to content tend to invite consideration of *what* is present: on the one hand, there is a question such as, "Is this person phobic?" and, on the other hand, a question more like, "What are this person's fears?" In this way, assessment theory offers a distinction between the assessment of constructs and the assessment of content.

The distinction between the two types of question also clarifies the distinction between Shapiro's indirect and direct methods of assessment. The existence of positive scores on the items of a standard questionnaire, such as "hatred of myself", or "feeling of guilt", or "inability to work", *indicate* by measuring it the presence of a something (depression, for example). In contrast, generation of personal items or statements, such as "not liking myself very much", "guilt about not doing more" and "fear of what may come up at work", *samples* that something by actually being part of it.

Part of what? Assessing content involves the sampling of some larger domain, for example, "emotional problems", or "issues that lead to the patient being referred", or "difficulties associated with being mentally ill". These domains resist conclusive or even persuasive definition. They are rather ones to be explored, described and represented as best one can.

The indicative procedure is in the loose sense of the word "diagnostic"; that involved in sampling might best be termed "descriptive". These relationships are summarized in Table 2.2. It is not a matter of the one type of assessment being "right" and the other "wrong". Rather, each has its uses. Depending on the stage work has reached, either one or other of the two will be of greater relevance.

The two tasks are simply different. Constructs are defined, rather than described. So it is inappropriate to tackle description by trying to improve on particular constructs or on a particular system of constructs, for example by advocating the adoption of a social or psychological set of constructs as an improvement on a medical set, as if there were a prospect here of finding a "better" one. This is because the issue is not about distinguishing the "social" or the "psychological" from the "medical". Instead, it is about disentangling separate strands within the framework of assessment theory.

Table 2.2 Distinctions between diagnostic and descriptive assessment (with a view to helping formalize and clarify differences between the measurement of constructs and the sampling of content)

Purpose of assessment	What happens	Relationship between test....	...and criterion	Nature of criterion	Function of criterion
"Diagnostic"	Patient responds and receives a total score on the "test".	This provides a measure which indicates...	...the degree of presence, or "strength" of the criterion	...which is a construct defined by its items...	...and which offers a diagnosis, predicting, discriminating and so on.
"Descriptive"	Patient generates some items.	This involves a sampling of...	the different areas of a criterion...	...which covers the content of something	...and provides a specific description of it.

Within assessment theory, the creation of a set of concerns as described in the next chapter belongs in the arena of content. The means proposed for achieving that requires some kind of structured interview. The practitioner avoids off-the-peg questionnaires of the prefabricated kind as a way of identifying concerns. To take this step though does not sound the death-knell for the use of assessment instruments of this type altogether. Standardized questionnaires are in the final analysis oriented towards classification, and, to the extent that a particular classification has been shown to be useful, they remain relevant.

In terms of the wider argument of the book, a *general* assessment task based on the assessment of *content* is being proposed here. This is distinguished from any number of *special* assessment tasks based, as often as not, on the assessment of *constructs*. In this book, the line of argument is that these special tasks often follow from the general one in pursuit of questions the general one has prompted. But this is a contentious position to adopt, because it is with special tasks of one kind or another that the contact with a service often starts. Routine procedures will be geared to answering questions such as the following:

- "Does this person meet the criteria for admission to our service?"
- "Is this person right for my approach?"
- "Has this person a serious mental illness?"

Where demand is high, where provision is specialized, where the service is "patchy" and where practitioners are isolated, the odds are that assessments will be special and not general. The general assessment task, although rarely completely omitted, may amount to little more than a box on a form marked "main difficulties" or even just "presenting problem". This distinction between general and special is taken up again in Chapter 5, where the usefulness of distinguishing general and special *work* begins to be explored.

Hesitant steps towards a concept of content

This section seeks to follow Shapiro's further thinking once he had adopted personal questionnaires around 1960. The method of personal questionnaires assumes the need to sample content de novo with each new patient. This is what is personal about it. The method accepts implicitly that it is no longer possible to assess using a fixed set of questionnaire items, ones previously generated and designed to assess the unchanging components of that measure, on which patients rate themselves on some kind of scale (for example, with a *yes, definitely*; or a *sometimes*; or a *four*; or a *hardly at all*). Instead, and in complete contrast, it has become necessary to work without a set of predetermined items, but with a clear sense of the content to be covered, within which patients are free to create their own items in their own words.

It is in pursuit of securing that clear sense of the content to be covered that the quest resumes. Shapiro's search after the nature of that content took the rest of his career. Indeed, he may never have completed it to his satisfaction. At the time I joined him, he was continuing to favour the notion that what he was looking for were *psychological dysfunctions*, and he had over the previous fifteen years or longer been working on various ideas of what the phenomena were that this term described.

A psychological dysfunction was a bit like an all-purpose construct; not a tight, well-established medical construct, but a loosely psychological one. He argued for a catholic approach to explanatory theory, shaped by the presentation of each individual patient: sometimes the psychological dysfunction might arise from a pathologically strong learnt association, sometimes from an unresolved conflict, sometimes from chronic frustration and so on. What he called psychological dysfunctions he first characterized as phenomena "causing considerable suffering", as "palpably out of accordance with fact" and as "maladaptive interaction, verbal and non-verbal" (Shapiro, 1963); later, he wrote of them as "distressing", as "disabling", as "socially inappropriate in the context of the patient's sub-culture" and as "incongruent with reality" (Shapiro, 1975b, 1985).

Something essential to this concept of psychological dysfunction was its link in Shapiro's mind with what he called "a systematic science of psychopathology" (Shapiro, 1975b). Inherent in the idea of psychopathology is the idea that there is something *wrong*. He was critical of psychiatric diagnostic categories largely on the grounds that these were not properly established (and wrote a number of papers on methodological issues in researching psychiatric depression). But he held for some years to the notion that patients should be seen as suffering from psychological dysfunctions, albeit that these dysfunctions were likely to be "relatively specific" to each patient.

He assessed them using the General Dysfunction Interview, regarding it as covering "quite familiar psychiatric ground" (Shapiro, 1975a, p.8). While he thought of the ground as broadly psychiatric, a person's personal statements of psychological dysfunction nevertheless had a distinctively individual feel. This reflected amongst much else "the inevitable complexities of natural phenomena" (Shapiro, 1985, p.5). Some years earlier, he had written this about the concerns of the clinical psychologist working as an applied scientist:

> The problems are those which are provided for the clinical psychologist by nature, as it were. The disorders of thinking, feeling, perception, behavior and physiological function are not deduced from any theory. Their appearance at the clinic often amazes and surprises the psychologist. In fact, there seems to be no aspect of human experience and behaviour which will not, in some exaggerated, diminished or repetitive form, present itself sometime or another as a dysfunction. (Shapiro, 1970, p.664)

Lodged in here is the notion of the psychological dysfunction as a reflection of a "disorder", something thrown up by nature to be assessed and treated. He writes elsewhere of the different *aspects* of a psychological dysfunction (self-reported, behavioural and so on); and this leaves a sense of a psychological dysfunction as something reified. If something has different aspects, it begins to assume an existence of its own. There is a something the different aspects are aspects of. Cone (1992) regarded this tendency to think of "superordinate constructs" as a legacy of trait-based views of emotion, views that suppose that these various different kinds of index measured the same *thing*. Even

Shapiro, so critical of trait-based personality theory, found it hard at times to shake off.

There is similarity between the concept of psychological dysfunction and Foulds' notion of personal illness that also dates from the 1960s and 1970s. Like Shapiro, he defines the personally ill by reference to notions of distress and relationship difficulty (Foulds with Caine, 1965). Like Shapiro, there is the sense in personal illness of a disorder of some kind. Unlike Shapiro, Foulds was prepared to propose classes and hierarchies of personal illness (Foulds, 1976).

While Shapiro held to the concept of psychological dysfunction, psychological dysfunctions supplied the content of what he was assessing and characterized that content in a psychopathological way. In the fullness of time, Shapiro dropped the notion of clinical psychologists as people engaged in developing a systematic science of psychopathology, preferring instead to speak of clinical psychology as "a branch of psychological science" (Shapiro, 1985). In his final paper, Shapiro (1989) had moved a little away from notions of psychopathology, at least from the implication that the clinical psychologist's job was limited to the investigating and treating of what was wrong. His description of "clinically relevant experiences and behaviour" in that paper is more of a mixed bag:

(1) Complaints
(2) Dysfunctions
(3) Malfunctions
(4) Disorders
(5) Symptoms
(6) Aversive experiences

In other words, dysfunctions were to be seen as just one thing the clinician might pick up and disorders another. More now was judged to be relevant; also judged to be relevant were what patients *brought*, matters like complaints and reports of aversive experiences and not just things patients *had*.

The underlying phenomenology seems here to be in the process of shifting from a phenomenology of disorders to a phenomenology of experiences. With the *bringing* comes the patient's direct experience of distress, while, with the *having*, that experience remained indirect, interpreted by someone else, in what Landfield years earlier had thought of as a confrontation between "personal urgency" and "professional reconstruction" (Landfield, 1975). It is easy now in retrospect to see how beginning to shift the terminology away from psychopathology towards demoting the concept of psychological dysfunction makes good sense. It was harder to see the good sense of it at the time and still harder to see how actually *everything* a patient describes and expresses is a bringing from the patient's point of view. One way in which matters might be taken from there, to arrive at a concept of content based entirely on the concerns that patients bring, is described in the next chapter.

CHAPTER 3

Data: Creating, Collecting and Reviewing

I thought psychologists measured things.

Older lady doctor to J.C., one evening in the staff canteen at Torbay General Hospital, 1986

This chapter draws out the implications of Chapter 2 for assessment procedure. In that chapter the idea of the need to sample, rather than measure, content was presented in a theoretical way. This chapter sets out a sequence of steps in harnessing content for practical purposes. It describes a way of assessing people's concerns and how personal questionnaires can be constructed from them. It shows how progress can be documented. Some attention is given to the way concerns can be reviewed and amended, as work progresses, and to the possibility of reflecting on process and outcome, as a practitioner looks back at what he or she has achieved over a period of time. By these means, it explains how the illustrative material later in this book came into being.

For now, the practices described are treated as having general application to a variety of counselling and clinical settings. The presumption is that there exists a common task with broad requirements, one that emerges from the decision to address content in settings where initial assessment priorities are mainly descriptive and exploratory and where the precise direction of the work to follow remains open.

The Traveller from Altruria

When I finished my clinical psychological training course at the Maudsley, I moved to the West of England where I had found a job on the outskirts of Bristol based at Glenside, an old Victorian psychiatric hospital. My time there over the next six years was divided between working on the wards, seeing outpatients in the hospital's psychology department and providing sessions to a couple of local health centres. From the first day I started to use Shapiro's procedures as laid out in the manuals that made up the two parts of *The Assessment of Psychological Dysfunctions* (Shapiro, 1975a) that I had come to know during my training.

I continued to see Shapiro in the years that followed, up until the mid-1990s but particularly in the early and mid-1980s when we were considering our collaboration on a book and then again after he and his wife Jean came to live in Bristol in 1989. Although we had many very valuable discussions, I feel now I was slow in my own labours to grasp many of the more important ideas relating to assessment theory, particularly the various implications of the pivotal distinction between content and constructs on which much of the argument of this book relies. Shapiro was very much at home with this material, although I don't think either of us was properly alert to the potential significance of differentiating, as I did at the end of the last chapter, between what patients *brought* and what they *had*.

As I see it now, people bring concerns (content) that may sometimes usefully or plausibly be understood by a practitioner in terms of having a disorder (construct) of some kind. All concerns are though in the first instance just concerns. At the time though, I was preoccupied with no longer being at the Maudsley and with the feeling that the psychiatric language of psychological dysfunction seemed less well to fit the new population I was seeing in community settings in Fishponds, Eastville and other parts of north-east Bristol. I found that sometimes patients would come not knowing what the problem was, or not knowing how to express it, or feeling they just shouldn't have a problem. I found problems were more often described as intolerable or unbearable than as intense or severe. And sometimes what seemed to make the problem so intolerable, or unbearable, was how the patient explained the problem to himself or herself. For example: "I am going to have a heart attack", or "I am going mad", or "It's my fault", or "It's just me" (Chalkley, 2004).

The practical question was how, if not in terms of the "quite familiar psychiatric ground" of the psychological dysfunctions interview, I was going to construct a new form of interview more suitable for the people I was now seeing. How, to put it more formally, was I to define what was to be sampled? What was my descriptive hypothesis?

The answer was offered to me in a timely and fortuitous way when Lyn Segal from the Brief Therapy Centre at Palo Alto came on a lecture tour to Bristol soon after the publication of the book *Tactics of Change* (Fisch, Weakland and Segal, 1982). In Chapter 1 of this book, the authors imagine a Martian visitor, sent to Earth to find out about psychotherapy and required to report back to Martian colleagues on his return. They pretend that the Man from Mars has been asked to report on "what an intelligent but naïve observer" like him would "perceive as common and characteristic if he could look in on an adequate sample – especially initial interviews – of actual psychotherapy sessions" (p.11). They justify this manoeuvre by saying that "though this may seem a superficial approach, it has the advantages of simplicity, concreteness, and minimization of presuppositions and inferences". In their view, the Martian would "over and over" have noted the following:

(1) A client expresses concerns about some behaviour – actions, thoughts or feelings – of himself or another person with whom he is significantly involved.
(2) This behaviour is described as deviant – unusual or inappropriate to the point of abnormality – and distressing or harmful, immediately or potentially, either to the "behaver" (the patient) or to others.
(3) It is reported that efforts have been made either by the patient or by others to stop or alter this behaviour, but they have been unsuccessful.
(4) Therefore, either the patient or others concerned are seeking the therapist's help in changing the situation, which they have not been able to change on their own (p.11).

In essence, the approach sees psychological problems as ordinary difficulties where attempted solutions to those difficulties have not worked and may actually have made things worse.

The radicalism of this proposal seems to lie in the notion of problems as building to a point where they are *taken* to someone somewhere. The interest is in what distinguishes them from ordinary problems, not in what causes them. This idea was very easy to extend. Instead of the report by the visitor from Mars, I with my literary interest in imaginary countries chose to adopt a fresh analysis. The new analysis comes from nearer home. It is one made by the Traveller from Altruria. This traveller is one of the series of visitors who from time to time have come to Europe and the Americas on a research mission from the still surprisingly little-known island continent in the southern oceans. William Dean Howells was the first person to write about Altruria; he did so in his books *A Traveller from Altruria* and *Through the Eye of a Needle* (Howells, 1894; Howells, 1907). Something of the background to these visits is given in Box E.

Box E: The Traveller from Altruria

The essayist and novelist William Dean Howells imagines a visit paid over the years 1892 and 1893 to the United States by Aristide Homos, a citizen of the great and enlightened island continent of Altruria in the southern oceans, which is never precisely situated in Howell's books. While people know about Altruria, or at least claim to know about it, Altruria discourages contact with the rest of the world ("the egoistic world"), assisted in this by an economic self-sufficiency unknown almost anywhere else. There are no direct sea links between America and Altruria, and indeed the voyage to Altruria only seems possible by opportunist changes of vessel mid-ocean. Altrurians have been visiting the rest of the world for many years, but Aristide Homos's visit is the first with any claim to be called "official".

His host in America is the romantic writer, Mr Twelvemough, author of comforting titles like *Glove and Gauntlet* and *Airs and Graces*, who – presumably at his own expense – puts up the traveller, Aristide Homos, at a hotel in the White Mountains of New Hampshire. Mr Homos' stay is a longish one and includes time spent in New York. He is something of a lion in society; the conversations faithfully reported by Mr Twelvemough, and later recorded in Homos' letters to his friend Cyril back in Altruria, include conversations with a banker, a professor and a society hostess, as well as a poor farmer and the farmer's ailing mother.

Altruria has known difficult times. Founded as a commune by an early Christian apostle (off route between the Holy Lands and Britain), the early "communist" impulse was lost in the period of rampant competitive capitalism known as *The Accumulation*. Recovery has taken the better part of a millennium. Even when the worst excesses of the period had been controlled, the old guard for long demanded "immunity and impunity". By the end of the nineteenth century, well advanced into the period of *The Evolution*, the nation has recovered the pleasure of doing a thing slowly and well.

It is remarked that during *The Accumulation*, "the insane were an army, an awful army of anguish and despair". Otherwise, the subjects of psychological and physical health and well-being receive no attention from Mr Homos, whose preoccupations (understandably for the period) dwell more on housing, noise, lack of light, domestic service, the plight of women and the cost of living. Now,

Box E: (Continued)

over one hundred years later, we can imagine another visitor, no doubt sharing with Mr Homos his sense of deep concern and polite indignation at what he finds and concerned at this point to explain to his Altrurian correspondent the phenomenon of seeking help for psychological difficulties, as he encounters it in a society still markedly less altruistic than his own.

The Altrurian's observations are more expansive than the Martian's. They are set out below as a descriptive hypothesis in nine sections, each section postulating a situation where ordinary difficulties become the kind of concerns one might encounter in a counselling or clinical setting. These sections represent loose conceptualizations that when strung together are intended to help the practitioner cover a certain amount of ground. Each section explains how the concern arises and then gives examples of what a patient might say.

Coping and Crisis: The concern arises because the patient feels *either* that he or she is no longer coping with difficulties, *or* a significant personal crisis is indicated. *I can't cope any longer; I'm in a state of total crisis; I feel frightened by my inability to cope; I am totally reliant on others to get by; I feel I am only coping on the surface; I feel overwhelmed by the number of my problems.*

Definition and Communication: The concern arises because the patient feels that he or she *either* cannot define *or* cannot communicate his or her difficulties in a way which is acceptable to him or her. *I have completely lost touch with my feelings; I feel I constantly deny there is a problem; I'm upset that I can find no way of understanding my difficulties; I cannot sort out whether I have a problem or not; I believe odd things are happening to me; I am unsure if I want to ask for help.*

Explanation and Appraisal: The concern arises because the patient finds his or her own explanation of the difficulties distressing; indeed the explanation is likely to be more distressing than the experiences (if these are still remembered) for which the explanation is sought. *I worry about what may be wrong with me; I fear I may be going mad; I'm terrified by the thought that I have a serious illness; I feel it's all my own fault; I feel I'm despicably weak; I believe I am a victim of my past.*

Response of Others: The concern arises because others' reaction (or lack of reaction) to the patient or the patient's difficulties aggravates those difficulties. *I have no one to talk to about how I feel inside; I feel no one believes what*

I tell them; I believe people are losing patience with me; I fear that I'm making my daughter's anorexia worse; I feel something bad is going to happen in my personal life; I am upset that other people think there is something wrong with me; I feel a failure in my relationships; I feel I distance people.

Unacceptable Feelings: The concern arises because the patient has difficulty accepting or tolerating some intense physical or mental experience, for example, a pain or mood: *I feel I am too angry; I cannot bear the sadness; I feel ashamed to be anxious so much of the time; I have great difficulty dealing with the tension in my neck; I can't face this loneliness; I am terrified of my voices; I am frightened when I feel myself leaving my body.*

Routine and Practical Matters: The concern arises because difficulties have amassed to the point where the patient perceives himself or herself to be no longer able to function in routine and practical matters. *I cannot get up in time to get to work; I find I am unreliable about collecting my daughter from school; my papers are in a state of total disorder; I cannot concentrate; I cannot bear to meet people; I wake up several hours early every morning; I am quite unable to eat enough to maintain my weight.*

Control and Identity: The concern arises because the patient has a distressing feeling that he or she is *either* not in control of his or her own feelings or actions (or fears this situation will soon arise), *or* in some other way that his or her existence as a person is under threat. *I have habits I can't give up although I want to; I get impulses I can't resist; I must always be in control; I fear I will lose all power to do anything for myself; I believe I must do what the voices tell me; I have distressing thoughts that just come into my head; I believe I'm many different people; I feel I have no sense of who I am.*

Desperation: The concern arises because the patient's difficulties have created a state of desperation. *I feel there is no future; I feel desperate; I feel completely hopeless; I want to kill myself; I feel like walking out on my family; I feel I will have to throw in my job; I feel like attacking someone.*

Solutions and Stuckness: The concern arises *either* because the patient feels attempts to solve his or her difficulties are stuck, *or* in some way the solutions tried are more problematic than the difficulties themselves: *I feel completely stuck; I feel I am not trying hard enough; I keep doing the same thing over and over again; I'm jumping from one solution to the next; I'm always running to my doctor for re-assurance; I avoid doing anything; I freeze like a rabbit.*

This is not a diagnostic interview. It has not been designed to place phenomena in classes, and the separate sections are not the product of any kind of cluster or factor analysis. This is because the intention behind the interview is descriptive, to capture the patient's concerns whole and live without categorization or division. The value of the interview, more a purposeful conversation, lies in the way it assembles a multiplicity of phenomena, the meaning of any particular statement of concern drawing on the meaning of the other concerns. (A point that will be returned to in later chapters is that single concerns make little sense by themselves in the absence of that kind of context.)

Most of the illustrations that follow in this book have used the Altrurian's observations as their starting point. The idea in generating this piece of make-believe is not surreptitiously to demarcate the "true" territory of psychological investigation. It is not even an attempt to begin such a process; rather, it is the attempt of one practitioner (myself) to be explicit about the heartland of his work, as he sees it at a particular time and place. Other practitioners will vary in the approach they take on this matter, reflecting their different trainings, orientations, client populations and work situations. This means that, to the extent other practitioners choose to think from first principles about the content of their work, as if they too were a visitor from distant parts, their view of its content will contain much that is a personal response to their particular circumstances.

Another way of looking at the matter is to treat the Altrurian's observations as an unvalidated theory about people seeking professional help; about what it is that brings people to a counsellor or clinician. But such a theory is one that resists conclusive evidence or definitive proof. David Smail illustrated this point by showing ways in which his patients' experiences of the world were beginning to be shaped by the new and disturbing social and environmental forces that were starting to define Mrs Thatcher's Britain of the 1980s. He summed it up this way: "One cannot… hope to say anything eternally true about the actual phenomena of our distress, the content of our pain. We can only fight a kind of running battle to keep track of it" (Smail, 2001, p.94).

Sampling a person's concerns

Having defined the potential terrain, the next step is to find a way of surveying it that will allow patients' actual concerns to be identified. Coverage cannot be limitless and so the activity involved is a sampling one, a search each time for a set of concerns that is *representative* rather than exhaustive. In the examples of the security guard and the baptist lay preacher (see Chapter 1), for instance, this led eventually to a selection of ten concerns each. But there is no limit set a priori on the number of concerns. Instead, patient and practitioner seek to explore the nature and extent of the patient's difficulties, while keeping the amount of material manageable.

How is the sampling to be done? The procedure I adopted was to use a relatively structured personal interview, including a bank of pre-set questions of my own choosing, from which I made a selection as the interview unfolded. I supplemented this by questions I devised on the spot. A selection from a larger set of such questions, designed to match the Altrurian's observations, is set out below:

Open Question

Would you try and put your concerns in your own words?

Coping and crisis

What made up your mind to seek help?
Do you feel frightened much of the time?
How well have you been coping recently?
How have things got worse recently?
Do you feel you are in some kind of crisis?
Do you feel under a lot of pressure?

Formulation and communication

Is there one particular problem?
Do you bottle things up?
Can you put your problems into words?
How do you feel about seeing me?
What is the thought in your head right now?
Do you think people are listening to what you have to say?

Explanation and appraisal

What do you think is the cause of your present difficulties?
How do you feel about yourself as a person?
Is anybody or anything to blame?
How does the past affect your present difficulties?
How do you compare with other people?
Do you believe you are weak, ... or vulnerable?

People and their responses

Who have you been able to discuss things with?
Does a relationship with anybody close contribute to your difficulties in any way?
Do you feel very cut off from people?
How are your difficulties affecting people you know well?

What do you think other people feel about you?
What has anybody said to you recently that has greatly upset you?

Discomfort and acceptance of discomfort

How do you feel in yourself?
What feelings seem to overwhelm you from time to time?
Do your feelings frighten you?
Do you have an overwhelming sense of frustration; or annoyance; or unfairness; or abuse?
What unpleasant physical feelings do you experience: tension? pain? fatigue? restlessness? breathing difficulties? dizziness? shakiness?
Do you have any strange or frightening experiences (like hallucinations or feeling things are unreal)?

Routine and practical

Can you get yourself organized on a daily basis?
What practical difficulties do you face?
Are there things that you can't face doing which you feel you should?
How are your concentration and memory?
How's your sleep?
How's your appetite?

Autonomy and control

Do you feel things have got or are beginning to get out of control?
What would you like to change but might find difficult?
What blocks you from doing the things you want to?
Are there any thoughts, or pictures in your mind's eye, which keep coming back to you and bother you a lot?
How does people's help sometimes not help?
Do you get urges or impulses that it is hard to resist?

Desperation

How do you feel about the future?
Do you feel desperate?
Have you thought of doing away with yourself?
Do you often feel like hitting somebody... or smashing something?
What else do you consider doing at particularly bad moments?
Do you feel hopeless?

Solutions and stuckness

How have you tried to cope up to now?
Do you feel stuck?... or trapped?

What do you find yourself doing over and over again without really wanting to?
Do you find you seek a lot of re-assurance from people?
Do you find yourself relying on food, or alcohol, or drugs to make life bearable?
Do you keep yourself terribly busy, or push yourself terribly hard?

Open Question (again)

Would you like to try again to put your concerns in your own words?

These questions (limited here to *just* the six that over the years I believe I most frequently asked from each section of the longer schedule) form the basis of the assessment interview used in the illustrative material in the following chapters. In further describing that procedure here, my intention is to give a sense of what I usually did in obtaining this material, not to provide a set of instructions on how to interview descriptively.

My customary practice was to do the following:

(1) Keep a printed sheet of the full set of questions beside me, having numbered each question for ease of reference in the margin.

(2) Record what the patient said reasonably fully, being faithful to the words he or she used.

(3) Suggest to the patient that questions were answered in terms of the last month, or a shorter period if the patient felt there has been too much fluctuation within the last month for a month to serve as a reliable basis for the description.

(4) Ask the open question, preferably at the end as well as the beginning of the interview.

(5) Then ask a *selection* of the questions in any order, at least one question from each section, recording the numbers of the questions I picked in the margin of my notes.

(6) Watch out for answers that might not represent concerns to the patient, and check them out by asking: "Is that a concern?" or "How does that concern you?" I would mark a "C" in the margin of my notes to show where I had done this.

(7) Be prepared to ask additional questions (devised there and then), always writing the question out fairly fully and putting an "X" in the margin.

(8) Expect the interview to last at least a full session and allow myself to let it run on for two, or three or even more sessions, where I judged this necessary and in some sense therapeutic.

Here is the opening part of a fictionalized transcript of an interview, as I might have tried to reconstruct it from the notes of a session. It gives an idea of how one can move around the interview, once familiarity with the pro forma has been established, once a numbering system for questions has been devised and once the habit of precisely noting the phrasing of answers has become second nature. Beyond this, the idea of the example is to show movement through the interview pro forma; the way questions will move backwards and forwards between sections; the manner in which supplementary questions are generated in response to things said; and the need to ask a patient from time to time whether something he or she has said is a concern.

JC. Would you like to have a shot at putting your difficulties in your own words?
Pt. I am constantly in a state of depression. The Citalopram has helped, but .... (*tails off*)
JC. How have you been coping recently?
Pt. Not very well. I feel I'm going down quite quickly. I've started to be less conscientious at work.
JC. Does that concern you? [C]
Pt. Yes, It's a sign of the way things are going .... I don't believe I can be helped.
JC. Is it like you almost want to do things to make things worse? [X]
Pt. Yes, but I don't want to be this way.
JC. Do you feel under a lot of pressure?
Pt. Not really.
JC. Do you bottle things up?
Pt. Yes, I do. Not consciously, but I am not very open about stuff. And I'm not very assertive, if it impacts on someone. I'll never say if I'm upset,... but then I don't realise I'm upset. I don't *do* anger. Suddenly, it surges. I can feel it in extremes. I don't express it. I probably direct it inwards. I'll always side with the victim. Not with me, though.
JC. Do you need a lot of re-assurance from people that they like you?
Pt. Yes!
JC. Is that a concern to you? [C]
Pt. Yes, I try and make people like me.
JC. How do you feel about yourself as a person?

Pt. I don't like myself.

JC. Got any idea why you don't like yourself? [X]

Pt. I don't like the depression, which seems like part of myself. It's the opposite of being reasonable or normal. And I don't like my body, which isn't like I want it to be – overweight, big. It's like there are two parts to me. The rational part is reasonable .... The feeling part, the depressed part, says I need everyone to like me. I'm lazy, selfish, self-obsessed, boring.

JC. How are your difficulties affecting people you know well?

Pt. Well, my husband is really pretty understanding. That's also a problem in a way. It's so unfair on him. So I usually try and hide how I feel.

JC. What do you think is the cause of your present difficulties?

Pt. I don't know.

JC. Is that a concern? [C]

Pt. Yes. I am always trying to find out.

JC. Do you sometimes feel you are weak or vulnerable?

Pt. Yes, weak. Yes, vulnerable .... to everything. Risk. Change. Even saying what I feel.

JC. What has anybody said to you recently that has greatly upset you?

Pt. My father-in-law said how clueless about current affairs I was. It was a turning point of a kind. O.K. I don't follow the news much. It's too upsetting. But he really is rather uncouth. I shouted at him. I never do that.

JC. Does that concern you? [C]

Pt. Yes. I hate to come over so sharply. People like me for my softness. I understand people too much. It's difficult for me to behave negatively towards someone. I want to be nice all the time; and now I can't be anymore ....

It is worth asking at this point whether processes and procedures quite as elaborate as these defining and sampling activities are really necessary. Do matters need to be this explicit and systematic? There are other ways of eliciting concerns. When papers first started to be written in the United States based on the undefined use of *target complaints*, the practitioner simply asked for one problem, and then another, until a list was built up (Battle, Imber, Hoen-Saric, Stone, Nash and Frank, 1966).

Robert Elliott, Carol Mack and David Shapiro devised a procedure called "Simplified Personal Questionnaire Procedure 9/99". It was available for a time on the Internet. The idea was to generate items from each of five areas, eventually limiting the patient to the ten he or she judged the most important overall:

- Symptoms
- Mood
- An area of *specific performance*, like work
- Relationships
- Self-esteem

Rather than view it as an interview, the authors saw the undertaking as a brainstorm. They encouraged the patient to generate as many items as possible. They had in mind an initial fifteen that could then be reduced down to the ten. If the brainstorm failed to produce the ten, then the practitioner might help the patient pick out items from a standardized screening measure.

I have tended to favour a tighter structure. This is in part a guard against the *After-Lunch Effect* or *Off-Day Syndrome*. But my readiness to work with a set procedure also reflects an apprehension that my own intuitive processes might need some curbing; it reveals my doubts about the wisdom of simply following my nose through clinical interviews and asking just whatever comes to mind. Reflecting on his own experiences as an applied psychologist with the Israel Defence Force, Daniel Kahneman concludes that "implementing interviewing procedures... requires relatively little effort but substantial discipline" (Kahneman, 2011, p.232).

Constructing and administering personal questionnaires

Whatever the procedure adopted, however structured or unstructured, whether interview, or brainstorm, or the most random of listings, at some point the material produced is scrutinized by patient and practitioner. They start to sift through the answers, picking out which add most to a sense of the overall landscape, to the sense from the patient's point of view that she or he has been at least well understood and from the practitioner's that she or he has been sufficiently thorough.

Sharing and assembling

Shapiro suggested a break at this point, the descriptive assessment to be set aside, the practitioner to go away and ponder over the notes of the session(s), underlining all the statements of concern, and then to bring back to the next session a set of items for practitioner and patient to discuss. But whether or not a break is first taken, the job to be done is the collaborative one of setting down the patient's concerns in the patient's own words.

Following are the additional steps I adopted at this point:

(1) Before further conversation with my patient, to go through what I had written in my notes and underline statements of concern the patient had made ("concern" meant concern to him or her, not to me)

(2) Next, now once more in conversation with the patient, with a fresh piece of paper to hand, to start to compose a *list of statements of concern* aiming to be *representative* of his or her concerns, presuming there to be too many to record all of them

(3) To stick as closely as possible to the patient's own words but be prepared to re-word things a little to make the statements more amenable to change, or more relevant to the aims of the work to the limited extent that the patient and I already understood them, but at all costs to be faithful to the essence of the patient's concern. "I'm the worst mother in the world" might become "I believe I'm the worst mother in the world". In some instances, though, a patient might feel that nothing less than "I am certain I'm the worst mother in the world" would do. (Shifting certainty to belief might sometimes be judged an important *treatment* task)

(4) To word each phrase as simply as possible. An example of the sort of sentence to avoid would be: "concern about my complete absence of any feeling of being available for other people"; actually, any sentence beginning with a negative created difficulty and was best avoided; better might be: "concern about always feeling unavailable for other people"

(5) Then to re-phrase (or "re-jig") each statement of concern so that it begins, or *could* grammatically begin, with an "a" or a "the" or a "my", for example: "(a) feeling of being at the end of my tether", "(the) difficulty I am having taking in anything you are saying", "(my) concern about the future". "Sense" and "feeling", and indeed "concern", are useful filler words. After re-phrasing, "I believe I'm the worst mother in the world" would now become "the belief I'm the worst mother in the world". (I could sometimes get away with just a noun: "hopelessness" or "frustration", for example; even so, it was usually worth trying to be a little more precise: "hopelessness about everything", "frustration about what's happening at work" and so on)

(6) To make sure I had avoided "ands" and "ors", for example: "concern about my stomach pains and headaches" (the rating becomes

difficult if the stomach pains improve, but not the headaches, or vice versa; so, if the inclusion of both stomach aches and headaches seems crucial, I might create two separate questionnaire items)

(7) To make sure too that each concern could readily be rated "considerable", "moderate" or "slight"

(8) Then to read the list out to the patient and ask him or her to check that each statement was *now, or had been recently, a considerable concern* and that I had the concern expressed right. It was important to make the patient feel I understood the concern correctly and that I wasn't just being polite

I would want if possible to have the items assembled within a session or two of the initial contact. If there were to be no questionnaire, just a set of items, then the steps from (5) onwards could in theory be omitted. One needed a questionnaire when it was clear that there would be contact over some length of time. Then, the items would need wording in a way that allowed for repeated assessment, the frequency of which I saw as a clinical and therapeutic decision to be made person by person.

The dilemma in practice was less *whether* than *how soon* to construct the questionnaire. Shapiro, much influenced by Rogerian ideas, was concerned that his approach to interviewing should facilitate the discovery of unrecognized feelings (Shapiro, 1979), implicitly a prolonged, open-ended process, lacking a definitive, final state. At the same time, he saw his procedure as a means of establishing whether progress was being made, and it is precisely this that gives rise to the idea of a personal *questionnaire*, this with its ring of something structured and systematic, suitable for administration at regular intervals.

There is a tension between these two impulses. On the one hand, there is the need to give ample time to a process of exploration, not necessarily one with a very clear end in sight. On the other hand, there is the wish to create an early baseline and so bear testimony to progress, or its lack (Hayes and Nelson, 1986), but this at the risk of curtailing a dynamic therapeutic process.

It is a familiar dilemma and one that leads to sharp differences of emphasis among individual counsellors and clinicians, and between therapeutic approaches. For the majority of patients, it may be possible to argue that the set of concerns established with the patient at the outset will provide a "good enough" description. (Sometimes the impression formed is of a set of discrete problems; sometimes different aspects of a single problem; usually something in between the two.) In many instances, the creation of the set may involve little refinement beyond the initial assessment. But individual questionnaire items may be badly phrased and need changing. This may not be apparent at the start but becomes obvious once the aims of the work become clearer, or perhaps "obvious" only once the work is finished. For example, I came in retrospect to realize that the statement included in one set of concerns: *feeling that effort doesn't make things better* had been poorly worded. The issue had been more to do with the patient's sense that she ought to try harder to accept things as they were and a better wording of the item might have been: *feeling of being under pressure to accept things as they are.*

Alternatively, this process of refining items later may be more a sign of treatment success than assessment failure. An exploration of the patient's difficulties may over time, perhaps over quite a short space of time, allow them to be re-cast in new, less entrenched ways. A patient who is certain that she is the worst mother in the world may become one who just holds a strong belief that she is. The longer and the more complex the work, the more likely it is that the content of a personal questionnaire will require revision. Sometimes, a personal questionnaire, as initially constructed, offers only a beginning, a first approximation in need of addition or refinement as fresh material surfaces. The following are some guidelines in managing this process:

(1) Add items which identify new concerns and which significantly expand or change the overall description.
(2) Substitute items which relate to old concerns and which represent a clearer or more accurate expression of them.
(3) Drop items that misrepresent the aims of the work being undertaken as these aims evolve.
(4) Do not drop items just because they have improved: they may get worse again.
(5) Seek to maintain a balanced questionnaire that is *representative* (rather than exhaustive) of all areas of concern and contains about fifteen items (plus or minus three).
(6) Consider re-interviewing from scratch where the episode of contact is prolonged and some fresh thinking seems necessary.

Administering and scoring

The administration of the questionnaires once constructed drew on an adaptation of a procedure first developed by David Mulhall called the *Personal Questionnaire Rapid Scaling Technique* or *PQRST.* This piece of clinical technology (Mulhall, 1976) required the use of a pink booklet consisting of a set of laminated pages that when turned revealed more and more of a loose score-sheet slipped inside the back cover of the booklet. On this sheet, patients made their ratings column by column. The National Foundation for Educational Research (NFER) produced this booklet with its accompanying manual for some years. David Mulhall and I adapted it for routine clinical use by reducing the number of ratings per item from ten to three. This gave a four-point scale. The adaptations were published as an article in the *British Journal of Clinical Psychology* under the title *The PQRSTUV: The Personal Questionnaire Rapid Scaling Technique – "Ultimate Version"* (Chalkley and Mulhall, 1991).

The pink booklet is now out of print. What it offered was a way of presenting items to the patient as a succession of forced choices. Once on each of the three laminated pages of PQRSTUV the patient would see reference to each of the questionnaire items. For example:

The first time:
Fear of my feelings – very considerable □
Fear of my feelings – moderate □
The second time:
Fear my feelings – moderate □
Fear of my feelings – very slight □
The third time:
Fear of my feelings – very slight □
Fear of my feelings – very considerable □

This paired comparison procedure meant that the patient had only to choose between the two statements laid out before her, rather than try and match her internal state against a choice of four "boxed" response categories in the manner of the more commonly employed Likert scale. Furthermore, it was possible to establish, given the sequence of comparisons, whether the choices the patient made were consistent with one another. (The three paired comparisons can be sorted in eight ways, but only four of them make sense. For example, it defies simple logic on a particular occasion to prefer the "very considerable" item to the "moderate" item the first time but moments later the "very slight" item to the "very considerable" item.)

It has become possible in recent years to use a procedure much like Shapiro's original one by taking advantage of the download offered by Stephen Morley from his website at the Leeds Institute of Health Sciences. Morley trained with Shapiro in the mid-1970s. The website has a link named *Personal Questionnaire*. This consists of a single folder called *EasyPQ*. The folder contains two PDF files, one a set of pro formas and the other a set of instructions. The development of *EasyPQ* was originally prompted by requests from members of the Leeds clinical psychology training course. The instructions end with an appreciation of Monte Shapiro as a clinician and include a link to the obituary Morley wrote for *The Guardian* newspaper upon Shapiro's death at the end of April 2000 (Morley, 2000).

Resuming this account of my own practice in handling ratings of concerns, such as those found in the following chapters, the final steps, after asking the patient to fill in the pages of the increasingly tattered pink booklet, have been the following:

(1) Ask the patient to make the self-rating.
(2) Transfer the ratings for the particular occasion on to a summary sheet.
(3) Record the median score.

Table 3.1 shows a summary sheet. The sheet records the session date, the session number, the rating period (usually for me the last week) and offers a number of extra rows at the bottom for additional information of one kind or another. Quite often, I have chosen to use these to record daily medication dosages, but in the example shown, I record before–after scores on CORE-OM (Connell, Barkham, Evans, Margison, McGrath and Milne, n.d.).

The summary sheet also offers a line for recording the median score for the ratings the patient makes on a particular occasion. The median has always seemed preferable to the mean as a way of obtaining an average score for a given session because it does not treat scores on different items as related to one another and so avoids the apples and pears problem. What does a "4" for sadness and a "3" on wrath add up to? Seven presumably. But seven what? Seven of what? Seven on what? There is no underlying construct or other variable to turn to, so no single scale or dimension on which items can be added and therefore no prospect of summing a total score from which legitimately to derive a mean by dividing by the number of items. In contrast, the calculation of a median doesn't involve any addition.

The intrusion of quantitative measurement at this late stage may seem brutal, almost a betrayal. Is this after all to be a quantitative rather than a qualitative type of assessment? No, it is not: the accuracy remains largely in the words and their faithfulness to the common language. The strategy is as described earlier: "qualitative with numbers". And its

Table 3.1 Seven sets of personal questionnaire ratings (showing scores on ten individual items and their median)

Session number	**8**	**11**	**14**	**19**	**23**	**27**	**31**
Date	**15 January**	**13 February**	**18 March**	**2 September**	**14 October**	**9 December**	**24 February**
Feeling of being lost in a world of my own	4	4	3	4	3	2	2
Sense of needing to block bad feelings out	3	3	3	4	3	2	1
Sense that I don't like myself very much	4	4	3	4	3	2	1
Feeling of fear that it will all begin again	4	3	3	3	4	1	1
Difficulty concentrating on anything	4	4	3	3	2	2	2
Tendency to wake many times during the night	4	4	3	2	3	4	2
Urge to cut myself	3	1	1	1	2	1	1
Furious feelings towards my stepbrother	4	3	3	2	2	4	4
Tendency to rely on distracting myself internally	4	4	4	4	4	3	3
Difficulty letting anything go	4	4	3	2	2	4	3
MEDIAN	4	4	3	3	3	2	2
CORE-OM	2.0						0.8

essence lies in the sampling of the sources of psychological distress, not in their measurement.

An alternative

This book is about counselling and clinical method rather than assessment technique, and there is a need to re-affirm its central thesis: that what needs most earnestly to be presented is a set of arguments about the importance of paying attention to content, to personal descriptions in ordinary language. Any procedure that fulfils this objective in a trustworthy and relevant way exercises a claim on a practitioner's attention.

The rest of the book presumes the existence of a personalized descriptive procedure of some kind, and this chapter has described one such procedure, the one in fact used in almost all the illustrative material that follows. Another such procedure is "Discan" (Singh and Bilsbury, 1989). Discan (Discretalized Analogue Scaling) differs from personal questionnaires in a number of respects. One difference is that Singh and Bilsbury manage without anyone like the Altrurian and suggest instead that practitioners make a choice among "suitable clinical unions of selected elements" (SCUSEs), a phrase they take from Wright and Feinstein (1992). These elements consist variously of a patient's symptoms, the complications and consequences of those symptoms, the poor quality of life endured by the patient and the patient's troubles coping and functioning. The list is not exhaustive but illustrative of the sort of material likely to be relevant, its type varying from patient to patient. One patient might present with just symptoms and another with a combination of symptoms and poor quality of life factors.

These SCUSEs provide a focus of therapeutic attention (FOTA). Bilsbury and Richman (2002) illustrate with one they call "restless legs". Here, the patient has listed a number of elements. He describes being "restless all evening and night; my knees begin to twitch in the early evening and don't stop; they awaken me in the middle of the night and I can't fall back to sleep" (p.26).

Where a personal questionnaire describes itemized concerns and judges at every administration the level of *each* concern in terms of the adjectives "considerable", "moderate" and "slight", Discan, having brought together the elements into a single prose passage, goes on to create similarly constructed but milder prose passages for less severe levels of concern. The language of these is personal too. "The manner in which they cascade from worst to best is unique to the patient" (p.21). In relation to the target complaint "restless legs", having specified level

4 (restless all evening and night, and so on), patient and practitioner go on to specify three further levels:

Level 3 (restless on and off). My knees begin to twitch in the early evening and continue intermittently. This may awake me in the middle of the night; then it is hard to fall back to sleep.

Level 2 (awareness of my knees). My knees don't actually twitch in the evening, but I feel I want to pull my kneecaps off. They don't usually awaken me.

Level 1 (not restless). I hardly notice my knees; they don't disturb my sleep.

Selective comparisons can be made between levels to achieve a rating; and because four rather than three levels are involved, a higher number of scale points emerge. However, the patient can also be asked to make judgements of whether they feel better or worse than just one particular level, and this adds still more to the number of rating points available.

Another difference between personal questionnaires and Discan is the way settings are established. Where in personal questionnaires settings are embedded partly within the particular item (for example, "fear of losing control of my feelings *in the office*") and partly by the rating instruction (for example, "*rate for the last seven days*"); with Discan, context is supplied by a single phrase which precedes the prose passages like "*when I go to bed at night*...", or "*generally over the last week*..."

Discan does much the same job as personal questionnaires, and this brief summary of it illustrates how the ideographic[1] (that is to say, the person-focused rather than population-focused) task of descriptive assessment can be done in more than just one way. In the remainder of this book, the illustrations, based as they are on my own practice, draw on personal questionnaire technique, but this technique represents just one among a number that share roughly the same intention.

Reviewing outcomes

Table 3.2 sets out a line of very basic outcome data for each of forty patients. The fourth column gives the number of *fours*, *threes*, *twos* and *ones* at the final assessment. A median score has been worked out from these in column five. The single numbers in that column represent

[1] Runyon (1983) quotes R.R. Holt describing the terms *ideographic* and *nomothetic* as "pretentious jargon, mouth-filling polysyllables to awe the uninitiated".

Table 3.2 Outcome data from the forty most recent personal questionnaires

1. Person	2. Comments	3. Number of sessions	4. Number of 4s, 3s, 2s and 1s at the finish	5. Median score From column 4.
1		9	2,2,8,6	Two
2		About 5	0,4,5,1	Two
3	Back in hospital within days	About 6	0,0,3,11	One
4		20	6,4,3,6	Three
5		31	1,2,3,4	Two
6		15	1,3,5,1	Two
7	Previous person re-contacted	13	0,1,1,4	One
8		32+FU	2,3,10,7	Two
9		15+FU	0,1,4,11	One
10	Withdrew	18	9,3,2,0	Four
11		About 8	2,4,3,5	Two
12		About 6	0,1,5,1	Two
13		19	11,2,2,0	Four
14		About 20	1,3,3,7	Two
15		45 + FU	5,3,2,6	Two
16		28 + FU	1,5,6,6	Two
17		41	1,2,7,4	Two
18		16	3,0,3,7	One
19	Withdrew	5	15,0,0,0	Four
20		12	10,1,0,1	Four
21	Moved abroad	30	10,6,0,1	Four
22		23	1,4,8,2	Two
23		24 + FU	1,0,0,11	One
24		14	1,4,0,1	Three
25		About 10	0,0,3,13	One
26		28 + FU	0,4,2,14	One
27		About 10	10,0,0,0	Four
28		29	1,0,3,9	Two
29		About 8	4,1,1,9	One
30		26	1,5,6,4	Two
31		6	0,0,2,11	One
32		8	0,0,0,10	One
33	Handed over before finish	25	6,7,1,3	Three

Table 3.2 (Continued)

1. Person	2. Comments	3. Number of sessions	4. Number of 4s, 3s, 2s and 1s at the finish	5. Median score From column 4.
34		17	9,4,3,4	Three
35	Still being seen by someone else	48	6,6,5,1	Three
36	Handed over before finish	About 30	9,3,2,1	Four
37	Handed over before finish	About 8	15,0,0,4	Four
38		10	0,1,7,3	Two
39		7	0,3,6,7	Two
40		32	0,4,10,5	Two

*Median size of personal questionnaires: 15 items; 1st quartile 12; 3rd quartile 17. Modal size of personal questionnaires: 14, 15 and 16 items equally. FU = Follow-Up.

a calculation of progress. As a summary, these outcomes represent as follows:

- A *Four*. Unchanged or worse overall (eight patients)
- A *Three*. Slight improvement overall (five patients)
- A *Two*. Moderate improvement overall (seventeen patients)
- A *One*. Considerable improvement overall (ten patients)

Each patient is usually a *four* to begin with overall and occasionally a *three* (if there has been improvement recently). Sometimes, the line of outcome data belies the facts. The most uncomfortable instance of this among the forty is the person in Row 3 who is summarily rated a *one*, in other words as “considerably improved”. In fact, she was not and had within days been re-admitted to the acute psychiatric ward. She explained to me later that she had described herself as considerably improved in order to remove herself from a therapy she felt she didn’t deserve. On the other hand, I felt there were signs that the person in Row 21, still a *four* after many sessions, was finally on the eve of some kind of breakthrough at the time of her move abroad.

The majority of patients (all but twelve) still had some considerable concerns at the finish. This is clear when one turns back from column 5 to column 4. In column 4, the numbers represent the following:

- Fours: very considerable concern
- Threes: moderate concern, but closer to considerable than slight
- Twos: moderate concern, but closer to slight than considerable
- Ones: very slight concern

On average (the median of the scores of all forty patients), the number of concerns remaining at *four* lies halfway between one and two (1.5). The range of the number of concerns remaining at *four* lies between zero and fifteen.

A more thorough review than this might now turn to examine what kinds of concern tended not to improve. It is of course only one form of review, offering numerically nothing about the process of reaching the outcome. That received scant attention from me over the years. But a quick study early in my early career suggested that improvement or lack of improvement in the overall level of concerns in the first four sessions was a good indicator of how much progress I was likely to make.

Something has been lost by the absence of standardized population-based measures. Among the illustrations that follow, personal questionnaire data have occasionally been shown supported by scores on standardized construct measures of one kind or another (Tables 3.1, 5.1, 5.4 and 6.4). But I have not routinely used standardized outcome measures and certainly not the same one on every occasion. Therefore, questions remain unanswered about how these forty patients compare with others, for example the large West Yorkshire outpatient sample, whose patterns of progress and outcome have been extensively surveyed using versions of Clinical Outcomes in Routine Evaluation (CORE), in practice-based evidence studies such as those by Evans, Connell, Barkham, Marshall and Mellor-Clark (2003) and Stulz, Lutz, Leach, Lucock and Barkham (2007).

This very basic review rests just on the sampling of relevant personal experience in the person's own words. Clinical researchers will at such a point quite possibly want to turn to hypothetical constructs, and experimental psychologists to psychophysiological instruments. As Daniel Gilbert recently wrote about measures of happiness: "Scientists who rely on the honest, real-time reports of attentive individuals often feel the need to defend that choice by reminding us that these reports correlate strongly with other measures... But in a sense, they've got it backward..." (Gilbert, 2006, p.66). A measure measures whatever the measure has been shown to measure. If a measure of personal concerns is wanted, then it is the measure of personal concerns that provides the anchor, and not some other measure. Gilbert concedes that we might be puzzled by somebody's reports, sceptical about their memory or unsure of their ability to use language as we do. "But when all our hand wringing is over, we must admit that [this person] is the *only* person who has the *slightest* chance of describing 'the view from in here', which is why [his or her] claims serve as the gold standard against which all other measures are measured."

CHAPTER 4

Psychological Concerns

I worked in a variety of settings (long-stay psychiatric wards, hospital outpatient departments, health centres and community mental health teams), gradually evolving a descriptive interview close to the Altrurian traveller's described in Chapter 3. In 1992, I found myself co-opted to the academic board of one of England's clinical psychology training courses, where by the end of the first meeting I was asked if I could teach "something on assessment". Assessment, back then, was not a popular topic among trainers or trainees.

It was soon clear to me that a "scientific" call for clarity per se would never be enough to engage the interest of most trainees; nor indeed would be some narrow notion of relevance, or "validity", within the framework of assessment theory. Trainees, barraged by a daily flood of new material and usually struggling to work out what to offer a particular patient they were about to meet again later that week, were really looking for something they could see would make an impact on their work. This was usually conceived quite concretely in terms of building relationships with patients and forming ideas about what to do. The same applies, writing now: arguments for content are unlikely to succeed until practitioners feel clear that greater attention to content through the sampling and itemizing of concerns will actually enhance the work they do.

Therefore, this chapter suggests ways that content, harnessed in the form of psychological concerns, can help practitioners. The five sections of this chapter argue roughly as follows:

(1) The process of establishing a person's concerns in their own words helps build a relationship between patient and practitioner.

(2) The use of the patient's own words enables the practitioner to gain a greater understanding of the meaning and context of what is being described.
(3) The attention to the patient's own words permits what is being *expressed* to be communicated, as well as what is being *described*.
(4) The provision of concerns in sets helps the practitioner think about content as a whole, and not draw over-rapid inferences from bits of it in isolation.
(5) The completion of the assessment exercise takes the practitioner and patient to a point of reflection where ideas and possibilities about how to take the work forward begin to suggest themselves (as then illustrated in chapters 5, 6 and 7).

Help in building a relationship

Attention paid to process, as will be later argued in this book, is not enough in itself to create work of the personal, systematic, accountable kind envisaged here. But good process is essential. So, before turning to how statements of concern describe and express content, it is worth reflecting on how talking about concerns with a patient becomes a vehicle for establishing the kind of relationship that needs to follow. Another way of thinking about this would be to ask what it is about the content of the conversation that might, from the patient's point of view, be perceived as supportive and personal.

- First of all, the content is personal to just this one patient. The set is not a long checklist where some problems are relevant and others not; neither is it a short listing of them where some problems have been remembered and others overlooked.
- Secondly, this personal content is *striven for*. The patient experiences someone else's care and diligence as the practitioner sets about the painstaking process of recording and checking the person's concerns. There is a concern on the practitioner's part to get the description *right*. This is as much a moral endeavour as it is a scientific one.
- Thirdly, while there is a structure to the procedures, they also have flexibility and can be modified in various ways, in accord with the patient's needs and interests: for example, modified in the order of topics, the questions asked, the amount of questioning and how the procedures are spread out over the early sessions. In other words, the practitioner adapts and modifies the procedures to suit circumstances.

- Finally, the patient stands to gain a sense of working collaboratively with the practitioner. Descriptive assessments are shared activities and personal questionnaires joint constructions, as far removed as possible from any notion of them as "instruments", devices administered in the pursuit of some menacing psychological abstraction or in obedience to the diktats of a remote department of state. The assessment, moreover, serves as a prelude and sets the tone for what is to follow.

Description in ordinary language

Chapter 2 described the early evolution of a concept of content. Then, Chapter 3 went on to explain how that concept, having been developed a little, might be operationalized. One may feel there has been a certain softening, a certain thawing out, as one moves away from the technical language of constructs, trait measurement, dysfunctions and relative specificity towards the more prosaic one of content and the sampling of concerns.

Concerns as rooted in ordinary language and human contexts

Now, it is necessary to reflect a little about the nature of these psychological concerns. To talk thus far about them as personal and specific reflects the way they are embedded contextually in the actual people, proclivities, situations and circumstances of a person's life. When content is personalized, context shines through: an unhappy affair, a definitive betrayal, a last chance, an ongoing divorce, uncertain employment status, an undiagnosed fibroid, a sick grandchild, serious financial hardship, long-standing illness, no job at all, the situation in Kenya, a lifetime of losses, economic migration, a despairing nature, an unfortunate oversight, a disadvantageous postcode, a family quarrel, increasing personal responsibilities, deteriorating sight, constant tinnitus, accusations of underachievement, a crisis of values, unexplained weight gain, a message from Xanadu, a near fatal yachting accident, a protracted recovery from zoophobia.

To do justice to context requires the precision and accuracy that can only be found in the patient's own words. However, by personalizing assessment, a way is found to tap the semantic wealth and syntactic complexity of the language available for people to draw on at times of difficulty. Shapiro managed this feat by being bold enough to challenge the conventional understanding of what constitutes a questionnaire.

His achievement can be turned to good use. There now arises a general loosening as ordinary words and phrases come naturally to supply the content of descriptive assessments, and sets of concerns begin to reflect the particularities of people's lives.

Before looking later at the force of concerns working in sets, here are some examples of how the greater freedom of vocabulary and grammar impacts upon them singly:

- Rather than be restricted to a *feeling of sadness*, a person might describe *a feeling of misery*, or *despondency*, or *bleakness*, or *wretchedness*, or *dejection*, or *gloom*, or *having a heavy heart.*
- A person might supply context by describing *despondency about his job prospects* or *a sense of wretchedness because of his status in life.*
- A person could, of course, simply talk about *concern about not being able to put my experiences into words*; but then someone else might describe *the frustration of trying to put my experiences into words* or perhaps *the embarrassment of trying to raise the things that preoccupy me.*
- Rather than *fear* (one item) and *anger* (another one), a person might want to put them together and describe *a fear of my anger.*
- Plenty of people might be distressed about *the unbearable pain of the past*, but someone further along the path to recovery might instead be concerned about *my need to hold on to the pain of the past.*
- One person might complain of *a sense of my gambling as out of control*, but another of his *belief that gambling is the only ok way to deal with my problems.* A third might speak to the practitioner of his *concern that you might try to stop me gambling.*
- Examples from later in this book where, like the gambler, a patient addresses himself or herself directly to the practitioner are: *concern that I am wasting Jack Chalkley's time and he's not telling me* (Table 4.2), and *my need for you to go extremely carefully with certain topics* (Table 7.3). Slightly less direct is *the feeling I have that the voice doesn't want me to talk to you* (Table 5.6).

Concerns as descriptive of experience

Something too needs to be said about the range of experience that comes as the broader notion of the concerns patients bring replaces the narrower one of the disorders patients have. Once this shift is made to assessing patients' experiences and the content of their concerns, disorders are replaced by *perceptions of* disorder, *and* these now arrive along with their "consequences and complications" (a phrase Bilsbury and

Table 4.1 List of concerns identified by Miss A., who lives with her parents and has a small child

Difficulty stopping washing my face over and over again once I have started
Feeling ashamed of myself after washing this way
Feeling of anxiety if I don't wash my face
Tendency to snap at my family after periods of washing
Feeling that I need to clean away everything not "right" with my face
Concern about the frequency of my face washing
Sense of myself as just existing
Concern that there is nothing I know how to do
Uncertainty about how to deal with my mum and dad when they interfere
Sense of not knowing how I feel about anything
Tendency always to be worrying about life in general
Feeling of being dirty when I fetch my daughter from the nursery
Concern that other parents know I am less together than I appear

Richman attribute to Alvan Feinstein). Sometimes, something disorderlike will fill a description. But it is no longer a construct; rather, it is a focus of content. Table 4.1 illustrates the effect.

While there is some ranging around the issue, six of Miss A.'s concerns refer to her washing. The washing provides the focus, but the concerns describe Miss A.'s distressing experiences of washing; they do not define the constituent parts of some washing condition or syndrome.

What, from this perspective, is one to consider a disorder, and what a consequence or a complication of it? With mental health, notions of disorder and illness are not so clear-cut as they are in physical health. They seem to merge with their consequences and complications. So often in mental health, it is recurrent and longer-term problems that are under consideration. These bring with them plenty of causes of additional concern: sectioning, hospital admission, misdiagnosis, the side-effects of medication, loss of earnings, relationship disruption, relapse, loss of social role, stigma associated with mental illness, discontinuities of service provision, suspension of benefits, homelessness, apparently arbitrary failure to meet eligibility criteria and the termination of services altogether. Of course, all this contains the possibility of further or greater illness as the patient loses confidence, identity and hope. Matters then start to circle and spiral.

Sometimes the sense of a disorder is largely lacking; at least the sense of a mental health disorder. The concerns in Table 4.2 provide an illustration. The original problem arose when Mrs B., a widow

Table 4.2 List of concerns of Mrs B., a seventy-year-old widow waiting for a cataract operation

Sense I will no longer be able to maintain my own home
Frustration at how little I can do at present with my eyesight so unclear
Belief that I ought to be saying everything's all right even though I don't feel it is
Feeling that my daughters can't take much more of me as I am
Feeling I will lose contact with my grandchildren
Concern that I am wasting Jack Chalkley's time and he's not telling me
Fear I will go blind
Need to scream at times
Belief that my behaviour remains unforgivable
Belief that I am losing my wits
Worry about what is going to happen to me, given how things are
Sense that everything is pretty desperate

living on her own, started to develop cataract. Numerous problems followed as a result, and these built up to such a degree and were of such a kind that for a time she was admitted as a patient to an inpatient psychiatric unit. One thing seemed to lead to another. The list of concerns has an almost storybook quality to it. Increasingly poor vision meant she was reluctant to tend to the garden or go rambling. Telling nobody to begin with, not even her daughters who lived locally and whom she saw often, she worried more and more about what was going to happen to her. She found it increasingly hard to perform tasks around the house. As she became more preoccupied, she found communication more and more difficult. She couldn't bear to allow her grandchildren to see her in the state she was in and began to think she was losing her wits. The sense of frustration as she became less capable, combined with her reluctance to seek any acknowledgement of her difficulties, and her ever-increasing worry about the future, all seem to be the factors that brought on her sudden outbursts of screaming. These outbursts confirmed in her view that she was losing her mind.

Expression as well as description

So far concerns have been treated entirely as *descriptive* acts of communication. But it is also possible to see them as *expressive* ones. Danziger (1976) argued that the words which pass between people are not just to be understood as a series of statements about how they are experiencing themselves, their bodies, their futures, other people, the world and so on, but are also to be understood as how people project their view of the relationship between themselves and the particular person they are speaking with. (Steven Pinker is offering a similar distinction when he writes: "People use language not just to transfer ideas from head to head but to negotiate the kind of relationship they wish to have with their conversational partner" (Pinker, 2007, p.3).)

Danziger distinguished these two aspects of communication as *representation* and *presentation*. He gives as an example the following: "If a husband says to his wife: 'This steak is burnt again', the quarrel that ensues is not over the correctness of the information conveyed but over the implication that she is a careless cook and a poor housekeeper" (pp.188–189). Representation is what we have been dealing with in the previous section on description. It operates on what Danziger (p.26) calls "the hoary model of human communication", according to which there is always a speaker, a listener and a referent that is talked about. (Here, information is passing from husband to wife about the state of a bit of meat.) Presentation, on the other hand, reflects the speaker's view of the nature of the relationship between the speaker and the listener. (Here, the man is assuming the familiar role of chiding husband, or at least trying to. The woman may, or may not, in her response permit the reciprocal role of hounded wife to be imposed upon her.) Danziger thinks that presentation usually constitutes the major purpose of the communication. One can talk without any real information passing between the parties but not without saying anything about the relationship between them. For the most part, "pragmatics" trumps "semantics".

The Palo Alto concept of "position" shares with Danziger something of this dual view of communication. In expressing their concerns in a certain way, rather than just describing them, patients *position* themselves in relation to the therapist, not just with respect to what the content of their concerns is but to what has caused those concerns, what is to be done about them, whether anything can be done about them and whether the particular therapist is the man or woman to be entrusted with the task (Fisch, Weakland and Segal, 1982). The patient makes an active bid to define reality in a certain way, rather than to just sit back and passively report on how reality appears to him or her.

Positional statements within the Palo Alto approach to *Doing Therapy Briefly* are seen as shaping how particular psychological interventions are to be framed and worded. Intriguingly, where Danziger holds to the traditional view that the therapist must listen not just to the verbal content of the patient's message but also to what the patient's words conceal, the Palo Alto view is that position is gauged by listening to the patient's exact wording.

> Whereas conventional psychotherapy places importance on listening for the underlying meaning of what the patient says, we emphasize the importance of listening to the exact wording of patients' remarks, because it is in the specific wording that they indicate their positions. (Fisch, Weakland and Segal, 1982, p.193)

An example is given in Table 4.3. Written in italics are those statements of concern which might also be construed as statements of position. As a position, they run something as follows: "I am helpless. Things are pretty much as bad as they could be; which people like you seem unable take on board. Consequently they don't understand, and expect too much of me. Don't be too sure that *your* ideas are going to help me either."

Should the concerns that have been picked out as position statements be prioritized as treatment targets? It may be that change to them depends on progress elsewhere. Perhaps such statements, as expressive communications, are not so much a series of individual concerns

Table 4.3 List of concerns of Ms I., an unemployed twenty-five-year-old woman living alone in her wealthy parents' house on the outskirts of town

Sense that time is running out for me
Sense of being completely lost
Lack of interest in anything
Feeling like a clockwork spring wound up all the time
Concern about older people in the neighbourhood disapproving of the people I need to hang out with sometimes
Sense of estrangement living in the respectable outskirts of the town
Feeling that I am bad news so far as my "friends" are concerned
Sense that no one ever, ever listens to my problems
Concern that you professionals don't appreciate the limits to how much I can change
Belief that my ability to take anything on board is permanently lost due to the drugs I have taken
Belief that I am as socially handicapped as it is possible to be
Feeling that I am paralyzed by shyness
Feeling of terrific injustice over what my parents did with the money my uncle left me
Tendency to give way to other people automatically and not stand up for myself
Feeling that I can only rely on drugs to dampen down my anxiety and depression
Feeling all is doomed around me

Table 4.4 List of concerns of Mr L., a thirty-year-old man recently promoted at work

Sense of being very sad a lot of the time
Feeling of hopelessness about everything
Sense of not knowing what I am doing with my life
Concern that I cannot control my feelings of anger about my father
Sense I am never going to achieve anything in any job I do
Uncertainty about whether I should be making as much as I am of my problems
Difficulty concentrating on my exercise routines
Concern that I am physically going down hill
Sense of emptiness about the recent promotion
Sense that deep down I am the problem
Feeling of being in two minds about whether I need help
Tendency to be zonked out for periods of time and not care about any of this
Fear that people will think less of me because of my beer drinking

to be addressed as a series of clues to how a set of concerns is best comprehended.

A second example is presented in Table 4.4. Here, the message is more along the lines of, "I'm really in two minds about seeing you, and at times may find it impossible to give myself over to the work, being on those occasions altogether past caring, and sensing in any case that there may not be anything legitimate to speak about at all, since the problem is just me."

Understanding and acknowledging statements of position affects how far change is possible, while ignoring them risks exacerbating the stuckness that characterizes the patient's predicament, as the practitioner becomes caught up in the same goo. Positions may need to be worked around rather than confronted directly. They shape the practitioner's response. They influence the language and concepts that the practitioner uses and may determine the purpose of the work. While counsellors and clinicians with experience may in some way come in time to absorb position material instinctively, it seems no bad thing for such material to be made explicit in a way that will assist efforts to begin to make sense of things.

A whole set to take account of

Daniel Kahneman's experimental work on heuristics, biases and overconfidence in making choices and decisions brings out the dangers of interpretation and judgement on the basis of too little information.

"At work here is that powerful WYSIATI (What You See is All There Is) rule. You cannot help dealing with the limited information you have as if it were all there is to know" (Kahneman, 2011, p.201). He goes on to warn that, "paradoxically, it is easier to construct a coherent story when you know little". The lesson from this, in the broadest of terms, is to seek to increase the information available.

Making judgements about a patient's state of mind, whether to intervene in a particular way and what will happen if one does or doesn't, are usually at the forefront of a practitioner's mind. One source of information will be content. The implication of Kahneman's findings for the practitioner would seem to be to base judgements and decisions on as much content as possible.

However, many such judgements and decisions involve predictions on the basis of some sort of explanation or understanding of the state of affairs. Here again, Daniel Kahneman (2011) warns about unrealistic expectations: "The ultimate test of an explanation is whether it would have made the event predictable in advance..." (Kahneman, 2011, p.200). By this criterion, he argues, most explanatory concepts in mental health will fail. An important lesson, he suggests, is for practitioners to grasp what kind of judgements are likely to be skilled ones and to have predictive power, and which ones not. The evidence he cites indicates that there is a marked contrast between practitioners' abilities to make long-term and short-term judgements:

> The correct judgments involve short-term predictions in the context of the therapeutic interview, a skill in which therapists may have years of practice. The tasks at which they fail typically require long-term predictions about the patient's future. These are much more difficult; even the best formulas do only modestly well, and they are also tasks the clinicians have never had the opportunity to learn properly – they would have to wait years for feedback, instead of receiving the instantaneous feedback of the clinical session. (Kahneman, 2011, p.228)

My own experience accords with this. I have found my ability to make predictions, certainly from single concerns, very limited. It is hard to imagine Kahneman being surprised by this. I would limit the concerns that I believed I had discovered for myself to have some predictive validity to just two, and this only in the short term:

- The existence of concerns about loss of *concentration* predicted lack of progress with psychological work and tended to encourage me to seek psychiatric involvement and medical review, which often led to the prescribing of antidepressant medication; where those actions led to improved concentration, the prospects for psychological work improved too.

- Similarly, concerns about *poor sleep* linked to a depressed presentation predicted lack of progress until successfully addressed, and also led me to seek psychiatric involvement and medical intervention; again, where those actions led to improved sleep, the prospects for psychological work improved too.

A number of other concerns I took on trust as pieces of clinical lore and treated as if they had predictive power, notably concerns about the *future* (for example, a statement like "there is no future"). Expressions of hopelessness caused me to consider the risk of suicide. To this might be added statements about *the problem*, where I came to respond in particular ways to statements like: "it's a silly problem" (more likely to be quite a serious one), or "it's just me – I'm the problem" (sometimes a difficult attribution to unpack and likely to require complicated work).

However, looking at *sets* of concerns in their entirety, one sees how a set contextualizes in a way that single concerns cannot. Consider the sets of items shown in Table 4.5 where two single items, first "constant thinking about killing myself" and then "constant voice of my old teacher in my head", are listed twice and depend for their meaning on the other three items in each group of four. It is hard to imagine a practitioner regarding the significance of the two items in each pairing as the same. The patients in the first pairing, both with thoughts of killing themselves, appear to be in quite different frames of mind. One seems ready to do it and wonders why he hasn't already. His other concerns seem purely practical, at least superficially so. The other patient worries *why* she is thinking about it and *that* she is thinking about it. In the second pairing, one patient is concerned to be hearing the voice and what it might mean; the other is concerned about the consequences both of doing and not doing what the voice is saying should be done.

Another way to illustrate much the same point is shown in Table 4.6. Here, you are to imagine the practitioner looking at Ms C.'s set of personal questionnaire results. The practitioner is wondering how much progress has been made. While there appears to be change for the better overall (in terms of the median score), not everything has improved. There has been improvement in the need to block bad feelings out, as there has been progress too with the sense of not liking herself very much. But there is no improvement in the concern about the feeling of rage towards her stepbrother; and there is only slight improvement in her difficulty letting things go.

Table 4.5 Contextual dependency of single personal questionnaire items

Constant thinking about killing myself
Feeling I should have done it long ago
Difficulty knowing what I should write in the suicide note
Worry that you might try and stop me
versus
Constant thinking about killing myself
Perplexity that I don't appreciate all that's good in my life
Huge guilt for continuing to think in this negative way
Fear for my children's wellbeing if I am gone
or
Constant voice of my old teacher in my head
Sense that there must be something terribly wrong with me to be hearing it
Confusion about what he might be trying to say to me
Distress that there is no one real talking to me instead
versus
Constant voice of my old teacher in my head
Fear of the consequences of disobeying him
The certainty that he will never leave me alone
Terror about what he wants me to do

Therefore, what determines whether sessions are safe to stop? Inevitably, there are many factors, but one of them will be how the items are understood in relation to one another. Feeling furious with a stepbrother may continue to be a concern and be rated as highly as before, but its significance seems less because the patient no longer feels the same need to block bad feelings out, or to cut herself (presumably in order to escape from the feelings). The meaning of any single item is near impossible to establish in isolation. Items are better understood in relation to other items. So, while it cannot altogether be a happy state of affairs to be so very angry with one's stepbrother, it is easier to carry that anger, and even perhaps to admit it, when it is not perceived as dangerous.

Material for reflection

The last section of this chapter addresses how concerns are to influence the work that follows their identification. Does content really

Table 4.6 Initial and final personal questionnaire ratings for Ms C., a teaching assistant in her mid-twenties

Session number	**8**	**31**
Date	**15 January Year I**	**24 February Year II**
Feeling of being lost in a world of my own	4	2
Sense of needing to block bad feelings out	3	1
Sense that I don't like myself very much	4	1
Feeling of fear that it will all begin again	4	1
Difficulty with concentrating on anything	4	2
Tendency to wake at various times during the night	4	2
Urge to cut myself	3	1
Furious feelings towards my stepbrother	4	4
Tendency to rely on distracting myself internally	4	3
Difficulty letting anything go	4	3
MEDIAN	4	2

help the practitioner and patient take things forward? Up to a certain moment, Shapiro seems to have seen his personalized assessments as merely tactical, as a technique to address the problem he found in ordinary, standardized ways of assessing. Solving that problem though had serendipitous consequences. A window was opened through which ordinary speech could be heard and people's worlds glimpsed. The possibility began to emerge that, in finding the tactic, he had also discovered a strategy and that what once had seemed just a technique was in reality better understood as a method. To provide clarity here in making the distinction between the two, *technique* is used in its sense of *means* or *device* and *method* to mean *system* or *approach*.

Perhaps, the distinction is a confusing one but nowhere near as confusing in the clinic as I found in the kitchen, from which experience I drew the lesson that the conscientious practitioner in fretting about technique should be clear that technique serves method, and not the other way round. See Box F.

Box F: Technique and method

Some years ago, suddenly needing to beef up my cooking for myself and my children, I came across two books by the French chef, Jacques Pépin (1976; 1979). One was called *La Téchnique* (its English subtitle being, "The Fundamental Techniques of Cooking: An Illustrated Guide") and the other *La Méthode* (its English subtitle being, "An Illustrated Guide to the Fundamental Skills of Cooking"). The first chapter in *La Téchnique* was called *La position du couteau*, or "Holding the Knife", and since in some sense this seemed fundamental to my purpose, being in something of a rush and unable to afford both books, I chose *La Téchnique*, despite noting the fact that the book went on immediately to discuss some esoteric topics, the first of which was in fact *ail* ("garlic"). Had my culinary instincts run counter to my priorities as a clinical psychologist though? At least, or so I believed, I had chosen my cookery book in a principled sort of way. Nineteen years passed until, my financial position having stabilized somewhat, I decided to go on line and search Amazon or ABE Books for the other volume. I was in luck. There was a copy in a bookshop in Southampton. When the volume arrived, I opened it and breathlessly surveyed the contents page only to discover that the first chapter of that volume was actually on the clearly still more fundamental subject of *L'aiguisage des couteaux*, or "How to Sharpen Knives", while the second chapter was on the absolutely fundamental matter of how to peel an onion (*Épluchage des oignons*). I have taken as a lesson from this experience that method is more fundamental than technique.

Reflecting on the content of the set of concerns

Having in the last section adopted the principle of working with the whole set of concerns, the next issue is what sort of inferences might one seek to draw from the set. Method in this context refers to how the particularities of a set of concerns provide a foundation for wider inferences and raising the kind of questions those inferences inspire. Questions pop up as the relationship forms; they occur as one begins to think about what has been described; and they arise in the experience of hearing how they have been expressed. Some examples follow:

- Am I being invited in? If not my patient, who else might be the real customer for my services? What kind of relationship seems to be emerging from, or is covertly implied by, our interaction?
- Do I see some recognizable pattern in the concerns? Is there a recognizable problem focus here? Something illness-like? Is it more a sense of a predicament of some kind? Should I be thinking more in terms of their consequences and complications than just particular disorders?
- Is something stuck? (If something is stuck, is it the person that is stuck, or rather the situation?) If it is the situation, are other people a part of it more than I am allowing, and should I be thinking more systemically?
- If it is something more illness- or disorder-like, is some kind of diagnostic entity, or perhaps some other kind of theoretical construct, beginning to emerge as a theme worth elaborating or exploring: for example, and more or less at random, literalism, or shame, or narcissism, or procrastination, or cognitive intrusion, or perfectionism, or learned helplessness?
- Alternatively, are these concerns less needing to be elaborated or explored in an intrapsychic way and viewed more from an interpersonal, or sociological, or cultural perspective?
- Do these concerns suggest the existence of particular intervention options available for discussion with my patient? Is the patient caught in an "attempted solution" in some unpleasant, unproductive way?
- Is there a call for urgent action now? Is there more immediate risk here than I have hitherto allowed for?
- Is work of a specialist kind required? Perhaps I am already inclining towards suggesting a particular type of psychological therapy?
- And later, in reviewing the work, the practitioner may ask: How am I doing? How are we doing? What's impeding progress? What point in the work have we reached? Where should we be going now? Should we be thinking of stopping?

The expectation is that the content of concerns will shape which questions seem most pressing with particular patients, what it is that needs to be explicated. Different questions will arise in relation to particular sets of concern as the work unwraps, unfolds and opens up. The questions are unlikely to be all equally pressing case by case. And the practitioner's training and experience will also affect their choice.

To reflect and to formulate?

At some moment, counsellors and clinicians start to have thoughts and form hunches about the material described and presented to them. When formalized, this process has in recent years often been referred to as *psychological formulation* or *psychotherapeutic formulation*. Making formulations shares with assessing content that bottom-up, particular-to-general quality that has just now been described as *method*.

Reflecting on what formulation might at heart be, Gillian Butler wrote some years ago: "The assumption that many clinicians of different orientations probably share about the psychological difficulties of others is this: at some level it all makes sense" (Butler, 1998, p.2); and Lucy Johnstone and Rudi Dallos (2006) actually subtitle their book on formulation: "Making Sense of People's Problems".

To make sense of things in a person-centred way requires making sense of things from the patient's position. Writing from a social constructionist point of view, Harper and Spelman (2006), in the book edited by Johnstone and Dallos on psychological formulation, stress "that passionate emphasis on the importance of listening to the words people say (as opposed to what we think they mean)" (p.100). "Who", they ask, "gets to define what the 'problem' is?" Another pair of writers on formulation in the same volume point out how far patients are from having a free hand in terms of what they can and cannot say, and emphasize how much care needs to be taken to secure the patient's "personal involvement and participation" (Miller and McClelland, 2006, p.133). They write that:

> the institutional context of clinical discourses is the "clinic" in its broadest sense, which shapes and is shaped by what can and cannot be said... From this perspective, it can be argued that in formulating we are located within a process of social control which has shifted away from overt forms of extended incarceration and the more brutal physical treatments towards subtler forms of control such as the processes and technologies of diagnosis, medication and therapy, but continues to serve the same ends. (pp.128–129)

They are concerned about the notion of the therapist as a technical expert. Proctor (2005) expresses something similar when she writes about the conflict between her roles as clinical psychologist (a role some of her colleagues might consider compatible with the language of formulation) and person-centred therapist (a role in which she, at least, would never countenance "formulating" or "pronouncing on" anyone).

Harper and Spelman favour "a process of ongoing collaborative sense making rather than one of developing objective or semi-objective descriptions of the causes of problems" (p.102). They warm to the words of Tom Anderson expressed towards the end of a two-day workshop he was giving in Liverpool; who had been described a patient, and then asked the question trainers dread: "What would you do in this situation?" To this, they report him replying after deep and lengthy thought: "Well, I would listen very carefully to what she said and then proceed from there." Agreeing that this is an understandable starting point for a respectable social constructionist to take, they conclude that, "it is really quite a challenge to develop our own formulation" (p.103).

Understanding the whole picture from the patient's point of view is rarely enough though. Danziger (1997) reviewing varieties of social construction shows compassion for conscience-stricken postmodern practitioners, fearful of seizing the initiative, but unsure how else to be effective therapeutically. Danziger provides them with a degree of legitimacy and solace:

> Therapeutic authority is not only arrogantly claimed [by therapists], it is also eagerly conferred by those on whom it is exercised. Help-seekers may even have good reason to collude in the construction of asymmetrical power relationships in a therapeutic context. (p.408)

It might make sense, therefore, to allow practitioners sufficient authority to put their knowledge and experience to the service of their distressed patients. What, at least, needs to be permitted is the attempt to make sense of a patient's *concerns*, and this may be more straightforward (and less contentious) than seeking to place those concerns within a formulation.

In thinking about concerns, one is, after all, thinking about just one class of assessment material. Formulation is potentially considerably more ambitious, bringing together different classes of information, and, understood from a multi-professional perspective, offering distinctive contributions from a number of disciplines. There are also to be reckoned with differences in how much emphasis is paid to formulation between different approaches to psychological therapy. The concept seems to sit comfortably within cognitive behavioural therapy, but to be seen as less crucial elsewhere. While the *Handbook of Counselling Psychology* (Woolfe, Strawbridge, Douglas and Dryden, 2010) also covers psychodynamic, humanistic and narrative approaches, the only references to formulation in the book occur in the chapter on CBT.

What though makes little sense from the present point of view is to seek to formulate without first taking account of a patient's concerns. Clare Crellin (1988) criticizes the practice of formulating before "hearing out the patient's narrative. This is actually neither logical nor scientific unless it is based on a purely technological approach to the client's problem" (p.26).

The matter of whether or not practitioners *should* then go on to formulate is a quite separate issue, one on which practitioners presumably will have differing views and one that lies outside the remit of this book to pronounce on. But it leads to a further thought: that one makes a *decision* to formulate, judging it on occasion a necessary or useful thing to do. It is no more mandatory than is diagnosis.

Accordingly, in what remains of this book there are *some* formulations, in much the same way that there are *some* diagnoses. In the next chapter, reference is made to formulation in the case of a patient hearing voices; in Chapter 6, a formulation is made in respect of a referral for psychodynamic therapy. In these examples, the concerns have helped arrive at something of an explanatory nature that fits the British Psychological Society's definition of formulation as "a hypothesis about a person's difficulties, which links theory with practice and guides the intervention" (British Psychological Society, 2011, p.2).

Proceeding from this point

In the end, what one might aspire to achieve from reflecting upon a set of concerns might be rather similar to what one might secure from pursuing a formulation: understanding, prioritizing, planning, predicting (short term more than long term) and reviewing, even if the activities involved lack formulation's greater thoroughness and formality.

In chapters 5 and 6, the various illustrations employed will bring out different ways of proceeding, taking the set of concerns in almost every case as a starting point. The sets contribute in different ways, for example:

- As a means of evaluation
- As a pointer to various matters needing to be covered
- As a set of options for a patient to consider
- As a guide to what to prioritize
- As a lead on where to turn
- As indicative of what might be going on
- As hinting that something else might be going on
- As a contribution to a formulation

- As symptoms of a diagnosis
- As furnishing material jointly to be chewed over
- As suggestive of how to relate
- As a source of ideas for intervention
- As helping define the nature of the work, or *naming* it
- As what wasn't uncovered at the outset and which needs painstakingly to be uncovered later

These functions combine and overlap, but usually there are a couple of phrases among them that best capture the precise nature of the contribution.

CHAPTER 5

General Work

This chapter explores the notion of *general work*, taking that to mean work where the primary focus is on content. General work can be very diverse. Emphasis is placed on this variety, it being content that defines a piece of general work, differentiates and names it.

Later in my career, I was part of a clinical psychology department that sought in various ways to take account of the broad nature of the one-to-one work it was asked to carry out. The conviction we held was that more was required of NHS psychologists than just the provision of certain designated psychological therapies. Many, perhaps most, routine referrals were of a "*Would You See So-and-So?*" kind, and, while there was certainly concern in taking up the discussion with the referrer to pin down what was really being asked, very often what the referrer wanted was a re-assessment from a fresh vantage point. With this re-assessment came the possibility in the referrer's mind of our going on to offer some coherent piece of additional work.

In other words, these requests were of a fairly general kind. They would lead on to specialist psychological therapy sometimes, and many of us had training in the modal therapies offered on the NHS: usually understood to be psychodynamic, cognitive behavioural, systemic and occasionally humanistic. But these "Would You See So-and-So?" requests also constituted a familiar if nameless *routine*, some kind of staple; and for some of us they represented a certain tradition, one which we sensed to be valuable but at risk of being lost as pressure mounted to funnel more and more patients into modal therapy. This chapter might be viewed as a response to that trend.

The distinction between general and special work

Of course, to describe work as a *routine* does not mean that it is easy, and arguably any mental health practitioner's routine activity is as hard, if not harder, to pursue than his or her specialist ones. There is missing the clear rationale and outline available for work falling within a well-developed specialist role. There may too be lacking the consultative and supervisory arrangements associated with the firmly established specialist activities to be found among the psychological therapies. The practitioner has to burrow his or her way through a thicket of complex material, to arrive at a notion of what needs to be done. And then do it.

Nonetheless, if not the easy part of their job, this kind of work can at least be thought of as what practitioners do *routinely*. It lies at the heart of what happens from day-to-day in the ordinary run of things, at least in those settings where practitioners are involved in regular one-to-one contact with patients. However, rather than continue to call this kind of work *routine* and further countenance the pejorative overtone of that word, it will henceforth be referred to as *general*. Likewise, rather than refer to its counterpart as *specialist*, with the unnecessary kudos attaching to that particular word, we will henceforth more often refer to it as just *special*. And in seeking here to pinpoint the distinction between the two sorts of work, rather than see the first as more intuitive and incremental, and the second as more modal and structured, the two will be distinguished by their assessment procedures.

To recap, Chapter 2 proposed a *general* assessment task based on the assessment of *content*. The personalized procedures involved were described in Chapter 3. This general assessment was distinguished from any number of *special* assessment tasks based, as often as not, on the assessment of *constructs*. The advantage of the distinction, so far as *general* work is concerned, is that it establishes each piece of such work on a secure content-based, phenomenological foundation. There is an advantage too in the distinction for *special* work: it allows special work to *be* special; a point to be taken up in the section on psychological therapies as special work that comes at the end of the next chapter.

General work so defined is in its essence varied. The variety arises from its personal nature, the way every piece is rooted in a patient's personal experience. Once one adopts this premise, it is necessary to be able to accommodate different metaphors and perspectives as patients describe and communicate their concerns in different ways. General work must avoid the hegemony of the single dominant idea explicitly or implicitly controlling the scene. Special work is different. There a single metaphor or perspective may well hold sway; and this holding sway really only becomes a problem where special work masquerades as general, as for example when a particular profession becomes too powerful or (in contrast) when resource shortfall and the lack of an affordable alternative encourage politicians and managers to press the extension of a particular approach beyond its natural territory.

But if hegemony is a danger, so is its opposite. This is the risk that the work will fail to take upon itself *any* metaphor or perspective at all and remain a timeless, shapeless, nameless entity throughout its duration. This namelessness is a particular risk in work that aspires to be patient-centred. There is always the possibility that it will drift, *just* consist of tracking and monitoring from session to session, attending to process, dealing compassionately and conscientiously with the issues of the moment; but *never* in conception be anything better than high-grade support or unbridled eclecticism. One needs to tackle the charge that the work is nothing more than a kind of *effluvium*, an outflow or stream of imperceptible particles.

What therefore is the service on offer to be beyond the tracking and monitoring of ongoing contact? Words that seem safe enough at first sight, like "therapy", risk being simultaneously both too vague a response and too much a standard one-size-fits-all one. What about psychological "education", "guidance" and "support", for example, as more accurate summaries of what the general activity involves, *sometimes*? Laying oneself open to the one-size-fits-all charge is particularly to be avoided by practitioners who continue to meet patients as individuals beyond the first few sessions. The work needs naming. Practitioners need to be clear about what they are doing, able to communicate it and when necessary able to defend it.

Nine named pieces of general work

The illustrations that follow aim to show the broad nature of a number of pieces of work that began with a personalized assessment. They also aim to give some idea of the possible range of a practitioner's use of the material deriving from it. Common to the different names is a phrase connecting an activity (for example, "offering", "processing", "collaborating over") to the focus of that activity (for example, "high-grade support", "a personal crisis", "a recurring psychiatric disorder"). The nine named pieces are the following:

- Emotionally processing a personal crisis
- Offering high-grade support
- Tackling a predicament

- Collaborating over a recurring psychiatric disorder
- Confronting obstacles on the path of development
- Finding meaning in psychosis
- Giving expression to the legacy of the past
- Soothing the savage breast
- Reversing an attempted solution

These illustrations do not represent an attempt at an exhaustive classification of a counsellor's or clinician's practice. Rather, the attempt is inspired by the sorts of ways in which over the years it has been possible to look upon some of the tasks that fall to me as a practitioner, those that are not special and fall more within the notion of regular psychological "casework". Sometimes the examples are really no more than a way of thinking about a particular piece of work after the event, an attempt to pick out the most striking from the variety of shifting positions in which patient and practitioner have found themselves with respect to one another over the course of their meetings. Other practitioners will, of course, find different recurring patterns in their own work and develop concepts and techniques to fit them. In doing this, there is the tension between, on the one hand, the need to do justice to the richness of the person as an individual and to the singularities of the situation and, on the other, to reap the benefits of circumstances and contexts with which the practitioner has become familiar and for which effective patterns of response have to a greater or lesser extent been found.

Emotionally processing a personal crisis

In this illustration, a list of concerns was constructed over a number of sessions and then administered as a personal questionnaire. The list and personal questionnaire results are shown in Table 5.1. The patient Mr E. was recovering well from a psychotic episode that had led to an admission under section in the weeks leading up to his first-year undergraduate history exams at university. The section had followed an "incident" at an undergraduate party, of which he had little memory. Someone he didn't know had called an ambulance, and he suddenly found himself on a psychiatric admissions ward. As much as anything else, he was distressed about his behaviour over the next forty-eight hours when he had used bad language with all and sundry and behaved as he saw it "untypically" towards two women members of the nursing staff and a psychiatric registrar (female). He could find no excuse for any of this, was wracked with guilt and considered his

Table 5.1 Personal questionnaire for Mr E., recovering from a psychotic episode

Session number	**4**	**8**	**10**
Date	**11/6**	**19/9**	**4/12**
Sense that my parents couldn't cope with my psychiatric admission	4	3	1
Feeling of no longer being worthy of my scholarship	4	2	1
Worries I may not prove able to finish my undergraduate course	4	3	2
Fear that my symptoms will come back	4	3	2
Continuing sense of shame about how I behaved on the ward	4	2	2
Sense that I can't get my side of the story of what happened across	2	1	1
Feeling that no one I know has a clue about how to be helpful after all this	3	3	2
Sense of still being traumatized by the section	4	4	2
Impossibility of talking about any of it with my college friends	4	2	2
Sense of being trapped by my diagnosis of psychosis	4	3	3
Concern about the possibility of being on antipsychotic medication indefinitely	4	4	2
MEDIAN	4	3	2
Raw score on the Trauma Symptom Inventory (TSI)	110	–	67

behaviour brutally to define him as "a psychotic". While he felt he had let his parents down hugely, he felt neither they, nor indeed anyone else, had the least notion now of how to be with him.

The follow-up to the admission took place on an outpatient basis when the patient had returned home. No fixed number of sessions was set, the view being that a better approach would be first to concentrate sessions, maximizing as far as possible the sense of time and availability, and then allow a slow process of attenuation as matters were worked through at the patient's own pace, the psychologist suggesting that things would probably improve rather more slowly than the patient expected, with the possibility of "relapses" (concerns worsening) along the way. The sessions roamed over the items in the questionnaire, individual sessions tending to concentrate on just one of the identified issues. Further items were added to in a way that defied clear demarcation between stages in the work, although there was a sense of a moment being reached when enough material had been assembled to furnish the conversation with sufficient areas of focus, providing the sessions with a representative selection of material, if not an exhaustive one. This approach (concentration in time of the early sessions – building up of material – working through it – attenuation – warnings of slowness and possible worsenings along the way) offers something of a paradigm for other cases, often ones involving loss.

What purpose did the list and the personal questionnaire derived from it serve? For the most part, the items represented particularly charged emotional matters that required airing, collectively expressive of the personal crisis. One or two were included that were slightly marginal to the crisis, but which the patient identified as recurring issues in times of difficulty. The set allowed the psychologist and Mr E. to look at matters in a bounded way. Use of the list as a questionnaire to establish whether progress was being made was kept limited, given the emphasis of the work on working things through slowly and the slightly paradoxical quality of the intervention ("more haste, less speed").

Offering high-grade support

Some portion of most psychological work involves high-grade support from time to time, notably when crises arise and must be addressed. However, in certain contexts, *much*, or even *all*, of the work is high-grade support. During these periods, the emphasis is on managing matters in the here and now, the content and quality of what is managed quite possibly shifting from session to session.

The concerns in Table 5.2 illustrates their potential immediacy in the situation of Mr F., a computer software engineer, homeless and sofa surfing as he and his Cypriot wife proceed through divorce proceedings, begin the sale of the family home and arrive at a mutual realization that there is neither the income nor capital available to sustain the family in its broken situation. Mr F. visits the house now only to maintain contact with his two sons, aged 4 and 2, but each time Mr and Mrs F. happen on each other, the tension between them becomes more unbearable.

Mr F. has been carrying a great deal of unexpressed emotion for a long time as he begins to see a counsellor for regular sessions. He is trying with great difficulty to cling to the belief that somehow he will find a way through it all and that life will not be terribly different on

Table 5.2 List of concerns of Mr F., in the middle of a divorce

Sense of the instability of my family situation
Need to keep very busy in order to hold myself together
Concern that my wife is trying to keep my children away from me
Feeling of being under huge financial pressure
Difficulty stopping money slipping through my fingers
Tendency to wake very anxious in the early hours
Terror that she might just up and go back to Cyprus with our boys
Sense of the unfairness of it all between us over the years
The stress of entering a war zone when visiting the house
Need to keep the lid tightly down on my stronger feelings
Terror that I might just lose control of everything
The difficulty of seeing my way through all this

the other side: his children still in the United Kingdom and in regular contact with him, his wife appeased, himself less frantic and with somewhere to live, and the money once more arriving in acceptable quantities from somewhere or other.

Tackling a predicament

Where the consequences and complications of a disorder are more to the fore than the disorder that gave rise to them, one might speak of a "predicament". With mental health problems, predicaments can develop very rapidly. This one though had built up rather slowly. In 1993, Professor J., a foreign-born teacher of English literature had moved to this country from Central Europe, where he had held a senior academic post, with his wife. He was then in his early forties. He subsequently suffered a deterioration in his mental health and had been in on–off contact with the CMHT for ten or so years. Something of a stalemate had developed between him and our team. He had been twice treated with CBT. Since then, the main intervention had been antidepressant medication. He felt some different kind of therapy was needed to get to the bottom of the problem, its "fundamentals", while from the team's point of view there was very limited other therapy on offer and doubts were voiced whether the patient was meeting increasingly tight referral criteria and notions of "serious mental illness". This resulted in a pattern of discharge followed by re-referral, often after a very short break, when the patient's GP felt the patient to be at risk of suicide. Professor J's concerns are listed in Table 5.3.

Table 5.3 Personal questionnaire for Professor J., a sixty-four-year-old former teacher of English Literature from Central Europe

Session number	**4**	**5**	**10**	**11**	**15**	**18**	**23**	**26**
Date	**3 April**	**10 April**	**5 June**	**12 June**	**10 July**	**11 September**	**23 October**	**11 December**
Belief that there is something fundamentally wrong with me	4	4	4	4	4	3	3	2
Distressing recognition that my emotions are in chaos	4	4	4	4	3	3	3	3
Fear I have repressed anger that may express itself badly	4	3	1	2	1	1	1	2
Sense of cowardice	4	3	2	3	3	2	1	2
Conviction that things will get worse	3	4	1	2	1	1	1	2
Conviction that life is completely meaningless	4	3	4	1	1	1	1	1
Feeling I want to have nothing to do with anybody	3	3	1	1	3	3	3	3
Feeling too much is expected of me by mental health people	4	4	1	1	3	1	1	1
Puzzlement that I don't do things that I believe might help	3	3	1	1	1	1	1	1
Need to pretend that my problems don't exist	4	2	3	2	3	2	1	<u>4</u>
Belief I'm worthless	3	3	3	2	3	3	1	3
Belief I'm here in England on false pretences	3	4	1	2	2	2	2	2
Belief I should never have left Uzdrowiskobad	4	4	3	1	2	3	3	3
Concern that work with you won't address fundamentals	4	4	2	2	2	1	1	<u>3</u>
Feeling that I am stuck	4	4	3	3	2	3	3	2
Sense of desperation	3	3	2	1	2	2	1	1
MEDIAN	4	4	2	2	2	2	1	2

The psychologist's remit in the team at the time was loose enough to accept a referral to see if there was some way the cycle could be broken. This part of the predicament is reflected in the personal questionnaire, particularly by the statements:

- Belief that there is something fundamentally wrong with me
- A feeling that too much is expected of me by professional people
- Need to pretend that my problems don't exist
- Concern that work with you won't address fundamentals

Professor J. was on benefits. There was therefore the complication that in getting better he would lose his only regular income and find himself exposed to the pressures of a declining employment market. This state of affairs is reflected in the further concern expressed in the questionnaire item: *sense of puzzlement that I don't do things that I think might help*. We agreed early on that this concern, *given his predicament*, was really quite understandable. Agreeing on this issue served to acknowledge that matters indeed had got stuck somewhere and avoided the risky therapeutic line: "Well, everything considered, I really think you are recovered enough to seek work now", which fell foul of Professor J.'s position that he had psychological difficulties, which were not understood, which were not being competently investigated and which the team were treating on the whole rather cavalierly.

There was more to Professor J.'s predicament. Having come to this country with what seemed the promise of a secure post, the job in question proved to be quite different from his expectations. He had resigned and subsequently failed to find anything remotely appropriate for someone of his accomplishments and standing. His wife and he had soon separated. So far as he knew she was no longer in the United Kingdom. His personal and professional life had never stabilized. He was dogged with questions about what had made him leave his own country and tended to see it as an action both rash and cowardly. We pursued this issue over a number of weeks, as a narrative following the course of his life. He spent the month of August staying with an old friend in Bologna (another emigré), where he revived his passion for modern Italian art, and on his return began once again to paint.

Did the work help? There was improvement overall in terms of the usual yardstick. The median dropped from *four* to *two* and remained there for many weeks. Good assessment though exposes weaknesses in treatment. Table 5.3 hints at some of the shortcomings. On this reading of it, the sessions didn't touch the issues of believing he was worthless, or ease the feeling that he didn't want to have anything to do with anybody. Much of the progress appears to come in the first half of the work, owing much, I sense, to the compassionate stance taken, which may at least claim to have been different from what had gone before and to have broken the circularity for a time. This is the hope, but one or two significant items worsen at the end, notably Professor J.'s need to pretend his problems don't exist; and despite the improvement in the belief that *there is something fundamentally wrong with me*, the concern about work with me *not addressing fundamentals* has been raised again. My feeling, in retrospect, was that I had not done enough to assure Professor J. that relations with our service would remain different henceforth. Somewhere, I had allowed myself to forget that the referral was deeply systemic. There was a problem between Professor J. and the team; and this had not been sorted out. This, more than anything to do with Professor J., was what was fundamentally wrong.

Collaborating over a recurring psychiatric disorder

The collaboration in this instance was with Dr P., a senior registrar in anaesthetics in his mid-thirties, who had suffered periodic episodes of depression, dating as far back as his time as a medical student. Having been placed on antidepressants a number of times by a series of general practitioners in different parts of the country and never having been referred for any sort of psychological work, he discussed with a psychiatrist colleague the possibility of seeing a clinical psychologist and exploring a different kind of approach. A cross-district referral was made.

The patient is concerned about another bout of psychiatric depression. Several items he chooses suggest it being already present at a certain level of severity: for example, *free-floating anxiety*, *great feeling of fatigue* and *difficulty with concentration*. Other concerns could be seen to fit with a cognitive therapist's view of features that maintain depression: *inability to settle for good enough at any time* and *sense of needing to put up a good front*.

Here, one sees how, while constructs are placed to one side at the descriptive stage in favour of content, they may re-emerge when that content is scrutinized. Where – as here – a construct like psychiatric depression does emerge, it can make good sense to see it as indicative of the patient's *position* and not just as the way things simply *are*. In talking about depression here, a practitioner is not only advancing a causal explanation of a certain kind, but encountering a patient's way of understanding his or her own experience.

Top of the list of Dr P's concerns during the first few meetings was concern about these bouts of depression. What was causing them? How were they best to be understood and addressed? The personal questionnaire (Table 5.4) catches something of this episode, covering ratings over the first winter (sessions 10 to 14), and perhaps best characterized by the items attracting ratings of *four* over that time: *concern about depression*, *free-floating anxiety*, *rumination* and *difficulty concentrating* (*four* each time), along with *tearful grief-like feelings* (*four* twice and *three* once).

Absolutely regular use of the personal questionnaire session by session might have helped see how things built up in the preceding weeks. But the questionnaire does catch the change for the worse between sessions 9 and 10. As a means of identifying causes in the sense of *triggers*, the questionnaire does not perform very well though. More frequent ratings might have helped a little, but the failure here to pick up an immediate trigger provokes a general observation I would make about personal questionnaires. When pursuit of content identifies the causes of concerns, it more often does so in the everyday sense of the phrase, not in the scientific one. It pinpoints the sources of the patient's distress, what it is that is giving rise to concern; it doesn't identify a set of antecedent conditions.

The patient's concerns are, nonetheless, a source of information. They feed the appetite. They stimulate ideas. We noted possible links between feeling stuck and colleagues not prioritizing his needs, and between feelings of fatigue and chaos. We could see how before the second Christmas, things seemed to build up, possibly due to pressure of work. But the profile of concerns was different from how it had been during the crisis the previous year. What also eventually caught our attention was the rumination item, the presence of intrusive thoughts about abandonment, which Dr P. felt he had let grow out of proportion and which he tended to deal with by seeking reassurance from his girlfriends. We worked on ways to view these thoughts so as to make the *content* of them less salient (for example, by postulating them to be the product of a wayward neural loop) and spent some time on mindfulness procedures as a further means of objectifying and distancing this particular material. At the finish, we noted that *inability to settle for "good enough"* was back.

The use of a personal questionnaire seemed here to support our collaboration and to provide material for the two of us to chew over. It documented something, and the documenting stimulated ideas. It did not give all the answers. A prompt medical response, structured activity, distress tolerance procedures and various other standard interventions contributed too.

Table 5.4 Personal questionnaire for Dr P., a thirty-six-year-old specialist registrar in anaesthetics

Session number	**5**	**9**	**10**	**13**	**14**	**16**	**17**	**19**	**21**	**24**	**27**	**29**
Date	**27 September**	**13 December**	**4 January**	**15 February**	**20 March**	**25 April**	**16 May**	**10 July**	**19 September**	**12 December**	**23 January**	**21 February**
Concern about bouts of depression	2	2	4	4	4	2	4	2	1	3	1	1
Free-floating anxiety	2	1	4	4	4	1	1	1	2	1	1	1
Ruminations out of proportion	3	3	4	4	4	3	3	4	3	2	1	1
Difficulty with concentration	3	2	4	4	3	3	2	3	2	1	2	1
Great feeling of fatigue	2	2	2	4	4	2	2	1	2	4	3	2
Tearful, grief-like feelings	1	1	4	4	4	2	3	2	2	2	1	1
Lonely, yearning feelings	2	2	2	3	2	1	3	4	2	2	1	1
Feelings of chaos	4	1	1	4	1	1	1	2	2	4	4	1
Inability to settle for “good enough”	4	2	2	1	1	1	3	2	2	4	4	4
Need to put up a front	3	3	4	2	1	1	3	1	1	3	1	1
Needs not prioritized by others at work	4	1	1	2	4	4	4	1	1	4	2	2
Sense of stuckness	4	1	4	3	3	3	4	1	2	2	1	1
Feeling of not knowing how to change	4	1	4	3	4	4	4	1	2	3	1	1
MEDIAN	3	2	4	4	4	2	3	2	2	3	1	1
BDI	18			27					16			11
Venlafaxine	150	150	150	225	225	225	225					
Mirtazapine							15	15				
Duloxetine								60	60	60	60	60

Confronting obstacles on the path of development

Mr G. was a man in his early thirties who at the time of his psychiatric referral to me for "anxiety and depression" had been in contact with services for two years. His troubles seemed to have started when he developed symptoms at work, such as shakiness, palpitations and nausea. He viewed these as life threatening, and continued to do so despite medical opinion that they could be plausibly explained as anxiety disorder. He continued to manage these symptoms on a fairly high dose of Fluoxetine (an anti-depressant) throughout the time I saw him.

Although he scored significantly highly on a measure of psychiatric depression (the BDI: consistently in the mid-twenties and indicative of "moderate psychiatric depression"), the items of his personal questionnaire adhered far less closely to the symptom profile associated with the psychiatric diagnosis than did those of Dr P. His concerns are listed in Table 5.5.

He described feeling estranged, lonely, at odds with society and somewhat daunted by his five-year older girlfriend's high-flying career with a City firm of stockbrokers. (They lived in the flat she owned, and

Table 5.5 List of concerns of Mr G., a twenty-five-year-old accounting technician living in his girlfriend's flat

Concern	Before	After
Concern about my physical health	4	2
Concern about lack of control over what goes on in my body	4	3
Concern about the effect of what's happened on my self-esteem	4	1
Sense of inadequacy in my present relationship	4	3
Sense of confusion about what is proper human contact	4	2
Concern that people think I am immature	4	2
Sense of pressure on all sides to just get on with it	4	2
Feeling of loneliness	4	1
Feeling of being physically exhausted	4	4
Difficulty getting up	4	3
Difficulty making commitments	3	2
Tendency to leave things to the last minute	4	3
Feeling of being undermined by my perception of how money operates	4	2
Sense of irreconcilable conflict between ideals and reality	3	2
Feeling of being completely lost	4	2
MEDIAN	4	2

she commuted to London daily.) While experiencing a sense of pressure from all sides to move on, he continued to feel exhausted, found it hard to get up, tended to procrastinate and doubted his ability to commit to a course of action. In summary, he said he felt completely lost.

I saw Mr G. for something over twenty sessions. Some improvement came during the autumn following a holiday in the Florida Everglades over several weeks. This time was quite stressful between him and his girlfriend, as they discussed their differences and in particular his indecision about whether to give up his job as an accounting technician with the local authority. However, over these weeks, he established that his physical symptoms, as they rose and fell, tied up closely with changes in the level of his anxiety over the same period. He therefore felt he had found evidence to support an anxiety-type explanation for his more somatic complaints.

There was some specialist work done here (CBT for health anxiety), but broadly the conception of his difficulties that we arrived at was developmental. He had sought to leave behind, and secure independence from, a rather unhappy home situation. He was orphaned young and brought up by an aunt and uncle whom he described as "rather cold and not particularly ambitious for me". As an adolescent, he had felt very beleaguered. Later, he found that he was required to carry a great deal on his own shoulders during a difficult period of transition. Initially, things had seemed certain and promising, and he was pleased to find work as an accounting technician with a local authority. In the event though, the job had proved to be complicated and fraught, as he battled with the rights and wrongs, and pros and cons, of taking a not very well paid job on "the outer reaches of the financial world".

He came to feel that more was attributable to the state of the world around him, and rather less was just *him*. While not all continued to be well between him and his girlfriend, he came to feel that some part of that lay in his wish to find in her something of what had been missing at home. So, as he saw it, his expectations had been pitched high. In terms of his relationship with me, potentially another problematic "grown-up", a turning point came when I apologized for an ineffective session a fortnight before. Suddenly there was greater freedom in the air, and we proceeded to a forty-minute discussion of clearing banks, their bookkeeping systems and what sorts of things count as debit and credit entries on their balance sheets. Thereafter, our collaboration continued to follow its course for some months, its quality much more that of two men discussing strategy for managing lives in an imperfect world.

Finding meaning in psychosis

The next patient, Mrs H. in her early fifties, had worked for many years as a renal nurse before she became psychiatrically ill following the death of a patient and the breakdown of her marriage after twenty-five years. She had been in contact with services for about twelve months at the time of her referral. She had had a single inpatient admission during that time. Following her referral to a hearing voices group, Mrs H. requested individual sessions and was seen not by me but by a colleague of mine sixteen times over the course of the next twelve months, while continuing also to be seen by other members of the recovery team. Her concerns are listed in Table 5.6.

Now no longer working, she explained during the assessment that she was hearing the voice of one of her managers from her old employer telling her that she was worthless and should kill herself. The voice was adamant that Mrs H. should not be wasting the valuable time of *competent* NHS staff in trying to keep her alive. Although the voice did not threaten to kill Mrs H., if Mrs H. disobeyed it, its tone was

Table 5.6 List of concerns of Mrs H., a former renal nurse in her early fifties

Concern	Before	After
Belief I am hearing my manager's voice	4	1
The feeling I have that the voice doesn't want me to talk to you	4	1
The belief the voice has complete control over me	4	1
The belief that the voice is right	4	2
A feeling of great fear in busy places	4	2
Need to avoid using public transport	4	2
Belief I was wrong not to have resuscitated my patient	4	2
Belief that I deserve to be punished	4	1
Belief I am only important as a support to other people*	4	2
Belief that I do not deserve to be cared for*	4	2
Feeling of sadness or anger about my colleagues not treating me well	4	1
Feeling of hopelessness about the future	4	1
Likelihood that I will kill myself some time soon	4	1
Shaking or trembling	4	1
A feeling that I have most of my grieving still to do*	4	3
MEDIAN	4	1

* These three questionnaire items were added at the end of the first month.

menacing. (This led my colleague to keep sessions short to begin with and to suggest an appropriate item be included in the questionnaire: *the feeling I have that the voice doesn't want me to talk to you.*)

My colleague and Mrs H. agreed on four goals:

(1) To work out why Mrs H. had become psychotic
(2) To reduce the power and control of her voice (and indeed – she hoped – be rid of it)
(3) To find her way back into employment
(4) To restore a sense of life's simple satisfactions and pleasures

Getting to the bottom of why she had become psychotic also exercised my colleague, who began to think about Mrs H.'s distressing experience in terms of Morrison's (2001) model of how hallucinations and delusions develop and persist. The model seeks to explain how an *intrusion* like the repeated hearing of a voice (quite commonly experienced by people not judged to be psychotic and in certain situations – sexual abuse, sleep deprivation or solitary confinement – quite usual) may become more frequent and subject to *interpretation* in ways that might suggest thought disorder. Whether though such interpretations actually are or are not considered thought disordered is a position a particular culture takes.

Additions and refinements to the set of concerns tracked the discussions between my colleague and Mrs H. as Morrison's model was explored. A collaborative written formulation was produced, not as the rounding off of an assessment but as part of "the hearing out of the client's narrative" (Crellin, 1998, p.26). This formulation stated how early experiences had led to her having a highly developed sense of responsibility for caring for others and a sense of self-worth and lovability tied in very closely with this role, and lacking any substance outside it. It made significant reference to the bullying she had experienced from a group of older girls at school that did much to develop a strong sense of vulnerability and even to foster a belief that the world was dangerous. Her value system nevertheless prevailed, providing her with some sense of worth and security, until the death of a patient and the breakdown of her marriage. Then, very suddenly, she faced the lack of any sense of goodness or deserving in her own right. To make matters worse, and the losses greater, as she became more withdrawn and fearful, such outside support as she had had disappeared when she was sacked from work and her friends there appeared to abandon her. Having no sense of personal self-worth outside the caring role, there was no strong sense of who she was, no quiet soothing internal voice to comfort her. The only internal voice now available to her was one expressive of the forces that had found her unworthy and decided to reject her. When she started to hear the voice, she tried to resist it. That seemed to increase its frequency, loudness and insistence, rather as happens when one tries not to think an unwanted thought and succeeds only in ensuring its more vigorous return. Effectively the voice assumed the qualities of the world she feared: powerful, alien, rejecting but ever present, threatening and *truly* epitomizing the way things *really were*.

This formulation was based on a certain understanding of the patient's difficulties and written from the patient's point of view. While it drew on a strong theoretical model, there was nevertheless room within it for the patient to exercise choice over how she wanted the work to be developed. It seemed in retrospect to have contained many of the seeds of the patient's recovery: the prospect of support and collaboration over time, the exploring of the past and its impact on the present and the preparing and testing of new ground and different possibilities as confidence built up and the patient started to take more and more initiative in tackling the various situations she had suddenly found so overwhelmingly difficult.

Giving expression to the legacy of the past

This example highlights the role played by descriptive assessment in working with Miss K., a retired civil servant in her mid-sixties, traumatized from childhood and with a significantly and problematically dissociative strategy for coping with it. The illustration involves some preliminary work done while the patient waited over several months to be seen for long-term work.

For various reasons, Miss K's dissociative strategy had been missed by professionals in numerous contacts with services over the thirty previous years. The pattern of her contacts had been intermittent. There had been a number of psychiatric admissions, usually involving a diagnosis of schizophrenia or manic depression. Treatment, subsequently, had been almost entirely with psychotropic medication, and any psychological therapy she received over these years funded privately.

This referral came after a gap in time of some years during which there had been a re-organization of services. After two or three meetings with Miss K., I wrote to the team recommending a search be made for a suitable therapist. It was essential that the person would be able to work over a good stretch of time with the range of interventions advocated in accounts of the treatment of complex post-traumatic and dissociative disorders, for example those considered by Chu (1998).

A copy of that letter ultimately found its way to a psychodynamic psychological therapist who was able to take on Miss K., agreeing to meet her for weekly sessions over two years.

This therapy was not immediately available and in the meantime, and for some weeks after the therapy began, Miss K. and I continued to meet. We decided to work on a description of concerns, continuing to see each other infrequently but regularly over this period. The principal aim was to find a way to give expression to Miss K.'s suffering over the years, and thereby to acknowledge it; another aim was to provide a possible framework for understanding and containing it. The result was the set of concerns laid out in Table 5.7.

We regarded this as a piece of work in its own right, one that *followed from* a diagnosis, rather than preceded it. The list gives some sense of Miss K.'s continuing experience of trauma and offers clues to the nature of her attempts as a small child to adjust intra-psychically to a very extreme situation. It suggests something of the later impact on her of dealing with the past in that way. It conveys what she took her experiences to imply about her and describes what for her had been the consequences of management and treatment by services themselves struggling with something terrible to contemplate, imperfectly understood and very complicated. The concerns expressed reflect particularly how her life continued to lack an ordinary present, any

Table 5.7 Concerns expressed by Miss K., a retired civil servant in her sixties physically and sexually abused through childhood

A sense of being in perpetual crisis
A feeling that I am under a life sentence of terror
A belief that I am in constant danger
A conviction that I am not the only one with keys to my property
Fear that I will be sectioned
Fear of yet more psychiatric mislabelling
Concern about the effect of neuroleptic medication being prescribed
The anguish as I appreciate my lack of a true sense of self
Inability to see my own face in a mirror without make-up
Disorientation caused by realization that I have a personality system with lots of not terribly well-combining parts
The disruption caused by the temporary disappearance of adult competencies
The sense of fusing past and present
The horror of breaking through amnesia
The problem of being triggered into complicated flashback
An underlying belief that I am totally worthless
The sense that I have been treated as an object
Intense, unresolved grief about the past

sense of continuity from moment to moment. Her experience of herself seemed disrupted by shifts of mood and bodily sensation. In recalling events, it seemed for her to be a struggle both to separate the recent from the distant past and to distinguish those voices that she experienced as her from others, which, while quite probably part of her, seemed external to her and persecutory. Her descriptions of shifting states of consciousness seemed consistent with switches between different parts of her, although she did not at this time experience herself as a number of distinct "alter" personalities.

There was a need in making the list to keep it free of jargon. Miss K. had read extensively on the subject of trauma, but significantly less about dissociation. This being the case, the construction of the list risked owing too much in its shaping to a psychologist's professional knowledge. A certain phrase in particular rested most uneasily with Miss K. This was the notion of a Dissociative *Disorder*. When some months after we had begun meeting the word at last inadvertently slipped through my lips, Miss K. commented on it frankly. The exchange went something as follows:

> The Psychologist (*confidingly but grandly*): I think it has been important to shift the burden of explanation from a psychotic to dissociative disorder.
>
> Miss K (*gently if insistently*): Dissociative Disorder? Really? Isn't dissociation more about order, . . . ordering, . . . re-ordering, . . . a very young person trying somehow to make sense of things?

The list was re-drafted a number of times before reaching any kind of acceptable, let alone definitive, state, reflecting not just the struggle to find her own way of saying things but also the way the start of the work with the psychodynamic psychological therapist had begun to open up fresh material and to amend her overall perception of her concerns.

Soothing the savage breast

The next illustration compares two patients, not entirely dissimilar in their presentation. Both are seeking help with techniques for coping with anxiety. The illustration plays with how subtly different sets of concerns may lead to the choice of quite different coping techniques. The first patient (N, a company executive aged 42) listed the following statements:

> Everything tenses me up.
> My body is reacting unpredictably.

All I do is think about how things might get worse.
I don't seem able to do anything constructive about it.
I'm unable to contemplate the slightest change.
I'm frightened of exhausting myself.
I'm anxious about what might be suggested to me.

The second patient (M, a company executive aged 43) listed these:

I'm totally stressed out about my life.
Things seem out of control.
My thoughts are all over the place.
I'm totally ineffective as a person.
I seem incapable of thinking about things properly.
I'm always in a mad rush.
I'm too worried to take anything in.

The point of the illustration was inspired by an article that appeared some years ago in *Behaviour Research and Therapy* entitled "To Soothe the Savage Breast".[1] It discusses ways to "reduce aversive mental states and emotional arousal" linked to "psychopathology, stressful events, and personal calamities" (Rosenthal, 1993, p.439). The procedures looked at are all "nonchemical counter arousal techniques", and as interventions they perhaps reflect a situation familiar to anyone asked to provide psychological alternatives to medication.

The article stresses the significant *number* of options that are available. It outlines and comments on "quite a range of procedures – some strange, some familiar – to calm and spare fantasied harm" (p.439). About twenty are covered. Among these Rosenthal considers imaginal relaxation, muscular relaxation, tai-chi, baths accompanied by soft music and bubbles, a few good jokes, acquiring a pet, new activities (at least an armchair contemplation of them) and help in developing an altered philosophy of life.

A key theme of the article is its objection to the "one-size-fits-all" approach taken to their selection. There *may* be techniques effective for nearly everybody, but if so they are rare. To the extent that such techniques are lacking, patients should be allowed to make personal choices among them "cafeteria-style" (p.446).

Can a person-centred set of concerns help a practitioner suggest to a patient what he or she might find most beneficial? Rosenthal feels

[1] "Musick has Charms to sooth a savage Breast/To soften Rocks, or bend a knotted Oak" (William Congreve. *The Mourning Bride*, 1697).

patients tend to have different "stylistic preferences" in terms of therapy. For example, he feels that while "imaginal relaxation may not comfort anxious, expressive 'worry-warts' ", it may "yet be acceptable to more reserved 'somaticizing' patients, afraid to move their muscles" (p.446). That would better fit Mr N., the first of the two patients described above, who tenses up and describes his body as reacting unpredictably. "Likewise", Rosenthal continues a sentence or so later, "will persons whose beliefs and values clash with introverted self-scrutiny try harder or comply better if an oscilloscope or a thermometer externalizes the task, moving the 'locus of blame' outside of their minds?" That would seem to favour physical relaxation as an approach for Mr M., the second patient, who confesses to being incapable of thinking about things properly and being too worried to take anything in.

Rosenthal calls for research to investigate what sorts of people pick which techniques, while reflecting that to date counsellors and clinicians have not shone in matching patients to their most favoured therapy.

Reversing an attempted solution

This final illustration draws on the notion of a concern or set of concerns as an attempted solution to a problem, but a solution rather worse than the problem it seeks to solve. This is the idea that cropped up earlier in defining "the terrain" back in Chapter 3 where the summary observations of the Man from Mars on the nature of mental health issues on planet Earth were noted. An "attempted solution" was understood there as a solution worse than the problem it was trying to solve (Fisch, Weakland and Segal, 1982). Examples of attempted solutions might be someone's avoidance of leaving their house in an attempt to stave off panic attacks, or somebody's reliance on regular if small doses of Valium to deal with insomnia, and leading in the one case to social isolation and in the other to dependence on a minor tranquillizer.

Sometimes, the source of the attempted solution is not the patient but those close to the patient who perhaps press for her to stay in or take the tablets. In the illustration that follows, attempts had been made over the years by family and friends, and above all by professional people, to reassure Miss W, who had great difficulty coping with a fear of being sick, that there was nothing really to fear from nausea or vomiting and that her anxieties accordingly were needlessly exaggerated. The concerns that were identified over the first few sessions are shown in Table 5.8.

Table 5.8 Concerns identified by Miss W., a games teacher in her mid-forties very frightened of vomiting

Concern	Before	After
Difficulty coping with feeling sick	4	3
Choking feeling in my throat	4	2
Frequent churning feelings in stomach	4	4
Feeling of fear in my whole body	4	2
Sense of my symptoms being intolerable	4	2
Sense of nowhere being safe	4	2
Impossibility of convincing myself that nothing is the matter	4	4
Worry about letting down the girls	3	1
Uncomfortable feeling of being alone with it	4	1
Sense of people being exasperated by me	3	2
Feeling that getting things across is very uphill	3	1
Sense of embarrassment at the ridiculousness of it	4	2
MEDIAN	4	2

Attempts had been made to make Miss W used to the experience of being sick by administering ipecac syrup to induce vomiting in an effort to prove to her that to vomit was in the final analysis "okay"; thoroughly unpleasant perhaps but not a threat to life or limb. Such attempts had not worked, and knowing this I was spared the need to pursue an in vivo behavioural course of action myself. Such a course of action might in any case be viewed as essentially yet another form of reassurance.

In Miss W's case, the failure of reassurance as a strategy can be seen in Miss W's futile attempts to convince herself that something basically rather unpleasant was in some sense acceptable: *the impossibility of convincing myself that nothing is the matter*. She was not helped by the intensity of the physical feelings. These included a churning stomach, choking feelings in her throat and what she described as a *feeling of fear in my whole body*. The *sense of nowhere being safe* conveys the inescapable quality of her experience.

Alongside these concerns are others hinting at how her distress was not validated by people close to her. She perceived people to be attempting to play down her anxieties or even to be dismissing them altogether. Told she need not or should not be worrying, she found herself worrying nonetheless. She felt alone with it all. She knew she exasperated people. Herself head games teacher in a secondary girls school, with the reputation of bringing the best out of every pupil in her charge, she possessed a strong sense of fairness and battled strongly for more sports and better facilities. Battling for herself she found considerably harder work. Getting things across seemed to be very uphill. By the time the G.P. practice she attended referred her, all parties (patient, doctors and the practice nurses) seemed to have reached a state of complete exhaustion.

In speaking of the intervention as "reversing" an attempted solution, the intention is to convey the sense of it as a 180° about turn: the replacement of reassurance by empathy rather in the manner of cognitive treatments for health anxiety (Salkovskis and Warwick, 1986). The thrust of the work was an attempt to understand and legitimize Miss W.'s feelings about being sick. Some of the most useful sessions were those that looked at her early experience of problems. As a young girl, Miss W.'s upsets about this and that were routinely ignored. For example, at school Miss W.'s parents didn't think it mattered that the milk she was made to drink was tepid or that she was required by the supply teacher to touch the frogspawn. And no doubt the mysterious root vegetables the school served up at lunchtime were entirely okay, or the school wouldn't be serving them up. When she complained, people told her she was the only one making a fuss. The result was that Miss W was left with a sense of things somehow being wrong and that no one cared a jot about it. Convinced that her concerns should be expressed, like Cassandra she knew that they would be totally disregarded.

The outcome of the work was positive. Most of the concerns, as originally identified, improved. She continued to be unable to convince herself that nothing was the matter. But that, of course, makes a degree of sense: it is only as one becomes clear about the nature of the task that the shape of a desirable outcome becomes clear. A referral, which first looked like one that waits upon the extent of symptom relief, instead becomes one that ends with a proper understanding of the source of the personal distress. Another reason for seeking a sizeable array of concerns at the outset is the uncertainty to begin with about which among them will prove to be the most meaningful.

Who does general work?

These nine illustrations have been offered as examples of general work, the foundations of which are laid down through a procedure in which assessments take content as their starting point and thereafter treat content as a point of constant reference. This work was described earlier in this chapter as *routine*. But it was stressed that *routine* did not necessarily mean easy.

The person to do it is *any* good practitioner versed adequately in its ideas and practices, in other words the sort of person for whom this book is written. It would be quite counter to the spirit of everything argued for here if general work were to become special, the preserve of assessment specialists. That would be as unfortunate as the tendency described in the next chapter for special work to be treated as general, as if it provided something fundamental, a general foundation. But there is a dilemma, and this arises because resources are limited.

My friend and colleague Raymond Chadwick expressed it to me recently as in the nature of a paradox that the difficult task of mental health assessment is often allocated to the least experienced people. It betrays an attitude towards assessment that sees it as no more than preliminary to the main event, when one might well take the view instead that assessment is indistinguishable from the main event, or indeed even *is* the main event. Does one "front-load" or "back-load" a service? In mental health, services tend to be back-loaded. Senior practitioners are wheeled out late in the day to re-assess only when things haven't worked or have gone seriously wrong. But how often do things not work, or go seriously wrong, because patients were poorly assessed in the first place?

CHAPTER 6

Framework for Psychological Therapies

In this chapter, the subject matter is work of a specialist, or (the term preferred here) *special* kind. Here, there is not the issue of naming that characterized general work. Decisions have been made, or are in the course of being made, that will direct activity towards recognized procedures and protocols. The work in prospect is adequately named already. In mental health, much of it currently falls under the banner of "psychological therapies", particularly the modal psychological therapies promoted in the NHS. And the examples in this chapter all relate to the psychological therapies, or to well-established, structured interventions of some kind.

What contribution does personalized assessment make to recognized procedures and protocols of the *special* kind? The thrust of the argument is that assessing content will sometimes direct the counsellor or clinician towards such procedures and protocols, and then when content is re-assessed, show the effect the work has had upon the patient's personal concerns. Content creates the *framework*.

The chapter is in three sections:

- The first section looks at the use of personalized assessment in suggesting the case for a certain type of psychological therapy (examples are given of content pointing towards psychodynamic and systemic therapies).
- The second section examines the use of personalized assessment during the actual course of psychological therapies (here, the examples explore the use of content during EMDR and CBT).
- The third section elaborates the nature of special work, clarifying how the psychological therapies are only one type of assessment,

although an important one, and clarifying too how in different ways the assessment procedures peculiar to different psychological therapies rely on some kind of foundation first being laid in general work.

Concerns and referral for psychological therapy

Not all special work is going to be amenable to this kind of descriptive underpinning. A psychological therapist might well feel that there was a fundamental division of role between the general and the special functions. He or she might adopt either way of working with a particular patient but regard a combining of the two roles with that patient as mistaken. In the next two illustrations, the situation imagined is the one where a practitioner, acting within a general role, decides on the basis of the patient's concerns to refer to someone else operating within a special role.

A referral for psychodynamic psychological therapy

In this example, therefore, the point of immediate interest is the value of the personalized assessment in identifying a case for the therapy rather than the uses of that assessment in what followed once the referral had been made. Here, the patient, Mr U., was in his forties and once an apparently very successful senior company executive, but living these last ten years removed (rather than legally separated) from his wife and family, and for the last four of them retired by his employer after increasing periods off work with "stress". A certain amount was known about his background and circumstances at the time the referral from his GP reached the CMHT, as there had been two earlier psychiatric contacts in the previous twelve months. Some of this information might have suggested to a practitioner that a psychodynamic approach was suitable, but for now, for the purposes of this book, the need is to discount that information and see if the referral makes sense on the basis of the concerns identified during the course of the two initial sessions, where the team member was reviewing what might be done following what was now the third referral.

The concerns identified are shown in Table 6.1. Having received the referral letter with them set out, the psychological therapist commented back to the referrer on the amount of abstraction and metaphor in the set. There is difficulty pinning the concerns down, even a degree of vagueness about them, while the sense of distress is nonetheless palpable: *sense of falling apart inside, hopelessness about how I am*

Table 6.1 A set of concerns of Mr U., a patient seen and referred on for psychodynamic psychotherapy

A sense of falling apart inside
Concern that I don't have any idea what's wrong with me
Difficulty explaining to people what I feel
The danger of even trying to think about my difficulties
A sense of confusion so great I can't begin
Worry that you are going unnecessarily to probe my past
A belief that people don't understand the world I see out there
The feeling that my wife doesn't take my point of view seriously
Feeling there's a glass pane separating me from "normal" people
Distress that people consider me unfit to do the job I love
Sense that sometimes my anger is so strong I feel like killing myself
Concern about my inability to concentrate on anything
My impulse to write off anything remotely good I do as rubbish
Belief that if I do anything for me I'll be severely punished
Feeling of exhaustion so strong I can't carry on
A sense of hopelessness about how I am going to find my way
The feeling that I can't stand all this any more
Belief I'm trapped (because anything I do will be wrong)

going to find my way. Much of the material clusters around the early sections of the personal interview: difficulties to do with identifying and articulating material, even internally to himself; difficulties with explaining it *at all*, difficulties communicating it and perhaps most of all concern about people's response to him and his difficulties, the categories "him" and "difficulties" not being that easy to separate.

In a later conversation with the referrer, the psychological therapist, having by now seen the patient for the first time, spoke about how the set of statements had brought to mind clinical features described in the work of Herbert Rosenfeld. From Rosenfeld's early papers, summarized by John Steiner (2008), there seemed to be reflected in the questionnaire the patient's sense of fragmentation, his sensitivity to the intrusiveness of a therapist and perhaps, in his reference to confusion, the chaotic nature of his experience of the world.

From the first of two papers Rosenfeld wrote on narcissism (Rosenfeld, 1964), my colleague picked out Rosenfeld's observations on the presence of a sense of frustration in personal relations and the lack of emotional contact. A suggestive parallel with Rosenfeld's observations in Mr U.'s set of statements is found in his belief that people don't see the world the way he does. Another parallel is discernible in

Mr U.'s feeling that there is a "glass pane" separating him from normal people.

Then, in this same article, Rosenfeld illustrated what he saw as a further familiar clinical feature, describing how one patient had lost contact with everything that had been discussed during sessions. Was such an obstacle to therapy to be foreseen in Mr U.'s remarks that he found concentration difficult and that he felt it to be dangerous even to think about his problems?

From the second of the two papers on narcissism (Rosenfeld, 1971), my colleague picked out the further references to resistance: that another patient of Rosenfeld's had said how he felt his mind drifting away from the consulting room and becoming so detached and sleepy that he could scarcely keep awake. "There was an enormous resistance, almost like a stone wall, which prevented any examination of the situation" (p.125). In this article, Rosenfeld also writes that "some of these patients become suicidal and the desire to die, to disappear into oblivion, is expressed quite openly and death is idealized as a solution to all problems" (p.123).

The questionnaire also brought out how Mr U. seemed to be sabotaged in his attempts to take matters in hand, particularly in his belief that if he does anything for himself he will be severely punished. Rosenfeld writes of how powerful these self-destructive impulses often are and how highly organized, "as if one were dealing with a powerful gang dominated by a leader" (p.125).

Of course, the idea that Mr U.'s concerns can be understood in terms of Rosenfeld's concept of narcissism, influenced as that is by Melanie Klein's theory of object relations and Freud's later concept of a death instinct, does not mean that that is the only way of understanding Mr U.'s difficulties or even that it was the right course of action to refer him for psychodynamic psychotherapy. The argument here is that from a psychodynamic point of view the case for the referral, based on the patient's concerns, is a plausible one.

A referral for systemic family therapy

The next patient was referred for systemic psychological therapy after the completion of a descriptive assessment. As in the case of Mr U., different people carried out the assessment and the intervention that followed. The patient, Miss V., was twenty-five years old. She had lately been referred to the multidisciplinary team, having recently returned home from university where she had found the degree course in religious studies much more academic than she had expected and

Table 6.2 A set of concerns of Miss V., a patient seen and referred on for systemic family therapy

Hatred of an unpleasant smell that comes from my father
Wish to shout out loud without being able at times
Difficulty expressing crossness to people I know well
Concern that I am too powerful a person within the family
Feeling that I need to protect my mother from my father
Constant upset about my parents being irreligious
Feeling unable to maintain my spiritual resolves because of my problem
Sense that my parents have nearly had their fill of it
Confusion that something like smell gets to me in this way
Concern that nobody understands how strongly I feel about everything
Feeling under pressure somehow to stay at home
Feeling I need my parents around to achieve anything
Feeling that deep down I am really short of confidence
Feeling of tremendous dismay at the state of the world

living away from home far more difficult than she had imagined. Her concerns are shown in Table 6.2.

She appeared to be caught in an uncomfortable place, finding it almost equally difficult to stay at home and to be away from home. The focal issue, which she had already presented to her university counselling service, was her sensitivity to smells, most of all to her father's smell, although she also had found herself acutely aware of her flat mates' smell (a man and a woman). The presentation seemed a little like the sensitivity to sounds described by people suffering from hyperacusis. Herself a devout Muslim, she came from a family split over religion. Her mother was religious and her father thoroughly secular. Miss V. felt she had never really got on with her father. He was a "larger than life" and very successful businessman, rather "jolly", but altogether nonplussed by his daughter's religious views and distressed by her sensitivity to how he smelt. Opinion varied among other family members over how much he smelt and whether the smell was pleasant or unpleasant. Her mother ventured out very little and seemed to Miss V. to be really rather "depressed and downtrodden". There were two younger siblings, but it was to Miss V. that her mother turned for support.

In thinking about making a referral to my family therapy colleague I was wondering about the chances of usefully working with Miss V. and her parents in some combination: whether her parents could be helped to look at the situation together, whether her mother could be encouraged to find support elsewhere than from her daughter and whether Miss V.'s relationship with her father could be improved, once there was less triangulation between father, mother and eldest child.

Dallos and Draper (2005) feel that modern family therapy gives greater weight than family therapy once did to the meanings, beliefs and perceptions of individual family members, while it continues to be alert to the function of symptoms, problem-maintaining patterns and contextual factors. Those concerns in Miss V.'s questionnaire that best indicated the nature of the systemic issues were perhaps her thought that she was too powerful a force within the family, her belief that she needed to protect her mother from her father and her sense of conflict between, on the one hand, feeling under uncomfortable pressure to stay at home and, on the other, needing her parents around to achieve anything.

This illustration provokes a thought about precisely how a line of questioning manages to arrive at a particular set of concerns. Of course, it depends in part on the attributes of the practitioner. For the procedure to serve as a source of ideas and act as guide at all a practitioner requires a modicum of relevant theoretical knowledge and a degree of personal and professional experience. This belies the notion of personalized assessment as an entirely innocent procedure, one where the practitioner simply absorbs the patient's answers, the questions being no more than the merest exhortatory prompts. There will usually be certain questions that a practitioner always asks, or at least likes to ask, but those apart there is the constantly pressing matter of the next question and where that comes from.

Concerns and the course of psychological therapy

So, where did my questions come from? They came from such special training that I myself had had, or from the special work of colleagues with which I had grown familiar over the years. In summary, arriving at the Maudsley in the late 1970s, my initial psychological therapy training was almost entirely behavioural and cognitive behavioural. This was an important time in the development of these approaches and I held firmly on to them throughout my ensuing career. Beck and his colleagues' book on depression reached the department in its prepublication typescript form towards the end of 1978, and Beck himself attended his first BABP (as it still then was) conference in Hull in the summer of 1983.

I worked for five years in a family therapy clinic where the dominant influences were communications theorists and practitioners like

Gregory Bateson, John Weakland and Milton Erickson and structural and strategic therapists like Salvador Minuchin and Jay Haley. In the mid-1990s, I came by accident on EMDR (Eye Movement Desensitization and Re-processing) just after the publication of Francine Shapiro's book (Shapiro, 1995) and returned to it in those years that EMDR supervision was available. And I was extremely fortunate in the later part of my career in always having close colleagues working with psychodynamic psychological therapy.

A short EMDR intervention

The patient Mr R., a commercial banker, had lost his French wife L. two years earlier. Mrs R. had died from a brain tumour, involving long and complicated surgery, an unpredictable time course and many acute crises. Mr R. was referred to me by his GP. The work sought to follow the standard EMDR protocol at the time (Shapiro, 1995). Its sequence over the four sessions unfolded somewhat as follows:

> *Session 1.* Personalized interview; construction and first administration of the personal questionnaire
>
> *Session 2.* EMDR phases 1 and 2 (client history and preparation) and phases 3 to 7 (desensitization and reprocessing – for one target)
>
> *Session 3.* EMDR phase 8 (re-evaluation of first target) and phases 3 to 7 (desensitization and reprocessing – for two further targets)
>
> *Session 4.* EMDR phase 8 (re-evaluation of all three targets); second administration of the personal questionnaire

Sessions 1 and 4 would have been about ninety minutes in length, and sessions 2 and 3 about two hours. The personal questionnaire results are shown in Table 6.3.

This example illustrates a simple combination of personalized assessment and specialist intervention, showing how occasionally a personalized assessment merely frames what is otherwise entirely taken up with a self-contained approach. The approach here is EMDR, perhaps best known as a treatment for trauma with sudden onset. This comes complete with its own rationale, thereby generating its own set of assessment routines. In EMDR, these assessment routines include as "phase one" an initial check on client safety; also a number of "phase three" assessments, each one for a separate target memory, where various components of the memory are measured in units of subjective

Table 6.3 Personal questionnaire results of Mr R., a banker treated with EMDR two years after the death of his wife

Session number	**1**	**2**	**3**	**4**
Date	**16/1**	**30/1**	**6/2**	**13/2**
Fear almost that L will come back	4	–	–	1
Fear of the nightmares	4	–	–	1
Feeling of being a shell of the man I was before	4	–	–	3
Sense of interior turmoil	4	–	–	1
Sense of still not having got over L's death	4	–	–	2
Sense of the outrageousness of it all	4	–	–	3
Worries for our two daughters in case they get it	4	–	–	4
Flashbacks of L's face at time of her death	4	–	–	1
A distressing memory from our last holiday together	4	–	–	1
Memory from the day of the second operation	4	–	–	1
Rotten temper	4	–	–	2
MEDIAN	4	–	–	1
EMDR given?		Yes	Yes	

discomfort or "SUDS" (Wolpe, 1991) from nought to ten. These provide a baseline score. The degree of success in tackling the memory is repeatedly measured, the aim being to reduce the SUDS score to something close to zero.

Only sometimes will a concern correspond to a target memory. Of the concerns listed in Table 6.3, just three images were targeted directly: Mrs R's face, the memory from the holiday (the actual memory was not disclosed to me) and the memory from the day of the second operation. The other concerns are better seen as just outcome variables than as both process and outcome ones, where *process* here refers to components of the treatment. A sufficient number of items are needed to get a picture of a patient's concerns, whereas the nature and number of targets depends on the theoretical or heuristic underpinnings of the intervention, here the notion of an "associated network" of "dysfunctional material" "chained" together in a "system" of memory "channels" that needs "cleaning out" (Shapiro, 1995, pp.147–148). Most of the items in the personal questionnaire are not part of this theoretical or heuristic underpinning, but they are there as a measure of whether the EMDR successfully addressed the patient's concerns.

The insistence on this distinction, one loosely between specialist interventions and casework outcomes, between special and general roles, is close to the heart of the argument for laying a personal and descriptive foundation to face-to-face psychological work.

Cognitive behavioural therapy for OCD

This example illustrates the use of the descriptive framework in following the progress of five months' cognitive behavioural therapy. It suggests the possibility of success in the tracking of interventions (particularly as here with an approach which is relatively explicit and structured). It ends by pointing to a flaw in the construction of the particular descriptive list.

The patient was Mr T., a man in his late twenties who had recently finished postgraduate studies in woodwind at a London music college. He was referred by the team psychiatrist for CBT to tackle an obsessional compulsive disorder involving thoughts of doing harm to children. He was afflicted with compulsive checking, miscellaneous rituals, counting and other urges aimed in various ways to neutralize anxieties. ("Neutralize" means in CBT terms to manage anxieties in superstitious or magical ways and thus avoid direct exposure to things that frightened him.) These were prominent in his music practices and rehearsals. A severe exacerbation of symptoms had occurred the previous autumn when Mr T. learnt of his girlfriend's risky sexual behaviour some months before they met. And then, in what again touched on the theme of danger in a different way, he had witnessed an accident at close quarters involving a cyclist.

In assessing Mr T., it became clear that almost whenever Mr T. saw an unaccompanied child, he began ruminating on the possibility that he might have harmed that child but be unaware of it. At no time did he ever *recall* an incident when he had harmed a child. At no time had he ever felt a physical or sexual desire to harm a child.

Once again, as with the EMDR example, the personal questionnaire items illustrate a mixture of personalized assessment and specialist intervention. The set of concerns in Table 6.4 combines items that are essentially just outcome variables with others, which also have a claim to be process variables and to be of some theoretical significance in respect of the therapy. In this example though, in contrast to the EMDR illustration, the therapy is tracked with greater frequency. The aim is to follow the development of the work over the course of time. As part of that, a question arises as to how far various different elements of the cognitive therapy intervention can be seen to impact on the set of concerns.

Table 6.4 Personal questionnaire results of Mr T., receiving CBT for obsessional thoughts of causing harm to children

Session number	**4**	**5**	**6**	**8**	**9**	**10**	**12**	**13**	**14**	**15**	**17**	**19**	**31**	**32**
Date	**10 March**	**13 March**	**19 March**	**2 April**	**16 April**	**21 April**	**7 May**	**14 May**	**22 May**	**5 June**	**23 June**	**9 July**	**22 June**	**6 July**
Preoccupation that something's happened	4	4	3	3	4	4	4	4	4	4	4	3	3	3
Fear it's something worse than OCD	4	3	2	1	2	2	2	1	1	1	1	1	1	1
Belief in everything my mind tells me	4	4	3	3	4	3	4	2	1	2	3	2	2	2
Worry about the cause of my uncertainty	4	4	2	3	3	2	2	2	1	2	2	2	2	2
Shameful feelings about my past values	4	4	3	2	2	2	3	2	3	3	3	2	2	2
Problem accepting "common sense"	4	4	4	3	3	4	4	2	2	2	4	2	2	2
Belief I am just letting myself off the hook	4	4	2	2	2	2	2	2	2	2	2	1	2	2
Need to feel convinced thoughts are not true	4	4	4	4	4	4	4	2	4	3	3	3	3	3
Fear of rejection	4	4	3	3	3	3	3	2	1	2	2	1	2	3
Unable to break free of whom I have been	4	4	3	4	4	3	4	4	4	4	4	3	1	1
Concentration difficulties	4	4	3	3	2	3	4	3	1	1	2	1	2	2
Fatigue	4	4	2	2	4	4	4	2	1	1	2	1	3	3
Concern not coping with my thoughts	4	4	3	2	2	2	4	2	2	1	1	1	1	1
Tendency to check more than is "OK"	4	4	4	4	4	4	4	4	3	3	2	2	2	2
Suicidal feelings	4	4	2	3	3	2	2	2	1	2	4	1	2	2
Sense of my life as very restricted	4	4	3	4	4	4	4	4	3	4	4	3	2	2
Fear of ending up in an awful place	4	4	3	2	2	1	2	2	1	1	2	1	1	1
Fear that CBT is brainwashing	4	–	3	1	1	2	2	2	1	1	1	1	1	1
MEDIAN	4	4	3	3	3	3	4	2	2	2	2	1	2	2
Citalopram (daily)	60	60	60	60	60	60	60	60	60	60	60	60	Nil	Nil
Rispiridone (daily)					1	1	1	1						
OCI-R		45										28		
Thought-Action Fusion		28										5		
Working (Various)	+	+		+	+	+	+						+	+

Many of the aspects of the therapy delivered drew on Rachman's later papers on obsessions (Rachman, 1997, 1998). The following account though is intended as no more than a brief summary of those strands of the work that seem helpful in understanding changes in the level of concerns recorded in Table 6.4.

The first session took place in February. In that session, the attempt was made to offer a framework in which Mr T. could understand his difficulties. It involved presenting Mr T.'s problems as symptoms of a psychiatric disorder (OCD). This is an important part of Rachman's approach, and was a particularly critical issue for Mr T., who did not come to the concept of OCD naively, but with a degree of scepticism about it. Mr T. was in fact a quietly sceptical man, and this scepticism extended to his view of himself. It gave rise both to concerns that he was suffering from something "worse than OCD", that OCD was really "brainwashing" and that, if he accepted the notion of OCD as the cause of his troubles, he would be "just letting himself off the hook". So, the therapist took time not so much to explain what OCD was, as to work through the case for viewing OCD as a convincing explanation in Mr T.'s case. The questionnaire suggests some progress had been made with this task by session 6. Some attention was also paid at the start to developing the idea of OCD as somewhat like a physical illness, needing conditions to be favourable for recovery, including possibly time off sick. The questionnaire hints at a link between work and fatigue. Taking time away from his job as a barman effectively took Mr T. away from a stressful and exhausting environment, where he checked a lot.

Less successful in the early stages were attempts made to distance Mr T. from his ruminative thoughts, either by exploring the nature of the evidence for them or by seeking to define thoughts as "just thoughts", mental events rather than truth. In fact, any gains in this area were hard to achieve. Ultimately, with the passage of time, he ceased to believe so strongly in everything his mind told him, his repetitive thoughts seeming less true to him and more "like a less good Beatle song, say 'The Ballad of John and Yoko' ". But at *no time* were the ratings for his *preoccupation with the possibility that something has happened* better than just slightly improved.

Things dipped quite badly at session 11 (badly enough for no time to be found to administer the questionnaire that day). After an earlier improvement, Mr T. felt once again that he was not coping with his thoughts. At this point, they seemed absolutely true to him and the mantra "a thought is just a thought" was not working. Moreover, the ratings for checking had not budged at all. A number of decisions were made in this session and the next, including one to see his GP about taking time off work and a second to use flashcards as a means of disrupting the urge to check. A third decision was to attack the presumption that he needed to be *convinced* that he had not done anything and instead rely more on looser notions like common sense. A wider perspective was sought by distinguishing an older Mr T. from a newer one: the old Mr T., slightly childlike, slightly cowering and requiring absolute certainty, the new Mr T, *already there* in conception, adult, active, adventurous, tolerant of uncertainty and really quite knowledgeable about the world.

The effect of these lines of attack seems plausibly reflected in the personal questionnaire results for session 13 onwards, which show improvements, sometimes sustained, sometimes fluctuating, among the following items:

- Belief in everything my mind tells me
- Problem accepting "common sense"
- Need to feel convinced thoughts are not true
- Fatigue
- Tendency to check more than is "OK"

After twenty sessions, a change of therapist was required when the first therapist (myself) retired. The second therapist (another clinical psychologist) took over and continued to see the patient every three or four weeks for the next year. The focus of the work changed at this point. This was partly because the second therapist approached the work with a somewhat different set of theoretical perspectives, partly because of the existence of additional concerns that had not been satisfactorily addressed so far.

The content of Table 6.4 suggests that moderate progress had been made overall by the first summer but also hints at matters unresolved and less obviously connected with obsessions and compulsions. This material is best represented by the items *unable to break free of whom I have been* and *sense of my life as very restricted*, items that had improved neither at session 6 nor at session 13 and so seemed separate from those that did improve. Exploring these over the later sessions brought to mind things Mr T. had said in earlier sessions, which might profitably have received more attention then and which perhaps needed better representation in the description of concerns: something of the explosiveness and violence which supplied the content of his ruminations seemed to connect with a number of statements dating back to a session in early March, which included him saying that he was "angry and frustrated", "strangled by constraints", "trying to fit in" and "desperate to be liked". This is where my colleague's work made its impact over the course of the next twelve months.

Psychological therapies as special work

This chapter has now looked at four illustrations of psychological therapy, psychological therapy having been introduced as a type of *special work*. What distinguishes special work? It was suggested in Chapter 2, and then again in Chapter 5, that a distinction between special work and *general work* could be drawn in terms of how the two are differently assessed. General work focuses on content: What content is present? Special work more on constructs: Is construct X present?

The definition of a construct offered earlier was "some postulated attribute of people" (Cronbach and Meehl, 1955, p.283). The subsequent examples have tended to be of mental illness classifications and categories. But constructs so defined might also include intelligence, racial prejudice, political attitude, as well as health status and functional disability. Wright and Feinstein (1992, p.1203) call constructs "complex phenomena containing multiple intangible attributes that cannot be easily isolated for a single measurement". And they quote Streiner and Norman (1989), who offer a vaguer definition than Cronbach and Meehl's: "A construct can be thought of as a mini-theory to explain the relationships among . . . various behaviours and attitudes."

So defined in relation to constructs, special work could be of many kinds and its assessment requirements complex. Risk assessment might be seen as special work. It involves thoughtful consideration of questions about the existence and degree of different sorts of risk. So might the assessment of a concept like "psychological mindedness". (Is that present, and if so, in what quantity?)

And, of course, psychiatric diagnosis can be understood in this way. The Present State Examination, as devised by Wing, Cooper and Sartorius (1974), asks questions about the *presence* or *absence* of 140 different symptoms arranged in 38 different diagnostic categories.

> The good clinician, when he undertakes a diagnostic examination, knows what he wants to find out. He makes a systematic exploration of the subject's mental state, in order to discover whether any of a finite number of abnormal phenomena are present. (p.vii)

The word "finite" is telltale. It is not a matter of what phenomena are present; it is a matter of whether *certain* phenomena are present.

A discussion of special work need not, therefore, be limited to approaches to various psychological therapies. But here it will be. *What* to assess is the issue; and what is assessed is in some sense *shaped by* the requirements and preoccupations of the particular therapy. These requirements vary from psychological therapy to psychological therapy. They make different and distinctive demands on assessment, as much distinctive of the different therapies as distinctive of therapy in general.

Jane Milton offers a clear and distinctive approach to psychoanalytical assessment in the NHS (Milton, 1997). She describes the procedure as "a disturbing and intrusive psychoanalytic investigation" (p.52), which seeks to obtain a good picture in a limited time of the patient's inner world and the way it functions, and which also serves to give the patient a good idea of the nature of the psychoanalytical process and whether this is something the patient would wish to proceed with. It approximates technically to an ordinary analytic session. There's a minimum of instruction. The patient is invited by a brief word to begin wherever they wish. No automatic social responses are given, for example smiles and attempts at chat. She describes the procedure as "invasive", not therefore to be undertaken without good reason, she thinks, nor to be conducted by someone inexperienced without careful supervision. In other words, the spirit of psychoanalytic psychological therapy pervades psychoanalytic psychological therapy assessment. The assessment reflects the sense of it as potentially quite difficult for the patient and the need for both practitioner and patient to be aware of this.

Hence the importance attached to selection in psychoanalytic psychological therapy, and its prominence among the answers to the question, "Why assess?" Milton identifies six requirements that need to be met, and they all relate to selection, particularly the importance of identifying for whom the therapy would be likely to be either harmful or useless. The six requirements are as follows:

(1) Patient and therapist physical safety
(2) Patient mental safety
(3) Patient privacy and dignity
(4) Indications for patient "suitability"
(5) Training needs of the therapist
(6) Economic considerations

In other words, one can see here a number of particular questions being posed by the therapist, who answers them by means of a process far removed from what Milton calls "the conventional social way". One imagines the personal interview outlined in Chapter 3 comes close in style and tenor to what she calls the conventional social way.

This view of what should be covered is uncluttered by the requirements of performing the general task of assessing content. To the extent that psychoanalytic therapists might value content, its assessment is someone else's job.

Now consider, in contrast, the predicament of CBT as reflected in the British Association for Behavioural & Cognitive Psychotherapies (BABCP) Core Curriculum Reference Document (Hool, 2010). The document lays out the BABCP's twenty-four assessment competences (Hool, 2010). This listing, rather than expressing an experienced practitioner's position on assessment priorities, puts forward a governing organization's formal statement of its comprehensive approach to assessment as it affects training. Its approach to assessment perhaps reflects CBT's greater exposure as a frontline, stand-alone service, particularly since the coming of the British government's *Improving Access to the Psychological Therapies* (IAPT) initiative.

At first sight, CBT provides a contrast. A great deal of assessment is asked for. But here again there is no place for content, or almost no place for it. (Attention focuses on the assessment of "problem episodes" once "preliminary problem relevant data" have already been "elicited".) Twenty-four assessment competencies are specified. Setting aside competences numbers 20 to 24, which relate to formulation and the process of making sense of assessment data after they have been collected, the twenty remaining fall into two categories: "semi-structured assessment" and "diagnostic classification of common mental health disorders".

The sense here is less that there is no need for content, more that there is no room for it. So much needs to be crammed in. Instead of being avowedly *special* (specialist), the curriculum is full of material that doesn't truly belong to CBT assessment at all; rather, it relates to the highly exposed context in which CBT operates: for example, "conducting a mental state examination", "assessing and managing risk", "awareness of the process of differential diagnosis" and "identifying common mental health disorders using DSM-IV-TR". In other words, questions that might be expected to arise in the course of *general* (routine) work, were it possible to acknowledge and treat that as operationally distinct, must here be handled within the framework of a complex therapy with demanding assessment priorities of its own.

These two examples illustrate hands-off and hands-on responses to the incursions of routine work upon the territory of the specialist. These responses arise in the absence of any clear distinction between general and special work. Both responses are understandable. One presumes the existence of a general assessment framework of some kind (its operation the responsibility of someone else), the other presumes its lack (and assumes responsibility for providing it). It is hard not to see both positions as in different ways necessary to their survival in the service contexts in which they now operate: one small and needing to man its defences against powerful forces outside, the other large, but already penetrated by those forces, and at risk of succumbing to pressures within.

CHAPTER 7

Hospital and Community

> It is important to note that complaints, even as they relate to organic or bodily pathology, can be defined as psychological phenomena.
>
> A.W. Landfield, *The Complaint: A Confrontation of Personal Urgency and Professional Construction*, 1975

Just as in earlier chapters, this chapter too offers a variety of examples of psychological concerns and work arising from them. In terms of the distinction operating in chapters 5 and 6, the nature of the work is general rather than special. The context has changed. The illustrations come from hospital and community medicine and deal for the most part with settings associated more with physical than mental health care. The assumption the argument makes is that concerns can be viewed as psychological phenomena, even where, as Landfield (1975) puts it, they "relate to organic or bodily pathology" (p.3).

Pain

The first illustrations of how the argument is extended to work outside adult mental health and recovery services draw on applications to patients suffering from intractable pain and attending the outpatient department of a district general hospital in the North of England. Pain management groups are familiar in this kind of environment. But here the work is that of a clinical psychologist colleague working one-to-one with a range of patients, using the personal interview procedure described in Chapter 3 of this book with minor alterations. The choice to appoint someone to work one-to-one reflected a perception in my colleague's team that, while pain management programmes with groups were useful, the range of patients for which they were useful had a fairly narrow bandwidth (bad enough to need it; good enough to be able to make use of it).

While my colleague's range of referrals is wide, the main point to be illustrated here is how two men with rather similar clinical presentations come across very differently when the content of their concerns is opened up. The concerns of the two men are listed in Table 7.1. Mr O., the first patient in his late fifties, had been a car bodywork mechanic and Mr Q., the second patient in his late thirties, a welder. Both had suffered work-related injuries, and both had been forced to give up their jobs some years before, Mr O. having retrained as a community support worker and managed thereby to regain employment for a time. Both suffered from neuropathic damage (that is, pain caused by damage to nerve pathways rather than pain carried along nerve pathways), following unsuccessful back surgery.

Reflecting on the presentations of these two men (both of whom he had assessed over a number of sessions) and the kind of explication or elaboration that the content of their concerns prompted, my colleague identified different themes. From Mr O.'s concerns, he picked out as particularly significant *a guilty feeling that I have been unable to give a hundred per cent in my new job, the feeling that how I am is unfair to my wife* and *the sense of frustration that I can't just get on with life.* Mr O. was a man devoted to his work, driving himself into the ground, who hated holidays and really wanted to give *more than* one hundred per cent. Devoted also to his wife, it was his opinion that a man not working flat out for his family was not a fit husband (a view it later proved to be not shared by his wife). Work had always been his thing, and from his father came the belief that in this life one simply manages, no matter what the obstacles.

From Mr Q.'s concerns, my colleague singled out *the belief that I'm always doing the wrong thing* and *a feeling that it is too risky to tell my wife how I feel.* The patient had in recent years come to blame himself for what he saw as a catalogue of mistakes extending back to a decision to postpone a visit to see his dying father and including a decision to delay surgery on his back, which he later consented to and probably should not have undergone then or at any other time. On the one hand, life was terribly unfair; on the other, it was all really his fault: he kept making mistakes and being punished for them.

In one illustration, the coming of chronic pain exposes the shortcomings of a set of assumptions, beliefs and strategies, which had previously served fairly well (a situation reminiscent of Ms W.'s attempted solution in Chapter 5); in the other, pain has a particular meaning, being simultaneously the product of powerlessness and responsibility.

Table 7.1 The concerns of two men suffering intractable pain following industrial injury

Mr O.
A feeling that things are very bad for me
A feeling of being tired all the time
The belief that I can only feel comfortable in bed
A feeling like burning rods being pushed through my thighs
The cramping pain in my foot
A feeling that there is nobody I can talk to
The feeling of not being a man anymore
A guilty feeling that I have been unable to give a hundred per cent in my new job
The feeling that how I am is unfair to my wife
The sense of frustration that I can't just get on with life
Difficulty finding any structure for my day
Difficulty with concentration
Concern about wakefulness at night
A desperate feeling occasionally that they'd be better off without me
Dependency on the drugs to get by
A sense of hopelessness
Mr Q.
A sense that things are stuck but might get worse
Concern that my wife will no longer be able to put up with me
A pain like I've been hit in the back
Throbbing up and down my spine
Difficulty keeping still, particularly at night
Difficulty keeping my temper
The belief that I am always doing the wrong thing
Difficulty concentrating on anything
Concern about not getting enough sleep
Feeling of fatigue all the time (despite seeming not to be doing anything)
A sense that I am less of a person than I once was
Concern about being very cut off from people
Lowness of mood
A feeling that it is too risky to tell my wife how I feel
The sense of being very dependent on my wife
The feeling that there is no one I can turn to

These two illustrations have different implications for how the work might be developed. At the same time, there are some features common to both presentations, where the differences between the way the two men word their concerns are for the most part minor: trouble with concentration; wakefulness at night or the sense of not getting enough sleep; fatigue or tiredness; and negative feelings about oneself as a man or as a person. These overlaps point to areas of work familiar to practitioners in pain.

The Intensive Care Unit

This section looks briefly at the work of a colleague who has spent many years working on the intensive-care unit (ICU) of another district general hospital, where from the start he has employed personalized, descriptive assessment methods including some use of personal questionnaires. His view is that, while the value of the specific and personal remains, the notion of comprehensive assessment of content and identified sets of concerns does not fit with the moment-to-moment nature of much of the work of such a unit. Concerns will sometimes change almost by the hour. Furthermore, some of this work will be done at the bedside, where the patient's physical condition and exhaustion will very possibly limit the contact to twenty minutes or so, while the range of intervention needs to be varied and necessarily opportunist, requiring, according to circumstance, presence, consistency, acknowledgement, reassurance, occasionally anxiety management and sometimes even persuasion.

Responsibility for the treating of the particular *illness* narrowly defined mostly lies elsewhere. Explanatory theorizing about its causes has limited relevance. Here, diagnosis usually carries weight and precision enough. Patients who smoke will generally be only too aware of why they are suffering from emphysema. But there may be work to do in helping someone accept that developing *necrotizing fasciitis* ("flesh-rotting disease") is a matter of tremendous bad luck and not a punishment for being a terribly bad person.

On the other hand, the sensitivity of the specific and personal approach in picking up the *consequences and complications* of the various medical conditions and surgical procedures is very clear. Here, my colleague might need to discuss the chances of a stoma bag in a bowel operation being reversible, or be asked to speak to a patient who, facing further surgical intervention, says she's had enough of "needles and things", or that she feels that it is all just no longer worth it. Later, post-operatively, a more comprehensive description of a person's difficulties may be possible. For example, Mr S., a forty-five-year-old self-employed gardener with multiple injuries following a road traffic accident, for which the other party, although entirely responsible, had received only a £100 fine and a few points on her licence, expressed the concerns set out in Table 7.2.

Table 7.2 The concerns of Mr S., a self-employed gardener, as assessed some time after his discharge from an intensive care unit

A feeling that I will never be the same again
A sense that she got away with it
An inability to let go of my fury
A concern that I will never have my physical strength back again
A fear that my body won't heal
Difficulty snapping out of this flatness of mood
A fear that I won't get my customers back
A worry that I won't be able to go sailing anymore
A concern that I will no longer be able to visit my sister in Ireland
A fear that, no longer able to work, I'll be entirely on my own

When I asked my colleague whether he used a descriptive framework in identifying concerns similar to the Traveller from Altruria's, he said he used something rather looser: broadly, a distinction of the biological (the illness itself and what could be immediately ascribed to the illness and its treatment, like loss of appetite, exhaustion and the stoma bag); the psychological (anguish, rage, nightmares, visions, risks and fears for the future); and the social (family, relationships, work and leisure). He re-iterated that matters usually arose very much one at a time and certainly had to be dealt with that way. He was convinced, nonetheless, that concerns are better understood in the context of other concerns.

Cancer and palliative care

The third area of application of these ideas is to cancer and palliative care. Here, I have over the last three years resumed contact with two former clinical psychologist colleagues now based in a large teaching hospital, where they practise, supervise and teach many of the kinds of idea covered in this book, in particular the practical application of personal questionnaires.

In a way, much more obvious than in the field of adult mental health and recovery, cancer and palliative care force practitioners to grapple with the patient's whole experience, rather than just treat the illness. The issue is addressed in James Brennan's book *Cancer in Context* (2004). The sense of cancer as something more than an illness comes over strongly in these chapters. To invoke Feinstein's language once again, there is the illness or disorder, and then there are its consequences and complications. Regardless of whether one is working inside or outside mental health, there is the case for finding a descriptive foundation for pieces of psychological work that reflects experiences associated with something broader and looser than just a concept of mental or physical *illness*. Given the level of psychological distress that characterizes them, those further experiences are no less deserving of the attention of professional services. Brennan writes: "We believe that it is possible to recognize profound human distress without having to define it as a form of mental illness." He continues: "Understanding people's state of mind is more important than knowing their 'mental state' " (Brennan, 2004, p.xxiii).

My colleagues would add that it is also possible to recognize the need for psychological work without having to define that work as some form of psychological therapy. This recalls the comment of the colleague in the ICU, where the range of intervention, he felt, needed to be varied (requiring, according to circumstance, presence, consistency, acknowledgement, reassurance, occasionally anxiety management and even sometimes persuasion). There is more opportunity for something structured and ongoing and less cause to be opportunist, but the same need for flexibility. This is not that easy a message to convey to new psychologist trainees on the unit, who may struggle to see how the psychological therapy they took to be the paradigm on their adult mental health placement has only very limited relevance on their cancer and palliative care placement, where the patients' highly distressing, highly contextualized situation, calls for something much more "bespoke".

Over the course of an analysis of some forty personal questionnaires, my colleagues looked at what concerns had been voiced. Their intention was to arrive at a view about what constituted appropriate interview coverage in this setting, somewhat different from the one that has furnished the illustrations in previous chapters. Rather than work with the circumstances of referral as the basis of the sections of a descriptive hypothesis, they came to feel it was more appropriate – there being no mystery about a person's reason for contacting an oncology service – to concentrate more on the course of the experience over time. Assessment, as they now normally approach it, includes an invitation to patients to tell the story of their illness. Requesting them to start from the first signs that they were unwell, the practice has been to ask them to help their interviewer imagine "what you have had to deal with and how it has affected you and the people you are close to".

From there, using its broadly chronological structure, one sets about exploring the suggested coverage of the interview. For example, as the patient talks about initial visits to the GP, there often comes a moment when it is possible to ascertain whether trust in this doctor (and perhaps others) has been diminished or strengthened. There is the same need, as on the ICU, to be sensitive and avoid making blunders like asking a hardened, life-long smoker why he thinks he has lung cancer. This is likely to be unhelpful, although it is important not to make assumptions about why people think things are the way they are, and many patients find other sorts of distressing explanation for why they have become ill. Outline coverage of the descriptive interview is set out below:

Diagnosis, treatment and trust: the patient's view of the extent to which the service offered has been logical and consistent; apparent contradictions in the medical story; experiences of poor or insensitive care, including lack of information; beliefs about the benefits and problems linked to the treatment that has now been recommended.

Mind and body: How the illness and the different treatments are affecting physical and cognitive functioning; physiological and psychological issues associated with such functioning.

Emotions, feelings and coping style: Exploration of what emotions and patterns of feeling have been present; establishing how these have been appraised or understood or managed by the patient; the sense of being unable to express things to people or of there being no one to express things to; tendencies not to report symptoms or tell family about the illness.

Changes, expectations and sense of self: How the patient sees and evaluates himself or herself; what won't ever be the same again; sense of loss of control; the perception that others are now treating the patient differently, and what effect this is having.

Practical concerns: varied, but including employment, housing, finances, childcare, visits and getting about.

Impact on relationships and loved ones: whether there have been changes in relationships with friends and relatives; how friends and relatives, especially children, seem to be in their own right, and whether they require support themselves.

Adequacy of supporting resources: social and non-social means of support; whether other people's responses are experienced as helpful or not.

Spiritual and existential issues: why the patient believes he or she has become ill; the patient's beliefs about the consequences of becoming ill (like the soul having departed from the body); the extent of religious or spiritual beliefs, and the impact of these on what the patient is facing now.

Endings, predictions and uncertainties: worries about the future; fear of the unknown, particular worries about the longer-term consequences of other concerns that have been identified; concerns about endings of one kind or another (both dying and discharge).

People are met at different stages along the path the illness takes. With the patient whose concerns are illustrated in Table 7.3, for example, the work assumes that quality described in Chapter 5 as "providing high-grade support". The psychologist has been referred a first-year teacher in an infant school, very much the rock of her family, who is suffering a series of medical and surgical interventions for metastatic breast cancer. The patient, widowed some years earlier, feels there has been undue delay and poor advice, and senses she faces a life that will be significantly foreshortened. Meanwhile, matters are taking their course, and at some pace: she faces numerous uncertainties and difficult decisions over the course of the coming weeks. She has particular worries about what to say to her elderly father, who refuses to believe that his daughter is dying. There has been little time to think about the more distant future: the patient's pre-occupations are with right now, or at least just with the time between right now and the next appointment.

The second illustration, Table 7.4, presents something of a contrast. Here, the patient is 30 and has had ovarian cancer. Now the prospects of her making a good recovery are quite reasonable. She will be seen regularly over the course of some five months while she begins to struggle with a sense of personal crisis that has intensified over the course of

Table 7.3 The concerns of Mrs X., a primary school teacher in her mid-forties undergoing medical and surgical treatment for breast cancer

My lack of trust in the medical team at the hospital
A tendency to over-analyse everything that's said to me by the medical team
Sense of not coping at all, especially when appointments are coming up
My need for you to go extremely carefully with certain topics
Feeling a need to push it all away
The impact my illness is already having on my father
The worry about upsetting my father still more if I talk to him properly about my cancer and what may happen
A fear that my whole family is falling apart around me
Concern that I seem incapable of thinking about anything but cancer
My difficulty making decisions of any kind
A sense of the pointlessness of going back to my job teaching the class
Feeling of desperation under the surface
Feeling I must put on a positive attitude for everybody, including myself
The uncertainty of not knowing what my medical treatment will bring next

Table 7.4 The concerns of Ms Y., a woman aged 30 recovering from ovarian cancer

Feeling angry towards my GP for not taking me seriously
Scared feeling that life is never going to be the same again
Belief that people won't want a relationship with me because I'm damaged goods
The feeling of pressure on me to be getting back to being normal
Sense that everything is a problem, now that I am tarnished
Growing sense of not knowing who I am anymore
Upset that other people have prospects but I don't
A mood of hopelessness
Irritation at what seems the naivety of other people
Belief that other people deep down don't care what I am going through
Feeling of my whole life being out of control
Difficulty in seeing a way forward from here
Terror of the future
Sense that I am trapped
Feeling I can't hold it together any more

her illness and has little abated despite the tide seeming to turn in her favour.

The psychologist sensed in some of the material, for example the statements *growing sense of not knowing who I am anymore* and *feeling of my whole life being out of control*, that there were issues that deserved longer-term psychological counselling or therapy.

"Failure to thrive" (poor weight gain in the very young)

This fourth example of how personalized assessment has been extended beyond mental health and recovery services tackles a service for very young children and their parents. I was invited by a consultant community paediatrician to devise an assessment system based on personal questionnaires suitable for a well-established, home-based, health visitor–led growth and nutrition team. This had been created as part of a larger multidisciplinary service for families in a poorer part of a northern English city. The notion of "failure to thrive" centred on poor growth and difficulties with feeding and mealtimes, but the professionals involved had for long recognized the wide range of concerns associated with that presentation. The children ranged in age from as little as six months to approaching five years. The parents tended to be the mothers, often quite isolated ones, and sometimes a mother and father meeting the health visitor together.

I met with the team for a training day. We concluded it with a long and extensive brainstorm to explore this new terrain and from this created a set of categories that would serve as the basis for a parent interview. The approach this time sprang from a recognition that here one needed new content based on a fresh descriptive hypothesis. From the brainstorm, the following set of categories and statements illustrative of those categories eventually emerged:

Feeding and Mealtimes: *Feeding is a nightmare! He doesn't eat. I dread mealtimes. I'm concerned about her diet. She's impossibly choosy. I never know how it's going to be. I don't want to take away the pleasure of eating. I am concerned about what they're giving him at the nursery.*

Impact on Family Life: *Food dominates everything. We never go out together as a family. He's depriving my other children of treats. We can't be a normal family. He's winding us both up. It's causing argument between my partner and me. My other children are being ignored.*

Explanations of What's the Matter: *I must be doing something wrong. It's all down to me and my problems. He's ruling the roost. My mother-in-law is spoiling her. I'm concerned not to know what's wrong. I feel something is very wrong. She must have some medical problem that hasn't been spotted.*

Solutions and Stuckness: *I have tried everything without success. It's all up to me. I just can't get him off the bottle. She doesn't seem to like what I cook her. I am concerned that my husband's way of dealing with it is so different from mine. I don't really have time to walk her to school. There's nothing I can do. I jump from one thing to the next. I'm going round and round in circles.*

Activity and Lifestyle: *He's always on the go! I've no control over how he spends his time. He's stuck on computer games. She seems sluggish. He hates any form of exercise. Nothing seems to interest her. There is no routine. Life is chaos. She just won't sleep.*

Professionals and People's Help: *Nobody's bothered. Too much is expected of me. It feels like nothing is helping. I believe people think it's my fault. They don't understand at the baby clinic. People tell me different things. People's suggestions just make things worse. They don't think I am looking after my child properly. People hassle me about it being a problem.*

Me and My Life: *I am really upset about it all. I waste so much time cooking. It's all such hard work. I feel guilty I did not notice this before. It makes me feel like a bad parent. I am beginning to hate him! I do not feel like me any more.*

> *I don't go out on my own. I blame myself for my child's weight. I feel I have failed as a parent. I feel overwhelmed.*
>
> Fears about future: *I am concerned where all this is going to lead. I can't see the way forward. I believe she's heading for an eating disorder later on. I fear what will happen to him at school. I am anxious about him being damaged in some way for ever. Maybe she will even die. I don't want my child to be different. I'm concerned about him always being small.*

The two illustrations in Table 7.5 give an idea of the sets of concerns that this form of interview might generate. Callum, the child in the first example, is just over two, and the parent is his mother; in the second example, Holly is three months short of her fifth birthday, and the parent, again, is her mother.

The illustrations are chosen to show how, while the concerns focus on food, they spin off in other directions. With Callum's mother, they highlight her sense of anxiety, isolation and self-recrimination; with

Table 7.5 The concerns of two parents arising from their children's response to food and mealtimes

Concerns about Callum – just over two:
My concern that mealtimes last too long
A belief that Callum is not eating a good diet
A feeling that Callum's diet is having a bad effect on his growth
Concern that Callum does not eat vegetables
The feeling that Callum won't eat, no matter what I do
The belief that Callum will make himself ill and end up in hospital
A worry that Callum may have ADHD like his cousin
A feeling that I have gone wrong somewhere with my child
A feeling of being ashamed of myself
A feeling of being a failure
Concerns about Holly – nearly five:
My concern that Holly won't eat
Concern that mealtimes are difficult
Concern that Holly's eating difficulties cause conflict between my husband and me
A feeling that I am being undermined by my husband
Concern about Holly's attitude
A feeling nothing works
Concern that Holly usually wins the mealtime battle
A feeling that I am losing control of Holly
A feeling that my mother makes Holly's behaviour worse because of the attention she gives her

Table 7.6 The most frequent sorts of concerns expressed by parents at a health visitor's first assessment (N = 34)

Concerns about the future	28
Concerns about type of food eaten	20
Concern about the negative effect on a parent's life	15
Mealtimes as stressful	13
Concerns about the amount of food eaten	12
Concern about ways of getting their child to eat	10
Concern that a child is not putting on weight	10
Feeling under too much pressure to sort it out	9
Concern that feeding is causing arguments between adults	8
Sense that life revolves around feeding	7
Concern about how professionals have been up to now	6

Holly's, the existence of interpersonal conflict and her lack, or loss, of any sense of being in command of the situation.

After the training day, the health visitor took on personal questionnaires as part of her routine. The work was documented as a piece of exploratory research over approximately two years and an unpublished (draft) report written by the health visitor, the consultant paediatrician and myself (Mulley, Rudolf and Chalkley, 2003). At that point, the initiative lapsed because of changes of personnel and before it had been fully established as a routine service.

The report began by loosely grouping the items of the personal questionnaires to give the team an idea of what sorts of concerns were more often described. These data are shown in Table 7.6. While families often describe concerns directly related to the type and amount of food their children ate or didn't eat, other concerns related more to stress, pressure, apprehension, the effect of what was happening at mealtimes, either in the parent's life or to the couple's relationship.

The report draws attention to the progress made in reducing the level of concern expressed by the thirty-four parents studied over the course of visits. At the first visit, thirty of these thirty-four rated the average level of their concerns *considerable* or *very considerable*. Some had just one subsequent visit, others two or more. Of the thirty who received a second visit, eighteen rated the level of their concerns *considerable* or *very considerable*. By the time of their last visit, only four still rated their concerns *considerable* or *very considerable*.

Twenty-two of the thirty-four parents involved in the study replied to a questionnaire asking about their satisfaction with personal questionnaires. The results are shown in Table 7.7. On these measures,

Table 7.7 Parents' views on personal questionnaires

	Agree	Disagree
It included my most important concerns about my child	22	0
Putting it together made me feel listened to	21	1
Listing the concerns made me feel clearer what they were	21	1
Using it made sure we focused on my concerns on each visit	19	3
It helped me see how my concerns changed over time	22	0
It meant that my concerns were addressed	20	2
It was easy to fill in	21	1

the parents' attitude towards the questionnaires was favourable. Over eighty per cent of parents agreed with each of items.

The report ended with some reflections from the health visitor herself on the use of personal questionnaires with the parents of these children. The team's decision to use personal questionnaires with these families in the first place was brought about by studies suggesting that poor weight gain in the very young might reflect continuing difficulties in doctor–patient communication in this area of paediatrics. (Elsewhere in paediatrics, studies tended to suggest that doctor–patient communication had already improved.)

The health visitor, a nurse specialist of considerable experience and training, felt that personal questionnaires were "very valuable" in improving communication, not just in identifying and understanding parents' difficulties but also in helping structure visits in such a way that the conversation returned to what the parent felt mattered most. "I have had a real sense of working with parents and starting from their perspective, not mine as a health professional."

To use them successfully proved harder with families who had been referred for reasons of professional rather than parental concern. Here, she thought there might well be parental concerns too, but it took considerable skill to draw them out. A final point she made, and one that perhaps recurs more often than any other when reservation is expressed about the use of personal questionnaires, is that they are "labour intensive". She did, however, feel that the time spent doing them developed the relationship and allowed things to move forward quicker. This prompts once more the thought that I am much wiser in my advocacy to present personal questionnaires as integral to a whole piece of work, or way of working, than I am to talk about "the PQ" as some elaborate, sophisticated and superior assessment "tool" or "instrument". In the study just summarized, speed of resolution seems to have repaid the effort of construction. This thought brings to mind the adage: "Long on assessment; short on treatment."

Forensic learning disabilities

This last section is based on conversations over a couple of years with a nurse colleague working on a men's medium secure forensic learning disabilities unit. These conversations threw up a number of challenges. In fact, it quickly became clear that in seeking to colonize this area of work for the content argument, he and I would be pushing the argument to its limits.

It is perhaps best to start by bringing out the sheer difficulty of the experience both patients, or perhaps here better "service users", and staff face. Over the course of their lives, service users may well have faced almost every handicap and stigma that human society can conceive and conjure up: poverty, lack of family support, inability to communicate, isolation, intellectual impairment, gang and institutional violence, all manner of exploitation (emotional, physical, financial and sexual), substance misuse, chronic physical illness (diabetes, for example), mental health problems, loss of liberty, lack of privacy, overcrowding and segregation.

Meanwhile, staff, especially nursing staff, are faced with attempting to reconcile the roles of custodian and carer. This arises because the service users have come into contact with the criminal justice system as a result of some offence they have committed. But they have then been diverted from this system because first and foremost they require care. Thus, nurses have dual responsibility. In exercising these roles, nurses are themselves exposed to trauma and secondary trauma: manipulation, harassment, sexually inappropriate behaviour, verbal abuse, threats, aggression and violence. To manage in such situations requires qualities of many kinds (ones like resilience, resourcefulness, reciprocity and reflection (Claxton 2002)). At times, it also needs the use of physical restraint, rapid tranquilization and, as a last resort, the use of a seclusion room; many of which courses of action are clearly at odds with the traditional notion of a caring role. Constant risk assessment and management can place a serious strain on the building and sustaining of therapeutic rapport.

In relation to content-based assessment, much of the above creates difficulties. The ward environment with its enforced proximity and constant presence to one another of client and staff, regulated only by partitions and keys and shifts, is entirely different from the outpatient or other occasional arrangement, which has quietly presumed itself to be the basis of contact thus far. With this comes a breakdown of assumptions about role, assumptions familiar from the sociological and social psychological literature. It is not just that care staff assume *more* roles within settings where the whole of life is squeezed into one place, but the particular roles that define the relationship between each client and member of staff are complex and varied. In other words, both social and psychological roles are matters in flux and contention.

In terms of the terminology of this book, difficulties arise too in finding a way to grasp what is being expressed or *presented* (see Chapter 4). There, understanding a patient's *position* meant gauging the client's view of what the problem was, what caused it, whether anyone could help and whether *you* the practitioner could help. Here, though, listening to the exact wording of what the client says may not give the key to position, at least, not in the way Fisch, Weakland and Segal (1982) defined it. This is because the client may well not be expressing a position in those senses of the word at all, but rather angling consciously or unconsciously to feel cared about, change the subject, end the encounter, convey ambivalence, sustain some level of undemanding contact, needle, claim respect, assume superiority, secure a privilege, create a distraction or just provoke a scene.

My nurse colleague illustrated the kind of situations that might arise where role and the responsibilities attaching to role are an issue, or where either no concern is expressed or a concern is expressed but its meaning is unclear. He first gave the example of one patient who arrived on the ward, who was diabetic, adamant that he didn't want to take insulin but offered no reason why and expressed no concern. Here, the concern clearly resided with staff not service user, and they were left wondering where they stood in relation to the person's capacity under the 2005 Mental Capacity Act.

Another service user had very limited speech and communicated mainly through his actions. He very rarely identified concerns but often "acted out" when something was wrong. With him, these occasions of shouting abuse at staff, self-harming, breaking chairs and so forth indicated he was concerned about something. What he was concerned about remained very unclear.

A third service user did talk to staff, and the content of these conversations suggested he might have concerns, but the content was difficult to interpret. On one occasion, his speech very indistinct, he appeared to be complaining about another member of the ward staff: "I don't like him. He wasn't nice to me." But what had the staff member done? This same service user later came to report his new stereo "broken".

The old stereo had broken the week before and been replaced. How had the new stereo become broken? Had the service user broken it himself? The mains lead appeared severed. Had someone else done it? If the service user had done it accidentally, had he severed it in trying to fix it? And if it was done deliberately, was this a way of conveying to the nurse that something else was broken or not right: a broken appointment or sick mother.

This leaves in jeopardy the notion of the one-to-one, patient–practitioner relationship as something transferable to the forensic learning difficulties setting. Instead, the closest approximation that can be hoped for is something like the set-up in the last section. There, a nurse specialist met with concerned parents; here, one might consider the possibility of concerned staff turning to a consultant to give voice to their worries about a particular service user. A possible basis for a consultative meeting arranged as a number of topics (eight), is set out below:

> Concerns related to the way this client behaves on the ward and the particular situations that arise from this: *His constant questions about leave. His regular complaints about other residents. The sense of chaos on the ward when he kicks off. Difficulty responding quickly enough to abrupt changes of mood.*
>
> Particular risks that concern us as a team arising from our understanding of his physical or psychological condition: *The danger he poses to children if he gets off the ward. The likelihood he'll try and escape again. The sense of greater risk from him when we are short staffed. Our concern about his consumption of sweets and fizzy drinks.*
>
> Concerns the client voices that we (or I) need to hear but may have missed in the past: *His concern he will be beaten up by J. His requests to see his sister that we feel compelled to block. His complaint that nobody cares for him.*
>
> Issues of context, translation and interpretation: *His lack of any speech at all. The meaning of his silences. Difficulty understanding what he means when he talks about his broken glasses. The troubling significance of his talking about seeing a child outside whom he would like to take care of.*
>
> Responses and attempted solutions: *Our tendency to rely on exclusion. Uncertainty about how to answer his questions about his next outing. The ineffectiveness of our response to his persisting requests for reassurance. Difficulty responding quickly enough to abrupt changes of mood. Need to take heed when he puts on that green jacket.*
>
> Concerns arising from the client's apparent response to physical and human resourcing and support: *His sensitivity to the present overcrowding on the ward. The slowness of the response from off the ward when he blew up last time.*

> *Difficulty managing him here on present staffing levels. The sense of greater risk from him when we are short staffed.*
>
> Impact of client on us (or me): *Our feeling of total frustration. Worry about our sense of rage at what he does to O. The menacing quality of his silences. A kind of numbed silence whenever he comes up in discussion. Temptation to insist that you (the consultant) fix things or get your hands dirty, when it's difficult with him or someone else.*
>
> Concerns related to future management: *Our sense of going around in circles. The inability to devise a management plan for him. Difficulty getting a clear view from the Home Office. Concern about the impact of impending discharge on his mentally ill mother.*

Various issues arise in creating a set of categories like this. The sequencing of them loosely follows the set of those for "failure to thrive": concerns about situations that might arise on the ward parallels concerns about eating and mealtimes; concerns about resourcing and support so far parallel those about the family's existing professional support. The intention as there, indeed as with all attempts to define coverage, is not to categorize the material, but to organize it with sufficient degree of overlap, or redundancy, between sections, so as to reduce the chances that important material will be missed. For example, "the sense of greater risk from him when we are short staffed" could (as illustrated) come up either in questions in the risks section or in the resources section; or, "difficulty responding quickly enough to abrupt changes of mood" could (again, as illustrated) come up either in the section on how a client behaves on the ward or in the section on responses and attempted solutions.

So far the procedure has not been put into action, and my nurse colleague has now moved on elsewhere. However, if something like this were to be routinely adopted, it would provide the opportunity for a structured case discussion between those immediately involved. Here, there is the possibility of a meeting that is neither box ticking nor a free-for-all, which teases out where responsibilities lie, focuses on the nursing staff, tolerates differences of opinion and validates nurses' concerns by taking them seriously, sometimes finding solutions to them and sometimes not.

CHAPTER 8

Ideas: From Practice to Philosophy

Some years back, I planned to write up my teaching as a short summary of Shapiro's individualized approach to assessment. Then that expanded to become a description of personalized assessment that would manage to bring together the systematic and the person-centred. Finally, the larger topic of *content* emerged. But with this more ambitious project, serving this aspirational concept, comes the need to situate the new argument in relation to other more established and better-known ones. In this chapter, therefore, a number of other positions are looked at. The treatment in each case varies, sometimes concentrating on exposition and seeking to show how these other ideas expand and enrich the content-based argument, at other times concentrating on what separates it from them, distinguishing what is original and different about it. There are four sections to the chapter:

- The first section deals with Carl Rogers and the person-centred approach. The person-centred approach fosters practitioners' awareness of the relationship between patient and therapist. It sees this as the vehicle of change, not the various skills, procedures and other *technologies* that are viewed as crucial elsewhere. As assessment counts as one of these technologies, Rogerian approaches struggle to find much use for assessment beyond the assessment of the relationship. Content surrenders to process with few shots fired.
- In contrast, George Kelly in developing Personal Construct Therapy found room for notions of technology, questioning the Rogerian position that relationship and technology are necessarily at odds. Kelly explored matters relating to assessment at some length. The

constructs of Personal Construct Therapy *are* personal ones and markedly different from the constructs encountered so far. Where Kelly differs from what I am proposing, the reason is often because content, or *the complaint* as he termed it, remains slightly marginal to his theory.

- The third section looks at qualitative and quantitative assessment issues through the work of Alvan Feinstein and at what he considered to be good and less good in the technology of clinical assessment, or as he tended to call it *clinical judgement*. In his view, assessment needs better to reflect the preoccupations of patients, to be stronger on words than numbers. When it comes to assessment *procedures*, these need to be more sensitive to what he called *clinimetric* notions like utility, practicality and directness, and not restricted to hybrid *psychometric* concepts like reliability and validity.
- Finally, Patrick Bracken and Philip Thomas further support the case for content. They offer a set of thoughts with a number of implications for an assessment technology aspiring to be humanistic. They carefully distinguish different traditions in continental phenomenology, in such a way as to help the discussion back to the particular and personal. They are understood to imply that the open air of ordinary language, not the subterranean confines of expert vocabulary, allows the fullest expression of the complex experience of human distress.

Assessing and relating

The notion of such a thing as a person-centred approach owes more to Carl Rogers than to anyone else. Rachel Freeth's (2007) book *Humanising Psychiatry and Mental Health Care* opens with sad reflections on how difficult it is to be person-centred in the modern National Health Service. "In many ways the person-centred approach is the antithesis of current mental health practice that is often, in my view, oppressive and dehumanized" (p.1). In the first of two forewords to the book, Brian Thorne writes about an environment where the humanity of doctors, nurses and patients alike is constantly endangered in the frantic attempt to keep chaos at bay (Thorne, 2007). In the other, Mike Shooter writes about the battle to establish the worth of the person-centred approach in the competitive world of commissioning, where success is judged on the throughput of patients, not on the quality of their lives. He continues:

> Small wonder that in the face of such challenges we have witnessed what a colleague has called "the endless retreat from patients". Some of us go

> into academic research, some into service management. Some of us climb the structure of our profession, some the slippery slope of NHS politics. (Shooter, 2007, p.x)

Don't be too sure either, Freeth herself quickly adds, that a claim to be person-centred, which originates from anywhere within that massive organization, really has any substance to it. Much of it is the rhetoric of service planners and personnel managers. This rhetorical abuse arises from a misunderstanding about what Rogers' contribution was: his contribution really should not be seen as another technique or set of techniques. Patient-centredness must not be viewed as just a glorified listening skill or indeed skill of any other kind. It is a philosophy and therefore something better described as an *approach* than a *therapy*.

This philosophical sense of the term comes over particularly strongly in Rachel Freeth's account. It sets a theme that recurs from time to time in this chapter: the tension between technology on the one hand and ethics on the other. The tension is most sharp here where Freeth and others argue that support for their approach is too weak in the NHS and again later where Bracken and Thomas argue as psychiatrists that powerful anti-humanistic currents within their profession are too strong.

How close to the spirit of the person-centred approach is this book's argument for content? A personalized assessment samples people's experience in the here and now. It embraces some kind of totality in the way it seeks to represent and comprehend a person's *whole* set of concerns rather than reduce or summarize matters in terms of one particular label, like alcoholism or narcissistic personality disorder. It refuses to impose a direction on proceedings beyond the exploration of content. And personalized assessment downplays the place of diagnosis, especially as a starting point for psychological enquiry.

A part of the Rogerian person-centred position though is missing from the present argument; and this is precisely the part that some, like Rachel Freeth, would see as the most important: the philosophy of the person. There has been no mention in this book so far of a person's innate tendency to growth and development: the actualizing tendency. This is a significant gap. "The actualizing tendency is the crucial concept at the heart of approaches to person-centred therapy" (Wilkins, 2010, p.29). "The starting point of all person-centred therapy must be the therapist's trust in the client's *actualizing tendency*" (Worsley, 2009, p.7). Simon du Plock, writing in the *Handbook of Counselling Psychology*, describes this as a fault line running through humanistic approaches. He is critical of the Rogerian insistence on self-actualization: "While we might agree with Rogers (1961) that potatoes invariably shoot in the direction of light, we should not confuse the growth of vegetables with the spiritual or psychological life of humans" (du Plock, 2010, p.134).

One is left wondering whether the argument for content will prove to sit more comfortably with the more phenomenological, existential European humanistic tradition of exploring how people understand their worlds, especially the more problematic parts of them, than with the American one based on self-actualizing and personal growth. But maybe there is no special place for content, even within an existential tradition. Irving Yalom, writing as an existential therapist in *The Gift of Therapy*, deals briskly with it in his introduction. " 'Content' is", he writes, "just what it says – the precise words spoken, the substantive issues addressed" (Yalom, 2002, p.xix). In the main body of the book, process gets forty chapters and content eleven, these latter being the existential topics of freedom, meaning and death. (But, says Yalom, the effective therapist should never try and force discussion of any content area; no more these than any other.)

At one time, this book's manifest preoccupation with assessment would definitely have consigned it to the long grass as far as Rogerian and post-Rogerian thinkers were concerned. Rather than stress the *complexity* of assessment, "Rogerians" have tended over the years to emphasize its *undesirability*; a tendency still not altogether suppressed and owing much historically to the equating of assessment with classifying, categorizing and diagnosing.

At its toughest and least compromising, the Rogerian position might be summarized as follows: "if anyone needs assessing, it is the counsellor, not the client!" Perhaps more representative of the standpoint of its practitioners today, the position might be expressed instead as follows: "assess the relationship, not the client."

> In practice many, if not most, person-centred practitioners do make an assessment of the likelihood that they will be able to offer a relationship . . . to the particular client, at the particular time, in the particular place even if they call it something else. This is something other than diagnosis and the emphasis is on the (potential) relationship, not the client. Under the right circumstances, the client will make constructive personality changes. Any limitation to this prospect is more likely to lie with the therapist . . . . (Wilkins, 2010, p.183)

This position is elaborated and qualified by Richard Worsley, who writes about the issues and pressures that arise as someone embarks on professional practice as a person-centred therapist:

> We are obliged to assess our clients, and yet we work within an approach that has been thought to scorn assessment as being too "expert". For those who espouse the role of expert, assessment can be a complex and time-consuming technical exercise... Yet to reject the idea of assessment completely is a misunderstanding, and an ethically dangerous one at that... It is not just an ethical issue but a technical one too. Each person is unique. People are unique in their processing, their ways of functioning and their life patterns. (Worsley, 2007, pp. 346–347)

He stresses the need to avoid mental health stereotypes, but adds: "assessment need not be about this classificatory nonsense." Instead, at its heart lies the question whether "this person and I" can enter into a therapeutic relationship. "Is there psychological contact between us?" He concedes that such a type of assessment will not be enough to meet all circumstances, and he says there is a need to be able to listen to the client from two places. "With most of my attention, I strive to accompany the client, but with a small part of my attention I seek to know what might get in the way of this contact" (p.347).

Assessment, therefore, is mainly about relating but includes the obstacles to relating. For a beginning therapist, especially, this idea may generate an internal conflict or at least present a "paradox". The paradox is that a beginner trying diligently to work within his or her competence, and less skilled in judging where its limits lie, will more often seek consultation. But the result of the consultation may be to be placed in the hands of "senior colleagues whose model involves thorough, formal and sometimes paper-bound assessments in agencies that are increasingly risk-averse" (p.347).

Worsley may have comprehensive risk assessments in mind here. These "formal and sometimes paper-bound assessments" do not sound like assessments of content. But content, which has so much to do with the implications of people being unique, comes close to the heart of the "technical" issue to which Worsley refers. As things stand, he seems, on my reading, to think either that people can't be assessed at all in their uniqueness or, to the extent that they can be, it is only by experts.

There seem to be various assessment dilemmas facing person-centred approaches, these less now about whether to assess and more about what and how. Perhaps the recognition of this will allow matters to shift from the idea of assessment as undesirable to the idea of it as complex. The catch is that by failing to tackle uniqueness, person-centred practitioners lack the means to assess the phenomena that lie at the heart of the approach: things seen through the eyes of the client.

Perhaps, one must reconcile oneself to the possibility that humanistic approaches will always favour process to the detriment of content. There is so much to be undone, so much in past process that has been inhumane. Something significantly more content driven comes with Paul Chadwick's *Person-Based Cognitive Therapy for Distressing Psychosis*. Chadwick is one of the very few practitioners to have made use of personal questionnaires in recent years and promoted their use (Chadwick and Lowe, 1990). The irony is that this person-based book comes out of CBT, the therapy described rather dismissively some years ago as "symptom-oriented, brief, and hence, reimbursable" (Yalom, 2002, p.xv). Chadwick draws on Rogerian principles, while saying that just to invoke Rogerian ideas is insufficient. The focus of the therapy is no longer on *symptoms*; it is on *personal distress*, and with that transformation comes the need to work with symptomatic *meaning*, "...or what is sometimes called content" (Chadwick, 2006, p.58).

Personal content or personal constructs?

In 1946, Carl Rogers left his post as professor and director of clinical psychology at Ohio State University. The person who replaced him was George Kelly. There are similarities between Rogers' person-centred approach and Kelly's psychology of personal constructs. Both approaches are the work of humanistic thinkers. Both these psychologists focus on people. Neither Rogers nor Kelly extrapolates from rats and pigeons. Humans are active. They have reasons and intentions. Like Rogers, Kelly's humanism embraces a theory of how man is in the world. In Rogers' case, this is as actualizing the self; in Kelly's case, it is as construing the world. Again, it is worth saying that, as with Rogers, Kelly's theorizing is at a level more ambitious than anything attempted in this book. And, rather as Rogers wasn't self-consciously a phenomenologist or existentialist, and apparently was surprised in fact to be called the latter, neither was Kelly in a rush to define himself as a phenomenologist or an existentialist, and indeed expressly denied he was the former.

However, there are differences between Kelly and Rogers, and it is in exploring certain of these differences that one can first begin to see a number of affinities between this book's arguments and Kelly's approach to what he eventually settled on calling *psychotherapy*.

The espousal of "technique"

Trevor Butt in his recent work on Kelly has brought out the sharp difference between Rogers and Kelly as humanistic thinkers. He quotes the following passage from Rogers to give a flavour of the sort of thing he feels might have put Kelly's back up:

> When I am somehow in touch with the unknown in me, when perhaps I am in a slightly altered state of consciousness, then whatever I do seems to be full of healing... There is nothing I can do to force this experience, but when I can relax and be close to the transcendent core of me, then I may behave in strange and impulsive ways in the relationship... But these strange behaviours turn out to be right in some odd way: it seems that my inner spirit has reached out and touched the inner spirit of the other. (Rogers, 1980, p.129)

These phrases, like "the unknown in me", "full of healing", "transcendent core" and "inner spirit", are, as Butt puts it, "the vocabulary... of the mystic and not the social scientist" (Butt, 2008, p.57).

There is more to this than the choice of language, however. Butt sees Kelly's approach as embodying "a new humanism", a willingness to embrace social science with zeal and in particular a readiness to take heed of some of "behaviourism's ventures". He draws attention to one of Kelly's later papers, where Kelly seems to seek to distinguish his sort of "humanistic methodology" from that of persons unnamed. He quotes the following passage:

> It would, in my opinion, be a serious mistake for psychologists who hope to raise man from the position of an unwitting subject in an experiment to a posture of greater dignity, to abandon technology. The spirit of man is not enlarged by withholding his tools... A man without instruments may look dignified enough to those who do not stand in his shoes, but he most certainly will be incapable of making the most of his potentialities. (Kelly, 1966, p.134)

Later, in the same paper, Kelly returns to the subject:

> This is not to say that the humanistic psychologist need be unconcerned with precision in his research... If precise measurement will reveal faint clues to what is going on, it should not be befogged by the global phraseologies of existentialism and phenomenology. (Kelly, 1966, p.139)

But he immediately adds that "the object of precision is to provide greater sensitivity to psychological processes not easily perceived, not to build impregnability into one's findings by adding decimal places". Then, in exploring this notion of greater sensitivity, he writes a couple of pages later about how the objects of investigation should be made "palpable" (p.141).

Nevertheless, Kelly's embracing of technique is striking. It is reflected in his approaches to counselling and therapy. Rogers sees the meeting with the person as the principal source of change in therapy. Kelly on the other hand sounds far more instrumentalist. Writing about the psychotherapeutic relationship specifically, rather than humanistic methodology generally, he asserts that "the psychotherapeutic relationship is designed to get things done" and continues: "Personal construct therapy is a way of getting on with the human enterprise and it may embody and mobilize all the techniques for doing this that man has yet devised" (Kelly, 1965, p.221).

With respect to the present argument, this rehabilitation of "technique" is important. To assess content too, one needs to be allowed to embrace technique. I really do question whether one needs to eschew it in order to be counted authentically personal or truly human! It seems small affront to the dignity of man or woman to seek to establish their concerns using a personal interview or collaborate further with them in creating a questionnaire, just so long as these activities are recognized as devices and do not become ends in themselves.

The legacy of pragmatism

What lies behind this assertion of the importance of technique? Butt sees a deep grounding in philosophical pragmatism. This is a strongly American philosophical tradition, one born in the troubled times that followed the Civil War, the era of the spoilsmen, a bold, bland, cynical epoch when the affairs of the country seemed to have passed into the clutches of the industrial entrepreneur (Hofstadter, 1948). This philosophical tradition was one that Kelly, much of whose early professional career was spent in the Midwestern states of Minnesota, Iowa and Kansas during the equally troubled years of the depression of the 1930s, came to embrace. Butt shows how Kelly's thinking draws on the American tradition of pragmatism associated with Charles Peirce, William James, John Dewey and George Mead (Butt, 2005).

What are the implications of *pragmatism* as one seeks to position the content argument in relation to Kelly's work? Butt sees two. First, there is phenomenology as seen from a pragmatic viewpoint: the world as experienced is a matter of individual perception, not absolute truth. Content, therefore, is constructed. People conceive what they know and shape it, rather than uncover and consume it. Kelly writes early in the first volume of *The Psychology of Personal Constructs* that people look at their worlds through transparent patterns or templates, ones that they create and then attempt to fit over the realities of which the world is actually composed. The fit is not always very good, but a poor fit is better than no fit because no fit leaves just an "undifferentiated homogeneity", out of which people cannot make any sense.

> Let us give the name *constructs* to these patterns that are tentatively tried on for size. They are ways of construing the world. They are what enable man, and lower animals too, to chart a course of behaviour, explicitly formulated or implicitly acted out, verbally expressed or utterly inarticulate, consistent with other courses of behaviour or inconsistent with them, intellectually reasoned or vegetatively sensed. (Kelly, 1955a, p.7)

A person is, in the ordinary course of things, more a construer of knowledge than a discoverer of it. Discoveries are occasionally made but more perhaps by physical scientists than by social scientists or ordinary mortals like patients and therapists. For the most part, ideas are actively construed and endure less because they are true and there to be revealed than because they are useful, being formed and then sustained or abandoned by human agency. Ordinary men and women, according to Kelly, are not just inventors of instruments but construers of knowledge too.

As one advances the argument for content over these pages, it is important not to forget to stress this "constructivist" aspect: how people organize their descriptions and presentations of material according to how they see their problems and how they then attempt to communicate them. It is not just a matter of their understanding of the material; it is also their understanding of how someone else will receive that material. The atmosphere of the consulting room is fraught with the intentions and anticipations of its occupants.

A second point Butt makes about Kelly and pragmatism, and which is relevant to the content argument, has a more existentialist feel to it. The world is experienced whole and live. A feature of pragmatic philosophy is its opposition not just to the dualism of mind and body or individual and society but also to the divisions of psychology into faculties like affect, cognition and conation, or feeling, thinking and willing.

As this book argues, when one captures the content of concerns of an individual, this wholeness is present. Concerns come in sets and provide descriptions. Content lies in the patient's realm, and while it may in time be the subject of academic scrutiny, and receive its due share of poking and prodding, it seems important to seek to bring out the unity, or at least the coherence, of a person's sense of their difficulties, rather than make it an exercise in compartmentalizing and categorizing. I think it is worth trying to look at the matter with fresh eyes, taking an outsider's view, such as that of the *Man from Mars* or the *Traveller from Altruria*. Time will tell whether the field of descriptive theorizing will prove fertile.

"Assessment" as a pragmatic concept

Given that George Kelly stands in a tradition of pragmatism and constructivism, and given so much mention of assessment over the course of this book, both assessment theory and assessment procedure, one should ask how *useful* a concept Kelly might consider *assessment* to be. Words become dichotomous constructs in Kelly's theory as they find their complementary pole. One might therefore also ask what lies at the opposite pole to *assessment*. A possible answer is *treatment*. Does a distinction between *assessment* and *treatment* represent something useful? Here, with *treatment*, one finds oneself grappling with a word that, whether or not useful, might in some quarters be viewed as undesirable, particularly in the context of person-centred work. "In fact, even to call the person-centred approach a 'treatment' would be to many person-centred practitioners, including myself, anathema" (Freeth, 2007, p.94). It seems altogether too resonant of the Age of Psychiatry.

Actually, Kelly – who likewise has little room for the word "treatment" – doesn't seem to have been very partial to the word "assessment" either. It makes no indexed appearance in *The Psychology of Personal Constructs* until Chapter 22. This is the very last chapter of a very long book, or rather a book in two substantial volumes. In fact, the reference to *assessment* only comes on page 814 of a work that runs to 861 pages. There, it is described "as a form of enactment". Kelly defines enactment as meaning tasks, "some of which are highly structured, some quite free, and some quite anxiety producing". Such tasks provide "relatively unstructured diagnostic observations". He traces them back to procedures of the British War Office Selection Boards but views them as deriving ultimately from "German military psychologists". This is not an altogether wholesome pedigree. The tasks are seen as having had no extensive use in connection with psychotherapy and to have been used mostly for "the selection of personnel for particular assignments" and for "research requiring the formulation of a comprehensive dependent variable".

"Assessment" may have been a word that had simply not come into its own. (There is still no mention of it at all in the index of the third edition of Anastasi's *Psychological Testing*, even though this standard work was not published until thirteen years later in 1968.)

Alternatively, *assessment* may simply have had the wrong overtones for Kelly, as *treatment* has had for Rachel Freeth.

Now, at least, the word is in common use in the Anglophone world. So, is it perhaps useful, after all? Kelly would still no doubt advise caution. "When a person uses familiar words he invokes traditional meanings." One risk, therefore, remains medicalizing. Another is not saying what the counsellor or clinician really wants to. "He usually ends up compromising between saying what he means and letting the listener hear what he is already prepared to hear" (Kelly, 1955a, p.129). But the trouble is that "if one is to communicate, one must use familiar words or else spend a great deal of time coining new ones". Kelly, with an acknowledgement to the man into whose shoes he had stepped at Ohio State, chose *client* instead of *patient*, but opted for *therapy* instead of *treatment* (or Rogers' newly coined term "counselling").

> We have submitted to the term "therapy", even though what we mean by "therapy" is quite different from what is commonly called "therapy"... [We] considered using the term "reconstruction" instead of "therapy". If it had not been such a mouth-filling word we might have gone ahead with the word. Perhaps later we may! (Kelly, 1955a, p.130)

In place of *assessment*, he opted for that word *diagnosis*, a word with plenty of traditional meaning and much additional baggage. In this book, I have stuck with *assessment* and have pressed the distinction between the assessment of content and the assessment of constructs. But to conjure with this term, more generally, is difficult. As soon as assessment lacks a polar opposite or resists definition, it loses its meaning or becomes so replete with meanings that it is in effect meaningless. Within a pragmatic personal framework, the word is more or less useful at different times, depending on the patient's understanding of it. Within a pragmatic professional framework, its meaning seems at least to be always shifting. And sometimes in person-centred work, especially, the word seems at risk of disappearing altogether. But if the term is finally to be abandoned, does anything need to be salvaged? One might wish to dispense with the term "assessment", but the need to gather together the experience of a patient's distress in a thoroughgoing, systematic way remains.

The complaint and its content

Kelly's practitioner, even if expected first and foremost to address the diagnosis of constructs, is required too to consider the patient's complaint, and this concept of the *complaint* does have something content-like about it. Kelly is not bothered with defining *complaints* at any length, and there is limited illustration of them. In various places, though, Kelly writes about the *nature* of complaints. At one point, he allows that a change of complaint might be heralded by the disappearance of the "principal symptom". This suggests that a complaint has constituent parts, rather as content is made up of a set of concerns. At other points, he explains that complaints are conventional things, that they are culture dependent, that they shouldn't be taken at face value, that they can be difficult to grasp and so on. And he does view the complaint as an extremely "important datum which deserves more attention than it usually gets" (Kelly, 1955b, p.163). It is not just the light the complaint sheds on the client's basic framework of ideas, or how the client's poor formulation of it hinders the client from finding a solution to it, but it is hearing out the complaint that allows the practitioner to establish rapport and build a co-operative therapeutic relationship.

Above all, it is complaints in Kelly's view that define the goal of therapy. Where Kelly's definition of a disorder is pitched at the level of the psychological system, the goal of psychotherapy is pitched at a phenomenological level. "We may say, simply, that the goal of psychotherapy is to alleviate complaints – complaints of a person about himself and others and complaints of others about him" (Kelly, 1955b, p.193).

> Some psychologists will not be very happy with this definition. Clinical psychologists are always being pressed to make some definitive statement of what ultimate value they pursue in their work. Such a statement would have to be pitched at the levels of a religion or philosophy, not at the level of a system of psychology. (Kelly, 1955b, p.193)

Kelly's interest, nonetheless, is principally in personal constructs, not personal concerns. Personal constructs lie at the heart of his theory and most – if not all – the other concepts on which he draws he applies to their service. He couches his concept of psychological disorder in terms of characteristics of a person's construct system. He gives expression to various emotions like threat, anxiety, guilt and hostility by way of what they mean about the operation of the personal construct system. Even his account of a complaint is seen as casting "light upon the complainant's basic framework of ideas... his basic manner of understanding, within which any reconstruction of his thinking about his problem must take place" (Kelly, 1955b, p.163).

Words before numbers

Bilsbury and Richman (2002) quote a passage from a tale – probably apocryphal and here paraphrased – about a famous physiologist and a famous psychiatrist in conversation at a time when rating scales were becoming fashionable in the 1940s. The physiologist had found evidence of biochemical change in the psychiatrist's patients and asked to see the psychiatrist's data. The psychiatrist handed the physiologist his voluminous case histories.

"Are there no numbers here on their behaviour?" asked the physiologist.

"No… But if you want numbers I'll make them up for you", cried the psychiatrist. And that very night, by some alchemical process, the psychiatrist, with the help of a male colleague named S——, turned the words into numbers as the two men converted paragraphs into tables and descriptions into ratings.

This section considers an attempt to slow down what Bilsbury and Richman term the "juggernaut of psychometrics". The juggernaut owes its mass and velocity to what Bernard Cohen has called *The Triumph of Numbers* (Cohen, 2006). In that book, Cohen traces the story from early times. He has an early chapter on numerology and mystic philosophy (subtitled "scientists at play with numbers"). There follows one on numbers in the Age of Reason and another on the new uses of numbers in the nineteenth century. In the last of these, he writes about the arrival of the "numerical method" in medicine. He describes the work of Pierre Charles Alexandre Louis (1787–1872). Louis obtained an M.D. in 1813 and then practised medicine in Russia, returning to Paris in 1820. He became associated with several hospitals in the city and produced quantified data in the form of the relative frequencies of various outcomes. His totals were employed to evaluate among other things the effectiveness of bloodletting in the treatment of pneumonia. Did patients recover or die? His data were obtained by *counting*. Cohen makes the comment that "this method seems so sensible that it is difficult to see why it was resisted by the medical establishment" (p.108).

Alvan Feinstein suggests reasons why in his book *Clinical Judgment* (1967). He comments that at a time when the foundations of medicine were being rocked in various ways, not least by the overthrow of the Hippocratic theory of the four bodily humours, "clinicians must have been stunned and furious to have blood-letting, their old standby in therapy, also taken from them" (p.221). The fate of Louis, reviled in his lifetime and forgotten for generations after it, should be a *caveat*, says Feinstein, to any practitioner who names no new disorders, develops no new therapies, neither lectures nor writes particularly well *and* dares question basic method to boot.

Feinstein, a former professor of medicine and epidemiology at Yale and a clinical biostatistician, whose writings included several books on method in clinical medicine, writes at length about the difficulties practitioners have faced in reconciling the art and science in their work. The difficulties arise "not because the clinician's human capacities impede science, but because he has failed to use his human capacities in a scientific manner. He applies scientific methods to analyse the patient as a case of disease, but not as a case of human illness" (Feinstein, 1967, p.29). He calls for the development of an "intellectual technology", defining this as "the methods of acquiring evidence and organizing clinical thought" (p.28). The barriers to the development of this intellectual technology are explored over the course of this book and a second one entitled *Clinimetrics* (1987). What he emphasizes over and over again are the difficulties to be faced in reconciling the aims of clinical medicine with those of its over-mighty supporting procedures.

Feinstein's particular preoccupation is with the place of measurement among the supporting procedures and its elevation into something more than a supporting role. "Ever since Kelvin stated the doctrine that measurement was a prerequisite of science", writes Feinstein, "biologists have been trying to measure, and clinicians have felt lost" (Feinstein, 1967, p.61). Practitioners have responded by either measuring what can be measured, not what ought to be measured or, despite knowing there are times they should not be measuring, by measuring all the same. Alternatively, believing that their clinical activities are too human and too complex for "science", they have failed to measure at all.

Essentially timid about numbers, many practitioners have eventually succumbed to their intoxicating effects. Thinking further about the fate of Pierre Louis, Feinstein surmises that it was not just that his ideas were unwanted by the clinicians of the epoch, intent on defending an entrenched orthodoxy. While *counting* was arduous, what actually did for Louis was the competition from a speedier and more alluring "numerical method"; this the method of *dimensional measurement*, well suited to the new ways of laboratory technology. This development made it possible to manage "without the laborious personal efforts needed to observe and count clinical numbers *à la* Louis" (Feinstein, 1967, p.224n). Feinstein rounds off his comments with a quote from Max Frisch's novel *Homo Faber*: "Technology is the knack of so arranging the world that we don't have to experience it." With the coming of dimensional measurement to medicine, technology won another round.

Associated with dimensional measurement are some of the more intoxicating numerical excesses of the Enlightenment. Cohen illustrates these with Francis Hutcheson's (1694–1747) "moral arithmetic". Here, Hutcheson scales numbers in a far more dramatic way, placing numerical values into algebraic equations and permitting himself to operate upon them computationally using not just addition but subtraction too, and even division. For example:

$$B = \frac{M \pm I}{A}$$

where "B" is a person's virtue, "M" his amount of public good, "A" his natural ability and "I" (the expense to) his private interest, all of these judged to be potentially quantifiable. In this, Cohen concludes, lies the notion of a human science "rooted in numbers", where apparent precision and accuracy of *measurement* enable a concept to be reduced to something numerical. "Not surprisingly, some leading thinkers of the time envisioned that all of human thought might be expressed mathematically" (Cohen, 2005, pp.71 and 96).

In modern-day terms, these excesses can be expressed as the abandonment of modestly scaled *nominal* data in favour of less modestly scaled *interval* data (Siegel, 1956). The former constitute categories without magnitudes (for example, just the plain numbers of men in the surgical beds of Hospital X at different dates) and the latter categories that can be measured and ranked with high precision (the individual blood pressures of those same men at those same dates). Feinstein's argument was not an argument against the use of numerical data. That, after all, would have come strangely from a biostatistician. And he was critical of the neglect of *ordinal data* in qualitative research (Feinstein, 1996). But he did question the promotion of this kind of dimensional measurement with its suggestion that a higher reality can be attained merely through the rattling of an abacus or the slithering of a slide rule or the clicking of an Apple. The problem as he saw it was that almost all the most important observations of pathology, and most of the symptoms and signs observed clinically, depend *first and foremost* on verbal description, on the use of words rather than numbers:

> There is no ordinary method of dimensionally measuring the firmness of a carcinoma, the fluctuation of an abscess, the croak of a rhonchus, or the rasp of a murmur. Yet each of these distinctions can be described precisely. There is no ordinary method of dimensionally measuring the locations,

> qualities, and other characteristics of the different types of pain produced by toothache, migraine, pleurisy, abdominal cramps, or *angina pectoris*. Yet each pain can be differentiated distinctly and precisely by verbal description. (Feinstein, 1967, p.63)

His conclusion in writing about the basis of clinical assessment was that instead of habitually seeking dimensional (interval level) measurement for symptoms, signs and other human properties that could not be dimensionally measured with precision or convenience, "clinicians must seek ways of improving the value of their own verbal clinical descriptions of these entities" (p.65). Precision depends on observation, not measurement. "Mathematics has no value in helping us understand nature unless we begin by understanding nature" (p.16). Only this way does a "scientific" (meaning a *systematic*) exploration of the clinical domain become possible, drawing on activities that restore the patient to his or her rightful place as a *source*, as well as a beneficiary, of the data used in the investigation.

Here in changed form re-surfaces the argument for a person-centred, personalized approach to assessment. Like the argument based on relative specificity (see Chapter 2), it is pitched in terms of accuracy. The criticism there of relying too much on general traits and diagnoses is counterbalanced here by concern about too much dependence on over-precise measurement. Indeed, the two are complementary: vague words and exact numbers. But, accuracy apart, an over-ready recourse to numbers also seems the very antithesis of a humanizing, patient-centred approach, as does a loose way with language.

Having asserted the primacy of words, matters shift to the sober deployment of numbers in the service of words. This is tackled in *Clinimetrics*, Feinstein's second book, which addresses the subject of metrics and indices. Here, he acknowledges at the outset that many patients and practitioners may be distressed that "art" produces measurement and that the process can be given so formidable a name as *clinimetrics*.

> The distress probably arises from the fear that formal clinimetric attention to these acts of measurement may threaten the few remaining features of humanistic clinical art that have managed to survive the technologic transformations of modern medical science. (Feinstein, 1987, p.1)

But like Molière's *bourgeois gentilhomme* who was astonished to discover that he spoke in prose, Feinstein points out that patients and practitioners don't realize that they constantly communicate with clinimetric indexes, even when they employ such banal, everyday phrases as *slight* headache or *some improvement* in appetite. So he has no further hesitation in stressing the importance of metrics but presses for a distinction between clinimetrics and psychometrics. Clinimetrics, like psychometrics, remains the domain concerned with indexes, rating scales and other expressions that are used to describe or measure symptoms, physical signs and other distinctly clinical phenomena. But Feinstein emphasizes the importance of devising metrics that keep in mind what patients and practitioners see as important to them. And here he regards the professional interests of practitioners and the group he calls *psychosocial scientists* appearing to divide: practitioners want highly personal data, may not be too concerned about dimensional measurement, but be greatly concerned with qualitative issues, while psychosocial scientists may well prefer to work from theory, pursue standardization as a goal, even "sometimes deliberately avoid a personal interrogation", and hanker after the dimensional scales used in other forms of scientific measurement (Feinstein, 1987, p.124). This preference is shown up by teaching methods that show greater interest in data analysis than in data quality (Feinstein, 1996).

Instead of uncritically relying just on the two concepts of *reliability* and *validity*, Feinstein picks his way through both these, downplaying some aspects of reliability, renaming it "consistency", and emphasizing content validity among the different types of validity, while listing a number of other desirable scale properties, important to practitioners as opposed to statisticians and social scientists, under the heading of a proposed third concept called *sensibility*.

Other people have offered "third" concepts of this sort. Bilsbury and Richman (2002) summarize much of this work. Near the end of their monograph, they turn to what they call the *stepsisters* of reliability and validity, that is to say valued properties of measures (some of them overlapping properties), described in the literature of the last forty years, notably:

- *Responsiveness*: scales which bring out change
- *Sensibility* (Feinstein's concept): scales which build in common sense along with pertinent clinical knowledge
- *Utility*: scales with advantages accruing from their use, like providing a clear interpretation and addressing meaningful clinical goals
- *Practicality*: scales that are reasonably brief, easy to score and can be used repeatedly

- *Suitability*: scales that are able to take account of intellectual ability, reading level, emotional state and other such characteristics
- *Directness*: the clinimetric word for the psychometric concept of content validity

Personal questionnaires need to be looked at critically in terms of such yardsticks, if they are to have any claim to be "qualitative assessments with numbers", where words have priority, but the more modest contribution of quantitative assessment is acknowledged too. To sum up: "the embrace of the numerical should not come at the cost of the word" (Goldblatt, 2013).

Heidegger not Jaspers!

The book *Postpsychiatry* by the psychiatrists Patrick Bracken and Philip Thomas appeared in 2005. Reflected in the title is the attempt "to imagine a form of medical encounter with states of distress, alienation and madness, which did not operate with the central assumptions that had guided psychiatry through the twentieth-century" (Bracken and Thomas, 2005, p.3). Their account provides a way of further developing a number of person-centred themes identified earlier in this chapter. These might be summarized as follows:

- The need in the patient's interest to heal the rift between the practitioner's art and the professional's science
- The need to understand that the way a person experiences his or her world – the content of that experience – is open and infinite, not finite and exhaustible
- The need to shield the patient from approaches where technical effectiveness comes at the expense of human relationship

We shall now look at these three issues in turn. Bracken and Thomas considerably expand the first issue. They see the rift as indicative of the extent to which things remain wrong, mainly in the profession to which they (the authors) belong, and to some extent in others (for example, my own), with which they are allied. The second issue, in Bracken and Thomas's hands, becomes a call for the overturning of the reductionist explanation of disorders in favour of the meaningful understanding of patients. The third issue is the need for technologies, including an intellectual technology like psychological assessment, to be watched carefully to make sure it is consistent with humane and ethical practice.

The growing sense of a schism

For Feinstein, there existed thirty or forty years ago a rift that separated the front-line clinicians lost for words from the armies of clinical specialists in possession of the numbers. While soberly argued, such a problem seemed serious enough then, if essentially a technical one: clinical and metrical. Now though the situation seems far graver. This is partly because the analysis offered by Bracken and Thomas is broader: sociological, political and philosophical, and partly because times have changed. In Bracken and Thomas's view, the schism arises because powerful interests impose ways of defining a person's condition that in some way are at odds with the person's experience of it. On the one side, the forces include the agencies of government through the imposition of national service frameworks and the drug companies through the funding of research activity. On the other side, stand the patients, silent in Feinstein's account, but these days silent no more.

Somewhere in between are left the clinicians, still straddling the divide. The divide between "town and gown" within the medical profession remains, but it has a most uncomfortable edge to it: much less the threat of a rift than the reality of a schism. With respect to psychiatry, Bracken and Thomas put it this way:

> We have found that psychiatrists who work mainly in clinical settings are more interested in (and open to) the challenges we present... Increasingly, they are working outside hospitals, and in their day-to-day work they meet with user groups and other non-medical organizations. Through such encounters, they have become sensitized to the ways in which many users of mental health services have experienced psychiatry as oppressive. Until recently, contact between doctors and patients only happened in clinical settings, and the power differential in these meant that the patient's views were often silenced. (pp.3–4)

In contrast, they say that while there are distinguished exceptions, academic colleagues, in general, appear less prepared to doubt and to question their assumptions. In fact:

> much of *academic* psychiatry has been moving in a very different direction. In parallel with other branches of medicine, psychiatry has been a major growth area for the pharmaceutical industry. Many medical academics have close links with the industry and there is evidence that many prominent research agendas have been developed on the back of these links. With few notable exceptions, most university-based psychiatrists are involved in some form of biological research (particularly genetic or biochemical), as reflected

> in the types of articles that are published in the British and American Journals of Psychiatry. (p.4)

With these genetic and biochemical explanations comes the temptation to reduce a person to a condition: a reduction, but not just any reduction, rather, a biological reduction, a reduction that, if not resonating with "depth", sounds "fundamental", almost final.

Here, one might be reminded of a statement of Heidegger's, namely:

> What good is all the explaining if what has to be explained remains unclear?

Does one really think, Heidegger continues, that what is unclear in *itself* can ever be clarified by a genetic explanation? "Whoever insists on a genetic explanation without clarifying the essence of what needs to be explained beforehand is like a man who wishes to reach a goal without having brought the goal itself into view" (Heidegger, 1987, p.213). In these passages, Heidegger is addressing the seminar of psychiatrists held at the Swiss doctor Medard Boss's home at Zollikon through the 1960s. To begin with, these seminars don't seem to have gone particularly well. The doctors had never encountered most of Heidegger's questions as questions. Boss describes the participants as "shocked, even outraged" that someone had permitted such questions to be raised at all. There were long pauses and silences. "It was as if a Man from Mars were visiting a group of earth-dwellers in an attempt to communicate with them" (Boss, 1987, p.xviii). (What? The Martian? Back again!)

Heidegger's is not Feinstein's language, but Feinstein in a late paper is in his own way quite as much to the point. He applauds "the majestic explicatory advances of molecular biology", but then adds that these "magnificent molecular achievements in explicating disease" don't offer a means for choosing and evaluating the interventions used in patient care (Feinstein, 1996, p.1339). The research is too distant to be related to clinical practice and patients' actual experience of illness, for which a different, or at least additional, basic science is needed.

It becomes much harder to ignore the need for that basic science, and what at root has to be explained, once patients begin to write about their experiences. That is another story.

The importance of dwelling on particularities and contexts

Bracken and Thomas are much concerned to explore the philosophical underpinnings of the troubles they diagnose. They describe the chapter dealing with this matter as the heart of the book. They believe that philosophy, particularly two quite different views of what constitutes the relevant phenomenology, helps with understanding the rift in mental health just described. In this chapter, the *reductionism* of the Age of Psychiatry is contrasted with *hermeneutics.* Bracken and Thomas think that these days hermeneutics is best understood as "approaches to human behavior and social organization that prioritize meaning" (p.14), that meanings are multiple, drawing on different perspectives and metaphors, and that what makes matters meaningful is context. Reductionism, by contrast, throws away meaning, narrows perspective (investing great power in a single expert view), kills metaphor and strips people's experiences of their historical and cultural referents.

> In psychiatry, a person might complain of feeling "empty", "without direction", "fed up" or simply "miserable". These feelings are often bound up with such things as unhappy relationships, difficult work situations or physical ill health. In the psychiatrist's formulation these feelings become "dysphoric mood", or "symptoms of depression". Painful thoughts about the possibility of ending one's life, with all the cultural, religious, personal and family implications and nuances that such thoughts invariably bring to the fore, become simply "suicidal ideation". Voices that discuss and comment upon the actions of the individual become "third party auditory hallucinations". (p.108)

This stripping down of language to some kind of common professional jargon fails to take account of what happens in the lives of persons, as they are actually lived:

> Painful thoughts, feelings and experiences are always woven in with other psychological, cultural and practical realities. In the course of the person's day-to-day life, such thoughts and feelings relate to particular situations and circumstances; they are often associated with longer-term worries and conflicts. They reach back to the past and look forward to the future. They also take place in the context of an embodied reality, a reality that wakes and sleeps and is subject to the rhythms of a personal physiology. (p.109)

The crux of the conflict, and perhaps the source of the rift, lies in a clash of approaches to phenomenology: on the one hand, Jaspers and, on the other, Heidegger.

Jaspers' phenomenology is a descriptive psychopathology. Its exposition makes for a very long but ultimately "finite" book. The spirit of it is well reflected in Wing, Cooper and Sartorius's (1974) Present State Examination. That, already referred to (see Chapter 6), seeks to make a systematic exploration of a patient's mental state in order to establish whether any of a finite number (140) of symptoms are present. Something of its spirit is also manifest in classification systems like DSM and ICD, where diagnoses are elaborated top-down in long lists. But the essence of it is the marking out of a set of phenomena "which become defined and capable of identification time and time again" (Jaspers, 1959, p.25), and requires the recognition of a "series of fragments from a person's total psychic experience" (p.27).

Heidegger's phenomenology seems different. It is much more like the *Lebenswelt* of Heidegger's teacher Husserl and of a world that, while not beyond systematic scientific scrutiny, resists any attempt to define and re-define it, or to break down and re-assemble it, in order to make it more scientific; "scientific" in such senses as stripped of "inessentials", neatly categorized, or even just arranged better. While the world as *Lebenswelt* may be studied scientifically, it is not a product of science. But it is in some sense a product of humankind, because the world as experienced is lived in human bodies, shared with other human beings and embedded in human cultures. Where Jaspers' phenomenology represents some kind of descent from the world to a relatively featureless psychological core, Heidegger's does not. His phenomenology rests on the surface, where it retains all the features of the common landscape, the open spaces and the seasons, a landscape created by people and which is inescapably theirs. When it comes to the expression of psychological distress, Jaspers' phenomenology has its own painstakingly abstracted special vocabulary, while Heidegger's floats in the limitless possibilities of ordinary language.

Later in the book, where Bracken and Thomas consider the distinction between evidence-based medicine (EBM) and narrative-based medicine (NBM), a distinction met earlier in their critique resurfaces: the contrast between the standard and the particular. Jaspers' phenomenology dealt with the general, stripping away the particular; Heidegger's was irretrievably enmeshed in the particular. Now the same distinction crops up again:

> EBM moves us from the general to the particular... This has to be so to make it possible to reduce the complex human experience of illness to the bare essentials... What matters in such an approach is not the individual, but the idealized outcomes of hundreds of thousands of individuals. Out of this, we develop generalized notions of effectiveness, widely suited to the greatest number. NBM operates in the opposite direction. It begins with the particular, indeed it may never leave it. (Bracken and Thomas, 2005, p.196)

All this said, it is easy to forget that Jaspers was writing about psychopathology and not psychiatry, something specialist rather than routine, special rather than general. On page 1 of the *General Psychopathology*, he distinguishes the two:

> Psychiatrists function primarily as a living, comprehending and acting person, to whom science is only one resource among many; for psychopathologists, however, science is the sole and ultimate aim of their work. Their aim is not the individual human being. Their aim is to know, recognize, describe and analyse general principles rather than particular individuals . . . We have to be content with a partial knowledge of an infinity which we cannot exhaust. As a person, not as a psychopathologist, one may well see more.

At a later point he writes: "The crude psychopathological categories which we use to classify and apprehend our subject-matter do not penetrate to human fundamentals" (p.426). And elsewhere he concedes that "for patients content is usually the one important thing" (p.59).

There remains then, in principle, psychiatry to take on the seeing more and the penetrating to human fundamentals. But there is some doubt in Jaspers' mind whether studying "the endless and confusing flood of life" (p.25) can be done scientifically. This admission would presumably have upset Feinstein in his quest after the additional basic science he spoke of.

Heidegger, unlike Jaspers, refuses to give up on thinking about the infinity we cannot exhaust. It is necessary to think about that first, *particularly*, Heidegger seems to be saying, if you want there to be a proper foundation on which to lay a science of the subject.

The nature and limits of an "intellectual technology"

Bracken and Thomas are concerned mainly with the present state of psychiatry, and save their harshest words for their discussion of drugs. They are on the whole too tactful to extend their critique to other professions and activities.

They do have some critical words to say about psychological psychotherapies, however. On the one hand, there is the lure of biological reduction and the descent to the molecules and genes; but, on the other, there is the lure of *cognitivism* and psychological reduction. This kind of reduction involves not a shift to a lower register (psychology to biology, biology to chemistry, chemistry to physics); rather, it involves a reduction in the sense of a simplification or narrowing, a risk in any intellectual enterprise keen on general explanations. With cognitivism, the reduction lies in the belief that it is mental processes that are at the root of what is the matter and that these mental processes are universal. This notion, at least if left unqualified, risks leaving patients with the idea that what they believe is quite simply wrong, if not actually meaningless. It removes the possibility of understanding what is happening in other ways "within shared human contexts" (p.152). In my view, this charge of reductionism, which seems to be levelled chiefly at cognitive behavioural therapy, seems a fairer judgement on early CBT, badly executed, than on more recent forms of it.

Bracken and Thomas make the additional point that the problem is not with technology per se, but with technologies that take over and monopolize. When one is dealing with intellectual technologies, less obviously technologies than the technologies of medication or computation, it seems one must be particularly watchful, even if the view is taken that technologies are necessary. The subtle power of *intellectual* technologies rests in their vocabularies, the easy recourse to explanatory concepts and so on, particularly objectionable in the context of the content argument being those that claim to explain matters without rendering an account of precisely what. These intellectual technologies include not just the psychological therapies but also what in technical language can be described as psychological assessment.

The technical word "assessment" doesn't capture the enormity of the undertaking very well. For a start, it doesn't capture its scope. The task involves creating a relationship and working within that relationship over time. What arises as content shapes the relationship and gives it focus and direction. The nature of the relationships that emerge is diverse and shifting, reflecting the range of content. Nor does the word "assessment" capture its moral nature. When Bracken and Thomas write about the relationship, they stress issues of value and meaning and regard the enterprise as above all an ethical one. To the extent that the enterprise is also about efficiency and effectiveness, this is a secondary matter for them.

Some of the richness, significance and morality of the clinical assessment are conveyed in Anton Chekhov's short story *A Case History*, to which Bracken and Thomas make reference later on in their book. Box G contains a summary of it. During the course of the tale, the doctor, Korolyov, and his patient Liza come to know each other better through a series of brief conversations over the course of a few hours, these meetings at first taking place at the patient's bedside. Chekhov records the patient's successive, somewhat faltering descriptions and expressions of what is upsetting to her and how these accumulate, so offering an increasingly full picture of her plight:

Box G: "A Case History" (1898) by Anton Chekhov

A house surgeon, Korolyov, is sent to answer an urgent call from a family who own a textile mill a short distance from Moscow. The countryside entrances him, but he pities the state of the workers who line his route as he approaches the mill. The patient, heiress to the unhappy estate, lies in bed upstairs. As he takes her cold, ungainly hand, she seems to Korolyov a poor, miserable creature, long used to doctors examining her.

"It's palpitations," she says. "I was frightened all night. I nearly died of fright. Do give me something to take." The doctor examines her and tells her he can find nothing wrong with her heart. She bursts into tears and his impression of her changes. Now he finds a gentle, suffering look, wise and moving, full of grace and charm.

The patient's mother prevails upon him to stay the night. Korolyov wanders outside, where for some hours he thinks about the unhappy lives of the mother and daughter, sustained by the mill hands working on the edge of starvation. He reflects on how the strong are bound to make life miserable for the weak, although it sometimes seems more as if some mysterious controlling force makes victims of both strong and weak.

He returns to his bedroom. Hearing noises in the next room, he goes in and finds his patient sitting in an armchair. He asks her how she is.

"All right, thank you." He feels her pulse. She looks at him and seems to want to tell him something. He asks her if this happens to her often.

"Yes, I feel depressed almost every night." Then, sudden banging begins outside. He asks whether the banging bothers her.

"I don't know. Everything bothers me here, everything," she answers. "I want to tell you what I think. I don't think I'm ill at all. Why am I worried and scared? It has to be so. Even the healthiest man can't help worrying if there's a burglar prowling under his window. I'm always seeing doctors," she continues, "but I don't so much want to talk to a doctor as to someone close to me: a friend who understands and says if I am right or wrong."

"Have you no friends, then?" the doctor asks.

"I'm lonely. That's the way things are. After all, I am free all day from morning till evening. I read in the daytime, but at night my head's empty – only shadows instead of thoughts."

Box G: (Continued)

"Do you see things at night?" Korolyov asks her.

"No, but I feel them…"

She looks at him so sadly and wisely that he feels she trusts him and shares his outlook. He thinks he knows what to say to her now: that she should run away from her mills and her roubles. But he doesn't know how to put it directly like that. The two of them talk a little longer. The sun comes up. He returns to his room and goes to bed.

In the morning everyone gathers to see him off, including his patient. She gazes at him sadly and wisely as before, with that same air of wanting to say something special, something vital, something for his ears only.

- The intensity of her palpitations
- The feeling of depression almost every night
- The sense that everything bothers her
- The feeling that things have to be as they are
- The lack of anyone close to her who understands
- The feeling of loneliness
- The shadowy feelings at night

Raimo Puustinen writes about this story in *The Journal of Medical Ethics*. He sees in the sequence of these concerns, and Korolyov's varying response to them (examination, diagnosis, comfort, advice, philosophy), an example of the many positions adopted by a good doctor, as he responds to the shifting positions of his patient. Puustinen attributes to Mikhail Bakhtin the understanding that the silent thoughts of a person will appear, and find firm expression, if there is a responsive other person willing to engage with them and able to comprehend the person as more than a biological object. "This responsive understanding creates a space in which unspoken voices take shape and become audible" (Puustinen, 2000, p.42).

Clare Crellin writing about formulation in *Clinical Psychological Forum* also refers to literary examples. She expounds how in Kierkegaard and in an unfinished early novel by Camus (*Le premier homme*), there is to be found a sense of something that eludes definition but which is valid about our experience. She speaks of how writing meanders, exploring first this aspect and then that in an attempt to elaborate and expand rather than to try and capture experience through a few explanatory devices.

Slowly, Chekhov's Dr Korolyov comes to form a view of the family's circumstances. The story presents us with what he chooses to say to his patient, but also tells us what he feels unable to say to her, that which perhaps lies beyond the limits of a physician's responsibilities. The visit ends, and there is a certain completeness about it. The conversation has had a degree of pointedness and particularity to it. Liza has not been *treated* in any ordinary sense of the word, but something significant has passed between the two of them. She has managed to say things she hasn't said before (even if she still seems to have more to say) and has in the process adopted a variety of positions. She has been *met*, and there has been conversation. But there is no rescue, and no resolution, as Korolyov leaves in his sunny carriage, thinking pleasant thoughts, the case closed, the world opening out before him once more.

CHAPTER 9

The Significance of Content

For patients content is usually the one important thing.
Karl Jaspers, *General Psychopathology*, 1959

What is the most powerful impetus that drives the content argument? Perhaps it is the ethical one. If it is indeed the case that ethics is where the content argument eventually rests, which seems on the whole likely, then it is tricky for practitioners to ignore Jaspers' opinion that for patients content usually is "the one important thing" (p.59).

The story, as it has been told here, does not begin with ethics, however. Instead, it begins in earnest with Shapiro's view of the value of precision, accuracy and relevance in the pursuit of clarifying one's ideas about phenomena as encountered in psychological work in the United Kingdom's National Health Service. Shapiro was an inspiring clinical psychologist and immensely sensitive to ethical issues, but the nature of his argument was certainly not first and foremost a moral one. If anything, the argument was more technical than ethical; it was one that hung on the notion of needing to improve the reliability and more particularly the validity of psychological assessments. The pursuit of better assessment, which was tracked over the course of Chapter 2 of this book, led eventually to a concept of content.

The significance for assessment

Feinstein referred to what is commonly called "assessment" as a technology, or more exactly as an intellectual technology. He intended nothing pejorative by that. But, while no doubt the domain of psychological assessment involves a gentler technology than that of drugs, it constitutes a technology nonetheless. Certainly, assessment offers practitioners much to take on board, to fuss over and to get right, as well as just get done. As with pharmacology, there is a certain amount to cause consternation or give offence in certain quarters as well: statistics, calculations, tabulations, standards, protocols, yardsticks and hoops, with the associated dangers of losing the patient in a litter of paper or in increasingly stringent selection criteria.

There is, therefore, the need to keep its use proportionate. To avoid the charge of hegemony, of over-dominance or undue influence, in the way that drugs attract that charge, a place needs to be found for assessment that is balanced. And one is confronted with the paradox that good assessment requires that matters are kept in balance: *personal*, not over-standardized, not too numerical, relevant to context and so on. Not *too* assessment-like, in other words.

The technical problems Shapiro found in routine psychological assessment led him and those who followed him to return to basic theory and seek a means to achieve greater directness. This directness involved a re-appraisal of content, as understood within assessment theory. In following the journey from there, there seem to have been two consequences:

(1) The assessment of content necessarily takes one into highly personal territory, where the product of the assessment process finds expression in ordinary language and in unique sets of concerns.
(2) The placing of each patient's concerns at the heart of the assessment encourages the focus to shift from identifying the various aspects of defined disorders to describing and expressing a person's broader psychological experience. It is as if in searching for accuracy Shapiro had stumbled across meaning.

One might say that assessment has as a result come closer to assessment of the "whole person". But, if so, it has done so not in some baffling, mystical way but in a manner sufficiently systematic and operationalized in its procedures, and sufficiently rich and metaphorical in its language, to have appeal to counsellors and clinicians of various dispositions and persuasions.

The significance for counsellors and clinicians

What began as "just assessment" now starts to touch on the practitioner's work as a whole. An assessment *technique* becomes something closer to a *method* of laying down a foundation for individual pieces of counselling and clinical work. What started as a necessary tactic seems now more akin to a significant strategy, a strategy in Feinstein's (1967) phrase for "acquiring evidence and organizing clinical thought" (p.28). The strategy as here described might be boldly summarized as follows:

> GIVE TIME TO WORKING OUT SYSTEMATICALLY WITH YOUR PATIENT IN ORDINARY LANGUAGE WHAT CONCERNS NEED TO BE ADDRESSED. EMBARK UPON THIS TASK IN THE EXPECTATION THAT WHEN IT IS DONE YOUR THOUGHTS ABOUT HOW TO ADDRESS YOUR PATIENT'S CONCERNS WILL HAVE BECOME CLEARER!

From such a summary, it is worth bringing out the way that the subject matter of this book has been more about the what-is-to-be-addressed than the addressing of it. In other words, the question is about *what* it is that needs to be understood, explained, treated and so on, rather than about *how* to understand, explain and treat it.

Content as fundamental

Psychological work based on content has been called in this book "general work". General work supplies a foundation in content. To the extent that counsellors and clinicians recognize the need for fundamentals of this kind, there is always general work to be done, and often it is *just* general work that needs to be done. General work begins with the content-based assessment, and while there may come a moment when there is a shift to some kind of special work, on many occasions the work remains general throughout.

In general work, the method is to dwell on the patient's psychological concerns, to linger over their description and expression, and to seek explication of them. The concerns shape in various ways how the patient and practitioner choose to take their understanding forward, assisted *on occasion* by some kind of diagnosis or formulation, and by the identifying or *naming* of what the patient and practitioner are trying to do. The naming defines the relationship as much as it defines the task, and there is much in general work that bears on process. But in content, there is to be found the person in context, in distress and in their own words.

It has been tempting at times to brand general work as "psychological casework", but "casework" has become something of a discredited term in recent years and perhaps does not convey well that the focus sought here is on the addressing of content, the distressing heart of things, rather than on matters of a more administrative nature: the discharging of statutory responsibilities, issues of capacity, consent and confidentiality, liaising and keeping communication channels open, reporting and accounting, and the maintenance of documentation.

In general work, the transition between the content-based assessment and what comes after it is subtle. Content remains the focus as psychological concerns are collectively or individually addressed. In contrast, there is necessarily something of a break to be experienced between the content-based assessment and what follows in the various kinds of special work that may be placed on the general foundation. Most of the examples of special work offered have been types of "modal" psychological therapy: psychodynamic, systemic and cognitive behavioural. EMDR provided an illustration of something structured, very much itself, which shares with the modal therapies the feature of having its own set of explanatory concepts, its own distinct procedures and protocols, and, perhaps most importantly, its own culture and traditions (trainings, conventions, hierarchies and disputes). These psychological therapies also have their own distinctive types of assessment, addressing issues pertinent to the particular therapy: maintaining factors, client safety, psychological readiness, core beliefs, target components, task understanding, task completion and so on. These do not to any great extent embrace content. With such therapies, it was suggested instead that content could provide a means of indicating the case for such therapies and then go on to offer a way of documenting and evaluating progress faithful to the person's concerns.

Many of the difficulties in mental health work seem to arise where general work is skipped over lightly, or skipped altogether, and special work substituted; as if it were possible by employing a familiar psychiatric intake procedure or an assessment for a well-established psychological therapy to bypass the discipline of identifying content. The argument of this book is not that general work is more important than special work; it is more that up to now there has been no rationale for any kind of notion of general work.

Content as the explicandum

Content, as what it is that needs understanding, explaining, treating and so forth, can be viewed as an *explicandum*. The word is defined in the *New Shorter Oxford English Dictionary* (1993) as "the fact, thing or expression to be explained or explicated". "Explication" with its sense of unwrapping, unfolding and opening up really does seem the single best word, a better word for what should be done with content than "explanation", which the dictionary defines in terms of making clear or intelligible. In other words, it is better to explicate content than to explain it.

Since this content, or explicandum, contains a person's highly charged and complex experience of distress, one may well choose to define the material as psychological, or judge it to be sufficiently psychological, to allow the possibility that in the explicating of it factors of a non-psychological kind can *also* be allowed into play. By choosing to *wrench* apart the explicandum from its counterpart, the explicans (the explicating part), one is better able to attend to and weigh the wide range of biological, social, spiritual, cultural and economic factors that bear on the person, allowing this and that and the other to come to mind: concepts, procedures, explanations, partial explanations, partial remedies. The manner of thinking will be varied: at different times analytical, experimental, practical, interpersonal, experiential, spontaneous.

In other words, if the explicandum carries the psychology, or at least some of the psychology, then the explicans is freer to go where it will and to allow that a person's psychological concerns can be seen and explicated in terms of this or that, or both this and that.

This *is* though indeed a wrench. "Our difficulty", writes David Smail, "is that we cannot by nature easily detach experience from explanation... Our private experience, far from giving us privileged information about the reasons for our troubles, is actually misleading, for overwhelming as it is, we are likely to attribute to it explanatory power it doesn't have" (Smail, 2001, p.370). We are left believing our mental and bodily shortcomings to be the cause of our distress, and we overlook the part played by impersonal social, economic and environmental forces, abstract and obscure as these are. Therefore, there can be a tendency, on the one hand, for patients to see what impacts on them powerfully but remotely as explainable as "just me", while, on the other, for practitioners there is the risk of succumbing to unhelpful, summary, circular, ideas, like "vulnerability" to psychiatric illness. In a special issue of *Clinical Psychology* dedicated to David Smail, Mary Boyle wrote about "the dangers of vulnerability". She reminded readers about a regular column in the weekend *Guardian* supplement that week by week picked on words that should be banned. "It may have been semi-serious, but there is nothing facetious in my suggestion that we should think of removing the words vulnerable and vulnerability from our vocabularies" (Boyle, 2003, p.27).

It is difficult for Smail to find *justification* for separating experience from the explaining of it. Experience for him is so much the product of the forces that explain it. And for him, it is a matter of better and worse explanations, a matter of being clear which forces really matter. Writing about the causes of distress, he says that it makes much more sense "to diagnose the ways the environment can be damaging than it does the people who are damaged by it" (p.281). Those external causes are just *so* powerful that one simply must write about them and counter the regrettable tendency to attend endlessly to the inner lives of people, where dwell constructs, vague, proliferating, seductive and pseudo-authoritative.

If one starts from experience, as Merleau-Ponty insisted one should, and holds off on what explains that experience, for a time at least, then to think about that experience in its own right becomes possible. Still, it is difficult to bring this off until there is some way of conceptualizing it. Once that step is taken, however, then there is much to explain,... or explicate. And the more there is potentially to explicate, the less disorders, dysfunctions and whatever else might be judged to be "wrong" with someone (whether their "illness", their "vulnerability" or just "them") will be permitted to hold sway and explain everything. Such notions as these simply won't explain enough. To put it another way, when you as a practitioner come to extend your focus from just the patient's psychological disorder to include the consequences and complications of it, you need to take more account of the whole range of factors that make the experience so dire and intractable.

Certainly, some concerns may still be viewed as symptomatic of a state of *such-and-such* or a *so-and-so* condition. That may sometimes still be the best way to view a sense of being in crisis, or of not coping, or of the impossibility of talking, or of seeing it all as just "me", or of a troubled relationship, or of unbearable feelings of shame, or of some practical difficulty, or of a loss of identity, or of feeling desperate, or of instantly needing to beat a retreat if anyone even so much as hints that anything is the matter, or of forever going round in circles. But often it may make a great deal more sense not to see such concerns in that way; rather, to regard them as only loosely associated with *such-and-such* or *so-and-so* or perhaps not connected with them at all. It is one thing to consider understanding the crying of Miss K.'s child parts as *an aspect* of a dissociative disorder and her despair about a life apparently lost as at least *linked* to it; *but* better, maybe, to recognize the disruption that brought an end to her many years of continuous employment in the civil service and precipitated her most recent crisis, not as the unmasking of her "vulnerability" or her susceptibility to "stress", but as the result of remote, powerful and impersonal forces, which re-designated her department an agency and offered her an hourly wage in place of an annual salary.

Turning to content, defining it broadly and distinguishing it as a psychological explicandum encourages matters to be explicated in all sorts of ways. The move does something to counter the sense of restriction, of claustrophobia, that Smail detects when practitioners, through their own choice or someone else's, limit their attention to the content of patients' heads, rather than seek to understand the content of their worlds. More comes into play when heads expand to become worlds. But there is a catch. As more content comes into play, more needs to be done with it. What about the patient's finances, housing, occupation and transport? The risk is that the general work involved in addressing content now becomes too stretched and diffuse. If there is only general work and no notion of a supporting comprehensive service comprising many elements – including various sorts of special work – one is left with Smail's disturbing vision of "therapeutic functions" confined to the consulting room and offering little more than comfort, clarity and encouragement, these being paradoxically "both highly essential and completely inadequate" (Smail, 2001, p.192).

Content and caring to know

The introduction to this book asserted, more than argued, the link between content and all sorts of other apparently highly desirable things, these being paraded there in anticipation of fuller treatment later: involvement, directness, sampling, surfaces, human contexts and ontology. They were seen as occupying one side of a divide, while constructs and their associates, detachment, indirectness, measurement, depth, philosophical and psychological categories and epistemology, were over on the other side. Counsellors and clinicians were portrayed as leaping across to the other side in indecent haste when the going got tough.

Most of these topics have cropped up in their pairings over the course of the chapters that followed. But not sufficiently the first of them: involvement/detachment. And this one seems as important as any of the others in establishing that what is being written about really has some claim to be "personal".

On the subject of involvement and the personal, it seems right to turn to the clinical psychologist Miller Mair (1989). Box H says something briefly about him and his book *Between Psychology and Psychotherapy*. Its first chapter and the last section of the second chapter are entitled "Caring to Know".

Box H: Miller Mair's *Between Psychology and Psychotherapy*

Between Psychology and Psychotherapy was published by Routledge in 1989 when Miller Mair was in his early fifties and was living and working in Dumfries. Having trained at the Maudsley in 1959–1960 and worked for some time in London with Don Bannister on personal construct theory and practice, he had returned to his native Scotland. In his introduction to the book, he says that he believes that we (by "we" he usually means clinical psychologists, but here he speaks more generally) boil down our experiencing to a dull normality.

The style of the book is in line with his beliefs about the nature of the quest. "We tend to banish what is tentative and growing in favour of what is solid and simply seen" (xiv). In his introduction, he outlines the book's subject matter, describing it as revised earlier work, followed by a personal story, followed in turn by work in progress. The book is full of reference to painters, poets, novelists and thinkers (Manet, TS Eliot, George Eliot, Owen Barfield).

His capacity for self-reflection is awe inspiring. But while frank about himself, he has much to say about his own profession, referring to it as "this vulnerable little discipline" (p.4). In fact, he writes about clinical psychology as "the patient". The sickness the patient suffers from is tied up with the patient avoiding self-knowledge and anxiously identifying himself or herself (it is usually herself), as a purveyor of a rather masculine "applied science". He hints that this is not real science. He wants the live spirit of inquiry, grounded in practice and "knowledge for yourself", not the dead hand of application and approved theorizing. Science, as seen the way the profession likes to see it, has favoured the technical in pursuit of conventional "necessities". Lacking the courage to tackle history, culture and the ordinary social world, psychologists ignore what comes invisibly and intangibly, indeed "everything that lurks in the darkness beyond the tribal fires" (p.283).

His "basic bet", as he calls it, is that intimate personal knowledge will teach us more than distant impersonal knowledge. He presses for a radical revision whereby the impersonal is subsumed within the personal. He calls what he is asking for "a conversational psychology".

The searching, introspective style of Miller Mair is very different from the tight ways of Monte Shapiro, typical as these latter were of the scientific clinical psychological writing of his period. The trouble these days is that it is possible to read Shapiro and find him very detached, even a bit stuffy, though his prose is often masterful. There's always the risk, says Miller Mair, that one will slip off into the impersonal. (A drift towards the standardized and the impersonal might seem already under way when personal questionnaires become PQs, as if PQs were of the same phylogeny as EPQs, OQs, BDIs, MMPIs, 16PFs and COREs.) Shapiro once advised me firmly to stick to proper "neutral" scientific expression and terminology. Failure to do so, he said, would "*irk*" the reader, who might view literary allusion, personal reflection or anecdote as attempts to curry favour, seduce or simply bamboozle. There had been a rumour at one time, I understood, that Shapiro was writing a book, but this turned out to be false. As Shapiro explained to me, the home ground of scholarly scientific writing in the Anglo-American tradition is not the book but the peer-reviewed journal article.

It does though feel to me that with Miller Mair one is beginning to come full circle, discovering in his writing here at the end of this book something of the same spirit as was to be found in Monte Shapiro's at the beginning of it. In Shapiro, one encountered attention to accuracy and relative specificity, preparedness to open up assessment to ordinary language, questionnaires constructed ex nihilo from descriptive assessments, a cautious approach to statistics, and the reproving of colleagues for not being interested in the actual state of affairs or failing to pursue investigations "intensively". (This word "intensively" is a perfect Shapiro word, one he employed entirely in a technical sense but which in lay speech conveys rigour, commitment and energy.) Yet in Miller Mair too, one finds reference to "passionate precision" and "precise particularity", "imaginative freedom of language", a call for "creative description", scepticism about "necessarily or often" turning to measurement, and concern about colleagues taking easy options and hesitating to "probe more widely".

In Miller Mair, though, there is no reference to "content". Perhaps, it is not difficult to see why. To re-iterate, in the literature there has been little or no *concept* of content. In the absence of a developed concept of it, content undefined may well seem to be at odds with process. When attempting to keep things free and flowing, turning to content may seem to risk making matters too static. The essential for Miller Mair was to keep things local and fresh and conversational, and, in achieving this, the live and active process of being in relationship to someone becomes the most important consideration.

But this conversational psychology of Miller Mair's is clearly difficult to bring off. And he does not pretend otherwise. In fact, he makes no bones about it. He points out that "being personal, or allowing others to be personal, means taking time, your own and the other person's time" (p.13). "It is easier to deal with people in terms of prepared procedures rather than allow more freedom and flow. All these easier ways may be useful, may often be enough. But sometimes they will not do" (pp.18–19). The practitioner is required to be in the midst of much that is not clearly labelled. Clues, hints and signs may be all that are available, and evidence and proof need to be forgone. To enter into someone else's experiencing, you need recourse to imaginative play and fictions of what may yet be realized. "And this brings you immediately into the realm of the possible and the unproven" (p.18). We cannot create safety for ourselves by dressing in the armour of some particular theory or bringing with us the weaponry and accoutrements of specialized techniques; instead, we must learn to trust ourselves. Not to do so lays you open to too "quick or slippery" a patient (p.17) who knocks you down and leaves you helpless like a knight who has been knocked off his horse.

I find myself wondering whether I cannot turn to content, re-assured by its claim to provide a *direct* connection to a person's distress; reassured by its preferred metaphor of the openness, richness and complexity of *surfaces*; and by its insistence on ordinary *human contexts* taking priority over (although not substituting for), the technical terminology of classes and categories.

Can though such a step be taken altogether in good faith, in the conviction that it is somehow enough? Involvement is *personally* demanding. Every now and again, as Miller Mair says, practitioners must require of themselves that they move in their own lives and not just shuffle off responsibility, stand aside or produce someone else. Thus, to suggest that the commitment to content is evidence of involvement with the person might be a claim that Miller Mair would not have found convincing. But where then might content find itself in the space between psychology and psychotherapy? Fairly early in his book, and rather briefly, Miller Mair writes about the importance of form. "Form provides the essential boundaries and structure for the creative act" (p.21). Perhaps this is how content is best seen, not as operationalized in procedures, rather as bounded by form.

The significance for evaluation and accountability

A significant part of the book's argument has concerned itself with data, in particular the nature of the evidence that is necessary to determine if, or how far, patients' distress has been addressed. It has been argued that addressing psychological distress and complex personal experience requires content to be prioritized in place of particular diagnostic constructs or composite constructs like serious mental illness.

The currency of the content of psychological distress is that of psychological concerns. This means that when a practitioner, one who adopts this framework, thinks about outcome, the likelihood is that he or she will think of it mainly in terms of whether concerns have eased or lifted. Is this adequate? And are there times when this is not appropriate?

Regarding adequacy, my view is that, while concerns represent the single best index available and should almost always be included as an index of outcome, reliance on one type of data exclusively is suspect. Too much can be pinned upon it, particularly if managers are looking for some simple yardstick by which to judge the effectiveness of a service. (On the whole, this has not been my experience of how managers behave however, which on the whole has been far more tolerant and open minded.) Mental health difficulties are almost invariably complex these days, at least those encountered in the statutory sector, and this is irrespective of whether a patient meets more formal definitions of "complex need" (such as enduring mental health problems involving multidisciplinary or multi-agency input).

The policy in the psychology department in which I worked was at one time to agree outcome criteria with the purchaser or referrer for all patients seen over more than eighteen months, this being judged to be the point where outcomes defined purely in terms of some single criterion, like reducing concerns and lessening distress, began to seem inadequate. At this point, additional outcome assessment would be considered: for example, the use of standardized construct measures where constructs had been defined, evaluation of the contribution of the work in the management of risk, or the degree of success in meeting the aims of the work where setting aims had been judged a valid intervention.

Regarding the appropriateness of content assessment, the practitioner is sensible to expect that some concerns will shift and others will not, and justified in thinking that, while the latter won't shift or haven't shifted, it was right nonetheless to include them in order to reflect the range and extent of someone's distress.

Ultimately, while content is important evidence, it is not the only evidence. Evidence must be practice based, and practice depends on context. The context that has been presumed on in the illustrations of this book, with the odd exception, has been one where patients come to some sort of outpatient setting, usually a clinic, see the practitioner and then go home again, where life rumbles on until the next visit. The arrangement is usually clear, the roles defined, the contact bounded. But sometimes the patient doesn't go home, and the place itself is certainly not quite like home. In some settings, there may not be the time or privacy necessary to explore a patient's concerns (the ICU, for instance); in others, the social roles assumed by the respective parties may hamper it (a patient "receiving" a CPN on a home visit or a primary worker supporting a resident in a community house). In some situations, the roles at times are so fluid or ambiguous that it is hard to know who is being who for whom. The implicit contract between "patient" and "practitioner" is frequently compromised in subtle ways, and sometimes not so subtle ones, and this makes conversation about concerns more complicated.

Whatever the context, the ethics of the argument in relation to evaluation and accountability require emphasis to be placed on the need to examine practice, to gauge the nature and extent of one's contribution, to recognize and not conceal its limits, and to look at refining ideas more generally and cumulatively across professions about where it is right and possible to make a difference.

The significance for psychology

Left to last is some further thought about the distinction between content and constructs. The argument for content must take into its sights the continuing reliance on constructs of disorder in the many textbooks so prominent in psychiatry and psychology education and training. This emphasis on disorders is understandable within psychiatry, where diagnosis is seen as useful and where the concern is more to improve its connection with the descriptive psychopathology that is deemed to underlie it, as argued, for example, by Taylor and Vaidya (2009); in other words, the object is to *improve* diagnosis and tackle what they see as the ineptness of existing diagnostic systems like DSM and ICD. Identifying classified disorders can be understood within the argument of this book as falling into the category of special work. It is harder to feel altogether easy about the support of such categorization in abnormal psychology, where writers often criticize diagnosis on many grounds but still seem bound captive to it.

In the early 1980s, Smith and Kraft asked: "DSM-III. Do psychologists really want an alternative?" (Smith and Kraft, 1983). They found that most of their sample of American counselling and clinical psychologists did, but there was confusion about what, and there were other factors present likely to guarantee the survival of DSM-III, this then the latest system of diagnostic constructs. The resilience of this diagnostic tradition is still evident in the profusion of undergraduate textbooks, particularly those of American provenance. Foyles bookshop in the Charing Cross Road stocked the following recently updated volumes in the weeks leading up to Christmas 2012:

Maddux and Winstead (eds). *Psychopathology. Foundations for a Contemporary Understanding*. Third edition, 2012.
Hersen and Beidel. *Adult Psychopathology and Diagnostics*. Sixth edition, 2012.
Durand and Barlow. *Essentials of Abnormal Psychology*. Sixth edition, 2013 (this still sealed in polythene awaiting the turn of the year).
Kring, Johnson, Davison and Neale. *Abnormal Psychology*. Twelfth edition, 2012.

The Foyles team had understandably decided to place these books in the shop's medical department. Later on line, I also found Comer's (2010) *Fundamentals of Abnormal Psychology* in its sixth edition. These textbooks are not exclusively aimed at apprentice psychologists. But their authors appear from the information available to be *psychologists*. In each case, the book's subject matter is organized around categories of psychological disorder and essentially the same set of categories of psychological disorder. In the United Kingdom, where home-grown textbooks are rarer than in the United States, there is to be found in the same vein Paul Bennett's Open University introductory textbook *Abnormal and Clinical Psychology*. It came out in 2003, and after 120 pages on "background and methods", the remaining 260 pages of the book are divided into chapters on "specific issues". These issues in fact are all categories of psychological disorder. Bennett is entirely frank and writes that "this book is generally organized around a set of diagnostic labels that can be ascribed to people with common mental experiences or who behave in similar ways – schizophrenia, depression and so on" (Bennett, 2003, p.9). In organizing his material in this way, he finds himself in good company.

Part of the explanation must lie in the tradition of *psychological approaches* to *psychiatric disorders*, which has provided so many valuable contributions to assessment and treatment in the decades since the Second World War and which has been significant in the growth of counselling and clinical psychology as professions. But there are a host of other factors that contribute to the attachment to psychiatric categories among psychologists. To take a practitioner's example, it doesn't make a great deal of sense to explain psychologists' continued attachment to psychiatric categories as resulting from a wish to understand madness primarily in terms of its biological substrate. However, the point is made by Bentall, Jackson and Pilgrim (1988) that some psychologists have seen an emphasis on the underlying biology of the condition as a useful, non-threatening way of persuading families of the need to manage their high levels of expressed emotion at home, while simultaneously reassuring them that the condition is deep down not their fault.

Nonetheless, a consequence of the amount of reliance placed on psychiatric categories has been that they have become so ingrained in the collective psyche that they seem less like concepts than facts. Generations of psychologists have lived and breathed this air. And the categories are so well established that they are hard to forego. For example, Harvey, Watkins, Mansell and Shafran (2004) argued for a transdiagnostic approach drawing on another set of concepts familiar to psychologists (attention, memory, reasoning, thought and behaviour) and treating these as a set of five cognitive processes, ones long recognized as having importance by clinical practitioners and researchers. At first sight, this new approach seems something completely fresh and different. But the phenomena that are bridged by these processes remain "the psychological disorders" as defined by Axis-1 of DSM-IV. Despite the authors' admission that they are in this way bound to "the system", and thereby obliged to exclude "clinically interesting phenomena (e.g. anger, hostility)", only by writing the book around the psychological disorders do they feel they can access the research evidence needed to evaluate the utility of the transdiagnostic perspective (pp.20–1). The sixty pages of references at the end of their book attest to the size of the body of research material at stake.

Even Richard Bentall's book *Madness Explained* (Bentall, 2003), which attacks prevalent psychiatric diagnostic constructs with flair and passion in Part One, seems at first sight to be re-admitting them one by one, stripped and chastened, in Part Three. They re-appear there brought to heel in the form of "smaller" constructs, like mania, delusions and hallucinations, more symptom sized than syndrome sized. But here Bentall, in re-admitting them, is not pressing for some new improved categorization *system*. The implication of his position is that the validity and utility of *particular* diagnostic constructs sometimes will, and sometimes will not, outlive their status collectively as parts of an overarching philosophy aspiring to define the entire field of mental health.

An earlier paper by Pilgrim and Bentall (1999) brought out the distinction between the systematizing and particular uses of diagnostic constructs. Conceived as parts of a system, these disease entities, like schizophrenia and psychiatric depression, are sometimes believed to provide the fundamental elements of an ever-increasingly sophisticated picture of how things *really* are. Pilgrim and Bentall reject this view as "medical naturalism", blind to the social forces and professional interests that can lead to phenomena being understood in this way. However, rather than substitute for it an out-and-out "social constructionism", and regard all constructs as socially and historically determined ephemera, Pilgrim and Bentall adopt the position called "critical realism" (Bhaskar, 1989). Adopting this perspective, account is taken of social and historical contexts in order to help us replace misleading or biased concepts with ones better established scientifically or clinically. Therefore, it is not reality that is to be viewed as socially constructed; it is just our theories of it.

Seen in this light, no longer regarded as parts of a reality defining system, some constructs are free to be viewed simply as better or worse than others and permitted to flourish or wither accordingly. Pilgrim and Bentall offer a number of illustrations where empirical evidence fails to support the validity of a particular construct, which in the absence of such evidence just soldiers on "pre-empirically" (p.271). In their article, the case they investigate is the medicalization of misery as psychiatric depression. The concept of depression in a number of instances seems to them superfluous. Their analysis of one study leads them to conclude that a better argument has been made there for saying oppressive men make women miserable than for claiming that oppressive men are "depressogenic" to women; and their reading of another seems to them to offer better evidence for disruption of circadian rhythms bringing early waking, fatigue and loss of appetite than for such disruption serving to provoke "affective disorders".

In relation to autism, another very prominent clinical construct and the subject of a recent special issue of *The Psychologist*, there is sometimes expressed the same worry that here also researchers and practitioners will seek to explain too much in terms of the particular construct. On the one hand, its aptness as an explanation is criticized: "It is more a description of the kind of explanation researchers are looking for than an explanation in and of itself" (Brock, 2014, p.751). On the other hand, there is nonetheless such fondness for an explanation of this (broadly cognitive) kind that there risks too little attention being paid to other types of explanation. In a letter to *The Psychologist* a month after the special issue, Sue Gerrard suggests that "researchers have tended to focus on commonalities and to overlook differences and somatic symptoms" (Gerard, 2014, p.802). She goes on to suggest an analogy with respiratory problems. All patients with respiratory problems have a number of symptoms in common. But it doesn't follow from this that all respiratory problems have the same cause.

In 2013, a textbook of abnormal psychology finally appeared which altogether avoids organizing its material around categories of psychiatric disorder. "Frequently", the authors write, "abnormal psychology entirely abandons psychology and turns to psychiatry" (p.11). Not this time though. The book by Cromby, Harper and Reavey (2013) is entitled *Psychology, Mental Health and Distress*. In writing the introduction to it, Richard Bentall expresses his relief at the arrival of a textbook that at last puts distress before diagnosis. In introducing the concept of distress, the authors write: "Distress is our term for the core subject matter of this book: the experiences associated with diagnostic categories such as schizophrenia and depression" (Bentall, 2013, p.6).

The authors see their book as covering "all the different kinds of difficulty or unusual experience associated with the hundreds of psychiatric diagnoses currently employed" (p.11). They have not just broken with the tradition of psychologists organizing the structure of their textbooks around diagnostic categories. They have managed also to pass beyond talking about the constituent "symptoms of" those disorders and speak instead in rather looser terms of "association with" them. Moreover, they have adopted a stronger patient perspective by choosing wholeheartedly to take on the terminology of distress and experience.

With this focus on distress and experience, it is tempting to see the concept of content as nearing attainment. Two developments would bring that closer still:

(1) The routine adoption of personalized assessment in order to allow content, as the concept is understood here, to become operationalized
(2) The further loosening of the ties that associate the experience of patients with those "hundreds of psychiatric diagnostic categories" largely to the exclusion of anything else

One way of further loosening these ties is to take up Feinstein's approach and proceed beyond *just* the disorders themselves to include their consequences and complications. Another is to start altogether afresh and create a new, more *fluid* subject matter based on the fresh observations of some fearsomely detached Martian or charmingly winsome Altrurian. In doing so, practitioners come closer to meeting their patients and the distressing experiences they "bring" and rid themselves of presuming upon the existence of disorders they "have".

Why a more "fluid" subject matter? Content is complex and personal, while constructs aspire to clarity and generality. Research hankers after the universal, while practice demands that matters remain local and fresh. To think coherently about descriptions of distress is harder than to devise definitions of disorder, to sample more laborious than to measure. Content is quick and slippery and resists attempts to pinion it; it certainly defies crude attempts to chop it up.

Yet, is it so hard to imagine that some years hence managers and insurers will want to bring things down to earth and include the quality of the contents of personal questionnaires in their decisions about whom to admit and whom to fund, rather than rely quite so heavily on the categories and abstractions of the *Diagnostic and Statistical Manual of Mental Disorders*? For now, it will be enough to bring to mind again the passage from Hermann Hesse's novel where Father Jacobus speaks of something "impossible, yet necessary and highly important" that involves "submitting to chaos and nevertheless retaining faith in order and meaning".

References

Anastasi, Anne (1968). *Psychological Testing*. Third edition. New York: Macmillan Publishing Co., Inc.

Barkham, Michael, Shapiro, David A. and Firth-Cozens, Jenny (1989). Personal questionnaire changes in prescriptive vs. exploratory psychotherapy. *British Journal of Clinical Psychology*, 28, 97–107.

Battle, Carolyn C., Imber, Stanley D., Hoen-Saric, Rudolf, Stone, Anthony R., Nash, Earl R. and Frank, Jerome D. (1966). Target complaints as a criterion of improvement. *American Journal of Psychotherapy*, 20, 184–192.

Beck, A.T., Ward, C.H., Mendelson, M., Mock, J. and Erbaugh, J. (1961). An inventory for measuring depression. *Archives of General Psychiatry*, 4, 561–571.

Bekhit, Nawal S., Thomas, Glyn V., Lalonde, Simon and Jolley, Richard (2002). Psychological assessment in clinical practice in Britain. *Clinical Psychology and Psychotherapy*, 9, 285–291.

Bennett, Paul (2003). *Abnormal and Clinical Psychology*. An Introductory Textbook. Maidenhead, Berkshire: Open University Press.

Bennun, I., Chalkley, A.J. and Donnelly, M. (1985). Research applications of Shapiro's personal questionnaire in marital therapy. *Journal of Family Therapy*, 9, 131–144.

Bentall, Richard P. (2003). *Madness Explained*. London: Penguin Books, 2004.

Bentall, Richard P. (2013). Foreword. In: Cromby, John, Harper, David and Reavey, Paula (eds). *Psychology, Mental Health and Distress*. Basingstoke, Hampshire: Palgrave Macmillan.

Bentall, Richard P., Jackson, Howard F. and Pilgrim, David (1988). Abandoning the concept of "schizophrenia": Some implications of validity arguments for research into psychotic phenomena. *British Journal of Clinical Psychology*, 27, 303–324.

Berger, Michael (2000). Monte Shapiro. Obituary in *The Independent*. 1st May.

Bernard, Claude (1865). *Introduction à l'étude de la médicine expérimentale*. Paris: Flammarion, 1984.

Bhaskar, Roy (1989). *Reclaiming Reality: A Critical Introduction to Contemporary Philosophy*. London: Verso.

Bilsbury, C.D. and Richman, A. (2002). A staging approach to measuring patient-centred subjective outcomes. *Acta Psychiatrica Scadinavica*, 106 (*Supplementum* 414), 5–40.

Boss, Medard (1987). Preface to the First German edition of Martin Heidegger's *Zollikon Seminars: Protocols, Conversations, Letters*. Edited by

Medard Boss. Translated by Franz Mayr and Richard Askay. Evanston, Illinois: Northwestern University Press, 2001.

Boyle, Mary (2003). The dangers of vulnerability. *Clinical Psychology*, 24, 27–30.

Bracken, Patrick and Thomas, Philip (2005). *Postpsychiatry: Mental Health in a Postmodern World*. Oxford: Oxford University Press.

Brennan, James, in collaboration with Moynihan, Clare (2004). *Cancer in Context: A Practical Guide to Supportive Care*. Oxford: Oxford University Press.

Brett-Jones, Jane, Garety, Philippa and Hemsley, Dave (1987). Measuring Delusional experiences: A method and its application. *British Journal of Clinical Psychology*, 26, 257–265.

British Psychological Society (2011). *Good Practice Guidelines on the Use of Psychological Formulation*. Leicester: Author.

Brock, Jon (2014). Combining the old and the new. *The Psychologist*, 27, 750–753.

Butler, Gillian (1998). Clinical formulation. In: A.S. Bellack and M. Hersen (eds). *Comprehensive Clinical Psychology*. New York: Pergamon.

Butt, T. (2005). Personal construct theory, phenomenology and pragmatism. *History and Philosophy of Psychology*, 7, 23–25.

Butt, T. (2008). *The Psychology of Personal Constructs*. Basingstoke, Hampshire: Palgrave Macmillan.

Chadwick, Paul D.J. (2006). *Person-Based Cognitive Therapy for Distressing Psychosis*. Chichester, West Sussex: Wiley.

Chadwick, Paul D. J. and Lowe, C. Fergus (1990). Measurement and modification of delusional beliefs. *Journal of Consulting and Clinical Psychology*, 58, 225–232.

Chalkley, A.J. (1994a). Problems related to sexual variation: Investigation. In: S.J.E. Lindsay and G.E. Powell (eds). *The Handbook of Clinical Adult Psychology*. Second edition. London: Routledge.

Chalkley, A.J. (1994b). Problems related to sexual variation: Treatment. In: S.J.E. Lindsay and G.E. Powell (eds). *The Handbook of Clinical Adult Psychology*. Second edition. London: Routledge.

Chalkley, A.J. (2004). The description of concerns. *Psychology and Psychotherapy*, 77, 207–230.

Chalkley, A.J. and Mulhall, D.J. (1991). The PQRSTUV: The Personal Questionnaire Rapid Scaling Technique – "Ultimate Version". *British Journal of Clinical Psychology*, 30, 181–183.

Chekhov, Anton (1898). A case history. In: *The Oxford Chekhov*, Volume IX Stories 1898–1904. Translated from the Russian and edited by Ronald Hingley. London: Oxford University Press, 1975.

Claxton, Guy (2002). *Building Learning Power*. Bristol: TLO.

Chu, James A. (1998). *Rebuilding Shattered Lives: The Responsible Treatment of Complex Post-Traumatic and Dissociative Disorders*. New York: Wiley.

Cliffe, Michael, Possamai, Anne and Mulhall, David (1995). Modified personal questionnaire scaling technique for measuring delusional beliefs. *British Journal of Clinical Psychology*, 34, 251–253.

Cohen, I.B. (2006). *The Triumph of Numbers.* New York: Norton.

Comer, Richard J. (2010). *Fundamentals of Abnormal Psychology.* Sixth edition. New York: Worth Publishers.

Cone, John D. (1992). That Was Then! This is Now! *Behavioral Assessment,* 14, 219–228.

Connell, Janice, Barkham, Michael, Evans, Chris, Margison, Frank, McGrath, Graeme and Milne, Derek. (n.d.). *Clinical Outcomes in Routine Evaluation – Outcome Measure. Guidelines for Use.* Version 1.0. Leeds, West Yorkshire: Psychological Research Centre.

Crellin, Clare (1988). Origins and social contexts of the term "formulation" in psychological case-reports. *Clinical Psychology Forum*, 112, 18–27.

Cromby, John, Harper, David and Reavey, Paula (2013). *Psychology, Mental Health and Distress.* Basingstoke, Hampshire: Palgrave Macmillan.

Cronbach, Lee J. and Meehl, Paul E. (1955). Construct validity in psychological tests. *Psychological Bulletin*, 52, 281–302.

Dallos, Rudi and Draper, Ros (2005). *An Introduction to Family Therapy. Systemic Theory and Practice.* Second edition. Maidenhead, Berkshire: Open University Press.

Danziger, Kurt (1976). *Interpersonal Communication.* New York: Pergamon Press.

Danziger, Kurt (1997). The varieties of social construction. *Theory and Psychology*, 7, 399–416.

Durac, Jack (1979). *Wine: A Matter of Taste.* London: Magnum Books.

Durand, V. Mark and Barlow, David H. (2013). *Essentials of Abnormal Psychology.* Sixth edition. n.p.: Wadsworth Cengage.

Evans, Chris, Connell, Janice, Barkham, Michael, Marshall, Chris and Mellor-Clark, John (2003). Practice-based evidence: Benchmarking NHS primary care counselling services at national and local levels. *Clinical Psychology and Psychotherapy*, 10, 374–388.

Feinstein, Alvan R. (1967). *Clinical Judgment.* Huntington, New York: Robert E. Krieger Publishing Company.

Feinstein, Alvan R. (1987). *Clinimetrics.* New Haven, Connecticut: Yale University Press.

Feinstein, Alvan R. (1996). Two centuries of conflict-collaboration between medicine and mathematics. *Journal of Clinical Epidemiology*, 49, 1339–1343.

Feinstein, Alvan R. and Horwitz, Ralph I. (1997). Problems in the "evidence" of "evidence-based medicine". *American Journal of Medicine*, 103, 529–535.

Fisch, Richard, Weakland, John H. and Segal, Lynn (1982). *The Tactics of Change: Doing Therapy Briefly.* San Francisco: Jossey-Bass.

First, Michael B., Frances, Allen, Widiger, Thomas A. Pincus, Harold A. and Wakefield Davis, Wendy (1992). DSM-IV and behavioral assessment. *Behavioral Assessment*, 14, 297–306.

Follette, William C. and Hayes, Steven C. (1992). Behavioral assessment in the DSM era. *Behavioral Assessment*, 14, 293–295.

Foulds, G.A. (1964). The certainty of personal relationships and the uncertainty of science. *Journal of Psychosomatic Research*, 8, 273–275.

Foulds, G.A. (1976). *The Hierarchical Nature of Personal Illness.* London: Academic Press.

Foulds, G.A. in collaboration with Caine, T.M. (1965). *Personality and Personal Illness.* London: Tavistock Publications.

Freeth, Rachel (2007). *Humanising Psychiatry and Mental Health Care. The Challenge of the Person-Centred Approach.* Oxford: Radcliffe Publishing.

Garety, Philippa (1985). Delusions: Problems in definition and measurement. *British Journal of Medical Psychology*, 53, 25–34.

Gerrard, Sue (2014). The end of autism? *The Psychologist*, 27, 802.

Gilbert, Daniel (2006). *Stumbling on Happiness.* London: Harper Perennial, 2007.

Goldblatt, David (2013). Clean Sheets. Review of Chris Anderson and David Sally. The Numbers Game: Why Everything You Know about Football Is Wrong. *Times Literary Supplement*, 6th September, 30.

Goldfried, Marvin R. and Kent, Ronald N. (1972). Traditional versus behavioral assessment: A comparison of methodological and theoretical assumptions. *Psychological Bulletin*, 77, 409–420.

Gordon, L.V. and Mooney, R.L. (1950). *Mooney Problem Check List.* New York: The Psychological Corporation.

Harper, David and Spelman, David (2006). Social constructionist formulation: Telling a different story. In: Lucy Johnstone and Rudi Dallos (eds). *Formulation in Psychology and Psychotherapy: Making Sense of People's Problems.* Hove, East Sussex: Routledge.

Harvey, Allison, Watkins, Edward, Mansell, Warren and Shafran, Roz (2004). *Cognitive Behavioural Processes Across Psychological Disorders: A Transdiagnostic Approach to Research and Treatment.* Oxford: Oxford University Press, 2004.

Hayes, Steven C. and Nelson, Rosemery O. (1986). Assessing the effects of therapeutic interventions. In: Rosemery O. Nelson and Steven C. Hayes (eds). *Conceptual Foundations of Behavioral Assessment.* New York: Guilford Press.

Heidegger, Martin (1987). *Zollikon Seminars: Protocols, Conversations, Letters.* Edited by Medard Boss. Translated by Franz Mayr and Richard Askay. Evanston, Illinois: Northwestern University Press, 2001.

Hersen, Michel and Beidel, Deborah C. (2012). *Adult Psychopathology and Diagnostics.* Sixth edition. Hoboken, New Jersey: Wiley.

Hesse, Hermann (1943). *The Glass Bead Game.* Translated from the German by Richard and Clara Winston. Harmonsworth, Middlesex: Penguin Books, 1972.

Hofstadter, Richard (1948). *The American Political Tradition.* Vintage paperback edition, 1954.

Hool, Nicholas (2010). *Core Curriculum Reference Document.* Bury, Lancashire: British Association for Behavioural & Cognitive Psychotherapies.

Howells, W.D. (1894). A traveller from Altruria. In: Scott Bennett, and Clara and Rudolf Kirk (eds). *The Altrurian Romances.* Bloomington, Indiana: The Indiana University Press, 1968.

Howells, W.D. (1907). Through the eye of the needle. In: Scott Bennett, and Clara and Rudolf Kirk (eds). *The Altrurian Romances.* Bloomington, Indiana: The Indiana University Press, 1968.

Jaspers, Karl (1959). *General Psychopathology.* Seventh edition. Translated from the German by J. Hoenig and Martin W. Hamilton. Manchester: Manchester University Press, 1963.

Johnstone, Lucy and Dallos, Rudi (2006). *Formulation in Psychology and Psychotherapy.* Hove, East Sussex: Routledge.

Kahneman, Daniel (2011). *Thinking Fast and Slow.* London: Penguin Books, 2012.

Kelly, George A. (1955a). *The Psychology of Personal Constructs.* Volume 1: Theory and Personality. London: Routledge, 1991.

Kelly, George A. (1955b). *The Psychology of Personal Constructs.* Volume 2: Clinical Diagnosis and Psychotherapy. London: Routledge, 1991.

Kelly, George A. (1965). The psychotherapeutic relationship. In: Brendan Maher (ed.). *Clinical Psychology and Personality: The Selected Papers of George Kelly.* New York: Wiley, 1969.

Kelly, George A. (1966). Humanistic methodology in psychological research. In: Brendan Maher (ed.). *Clinical Psychology and Personality: The Selected Papers of George Kelly.* New York: Wiley, 1969.

Kring, Ann M., Johnson, Sheri L., Davison, Gerald and Neale, John (2012). *Abnormal Psychology.* Twelfth edition. Hoboken, New Jersey: Wiley.

Kuppner, Frank (1990). *A Concussed History of Scotland.* Edinburgh: Polygon.

Landfield, A.W. (1975). The complaint: A confrontation of personal urgency and professional construction. In: D. Bannister (ed.). *Issues and Approaches in the Psychological Therapies.* London: Wiley.

Maddux, James E. and Winstead, Barbara A. (2012). *Psychopathology. Foundations for a Contemporary Understanding.* Third edition. New York: Routledge.

Mair, Miller (1989). *Between Psychology and Psychotherapy.* London: Routledge.

McNair, Douglas M. and Lorr, Maurice (1964). An analysis of mood in neurotics. *Journal of Abnormal and Social Psychology*, 69, 620–627.

McPherson, Frank and Le Gassicke, John (1965). A single-patient, self-controlled and self-recorded trial of Wy 3498. *British Journal of Psychiatry*, 111, 149–154.

Merleau-Ponty, Maurice (1945). *Phenomenology of Perception.* Translated from the French by Colin Smith. London: Routledge Classics, 2002.

Miller, Joe and McClelland, Lynn (2006). Social inequalities formulation: Mad, bad and dangerous to know. In: Lucy Johnstone and Rudi Dallos (eds). *Formulation in Psychology and Psychotherapy: Making Sense of People's Problems.* Hove, East Sussex: Routledge.

Milton, Jane (1997). Why Assess? Psychoanalytical assessment in the NHS. *Psychoanalytic Psychotherapy*, 11, 47–58.

Mitchell, Kenneth R. (1969). Shapiro's single case repeated-measure design applied to the individual client in counselling. *Australian Psychologist*, 4, 20–35.

Morley, Stephen (2000). Monte Shapiro. Putting clinical psychology at the service of the patient. Obituary in *The Guardian*, 2nd May.

Morrison, A.P. (2001). The interpretation of intrusions in psychosis: An integrative cognitive approach to hallucinations and delusions. *Behavioural and Cognitive Psychotherapy*, 29, 257–276.

Mosier, Charles I. (1937). A factor analysis of certain neurotic symptoms. *Psychometrika*, 2, 263–286.

Mulhall, D.J. (1976). Systematic assessment by PQRST. *Psychological Medicine*, 6, 591–597.

Mulley, Bernadette, Rudolf, Mary and Chalkley, Jack (2003). *Personal Questionnaires – A Better Way to Listen to the Concerns of Parents Whose Child is Failing to Thrive.* Children's Services, Belmont House, East Leeds: Unpublished Typescript.

Nelson, Rosemery O. (1981). Realistic dependent measures for clinical use. *Journal of Consulting and Clinical Psychology*, 49, 168–182.

New Shorter Oxford English Dictionary (1993). Fourth edition. Oxford: Oxford University Press.

Parry, Glenys, Shapiro, David A. and Firth, Jenny (1986). The case of the anxious executive: A study from the research clinic. *British Journal of Medical Psychology*, 59, 221–233.

Pépin, Jacques (1976). *"La technique". An Illustrated Guide to the Fundamental Techniques of Cooking.* English language edition. London: Macmillan Papermac, 1982.

Pépin, Jacques (1979). *"La méthode". An Illustrated Guide to the Fundamental Skills of Cooking.* English language edition. London: Macmillan Papermac, 1982.

Phillips, J.P.N. (1986). Generalized personal questionnaire techniques. In: P. Slater (ed.). *The Measurement of Interpersonal Space by Grid Technique.* London: Wiley.

Pilgrim, David and Bentall, Richard P. (1999). The medicalisation of misery: A critical realist analyst of the concept of depression. *Journal of Mental Health*, 8, 261–274.

Pinker, Steven (2007). *The Stuff of Thought. Language as a Window into Human Nature.* London: Allen Lane. Penguin Books, 2008.

du Plock, Simon (2010). Humanistic approaches. In: Ray Woolfe, Sheelagh Strawbridge, Barbara Douglas and Windy Dryden (eds). *Handbook of Counselling Psychology.* Third edition. London: Sage.

Proctor, Gillian (2005). Clinical psychology and the person-centred approach: An uncomfortable fit. In: Stephen Joseph and Richard Worsley (eds). *Person-Centred Psychopathology.* Ross-on-Wye, Herefordshire: PCCS Books.

Puustinen, Raimo (2000). Voices to be heard – the many positions of a physician in Anton Chekhov's short story, "A Case History". *Journal of Medical Ethics: Medical Humanities*, 26, 37–42.

Rachman, S.J. (1997). A cognitive theory of obsessions. *Behaviour Research and Therapy*, 35, 793–802.

Rachman, S.J. (1998). A cognitive theory of obsessions: Elaborations. *Behaviour Research and Therapy*, 36, 385–401.

Rippere, Vicky and Williams, Ruth (1985). *Wounded Healers.* Chichester, West Sussex: Wiley.

Rogers, Carl (1961). *On Becoming a Person.* London: Constable.

Rogers, Carl (1980). *Way of Being.* Boston, Massachusetts: Houghton-Mifflin.

Rosenfeld, Herbert (1964). On the psychopathology of narcissism: A clinical approach. Reprinted in: *Rosenfeld in Retrospect: Essays on his Clinical Influence.* Edited by John Steiner. Hove, East Sussex: Routledge, 2008.

Rosenfeld, Herbert (1971). A clinical approach to the psychoanalytic theory of the life and death instincts: An investigation into the aggressive aspects of narcissism. Reprinted in: *Rosenfeld in Retrospect: Essays on his Clinical Influence.* Edited by John Steiner. Hove, East Sussex: Routledge, 2008.

Rosenthal, Ted L. (1993). To soothe the savage breast. *Behaviour Research and Therapy*, 31, 439–462.

Rowland, Len (1985). Assessment. In: Bradley, Brendan P. and Thompson, Christopher (eds). *Psychological Applications in Psychiatry.* Chichester, West Sussex: Wiley.

Runyon, W.M. (1983). Ideographic goals and methods in the study of lives. *Journal of Personality*, 51, 413–437.

Salkovskis, Paul M. and Warwick, Hilary M.C. (1986). Morbid preoccupations, health anxiety and reassurance: A cognitive-behavioural approach to hypochondriasis. *Behaviour Research and Therapy*, 24, 597–602.

Sandler, J. (1954). Studies in psychopathology using a self-assessment inventory: 1. The development and construction of the inventory. *British Journal of Medical Psychology*, 27, 142–145.

Scruton, Roger (1986). *Sexual Desire. A Philosophical Investigation.* London: Continuum, 2006.

Shapiro, D.A., Caplan, H.L., Rohde, P.D. and Watson, J.P. (1975). Personal questionnaire changes and their correlates in a psychotherapeutic group. *British Journal of Medical Psychology*, 48, 207–215.

Shapiro, Francine (1995). *Eye Movement Desensitization and Reprocessing. Basic Principles, Protocols and Procedures.* New York: Guilford Press.

Shapiro, M.B. (1951). An experimental approach to diagnostic psychological testing. *Journal of Mental Science*, 97, 748–764.

Shapiro, M.B. (1957). Experimental method in the psychological description of the individual psychiatric patient. *The International Journal of Social Psychiatry*, 3, 89–102.

Shapiro, M.B. (1961). A method of measuring changes specific to the individual psychiatric patient. *British Journal of Medical Psychology*, 34, 151–155.

Shapiro, M.B. (1963). A clinical approach to fundamental research with special reference to the study of the single patient. In: Peter Sainsbury and Norman

Kreitman (eds). *Methods of Psychiatric Research. An Introduction for Clinical Psychiatrists.* London: Oxford University Press.

Shapiro, M.B. (1964). The measurement of clinically relevant variables. *Journal of Psychosomatic Research*, 8, 245–254.

Shapiro, M.B. (1966). Generality of psychological processes and specificity of outcomes. *Perception and Motor Skills*, 23, 16.

Shapiro, M.B. (1969). Short-term improvements in the symptoms of affective disorder. *British Journal of Social and Clinical Psychology*, 8, 187–188.

Shapiro, M.B. (1970). Intensive assessment of the single case: An inductive-deductive approach. In: P. Mittler (ed.). *The Psychological Assessment of Mental and Physical Handicap.* London: Methuen.

Shapiro, M.B. (1975a). *The Assessment of Psychological Dysfunctions: A Manual with Its Rationale and Applications.* Parts One and Two. Unpublished Typescript, Institute of Psychiatry, University of London.

Shapiro, M.B. (1975b). The requirements and implications of a systematic science of psychopathology. *Bulletin of the British Psychological Society*, 28, 149–155.

Shapiro, M.B. (1979). Assessment interviewing in clinical psychology. *British Journal of Social and Clinical Psychology*, 18, 211–218.

Shapiro, M.B. (1985). A reassessment of clinical psychology as an applied science. *British Journal of Clinical Psychology*, 24, 1–11.

Shapiro, M.B. (1989). A phenomenon-oriented strategy in depression research. *British Journal of Clinical Psychology*, 28, 289–305.

Shapiro, M.B., Marks, I.M. and Fox, B. (1963). A therapeutic experiment on phobic and affective symptoms. *British Journal of Social and Clinical Psychology*, 2, 81–93.

Shapiro, M.B. and Ravenette, A.T. (1959). A preliminary experiment on paranoid delusions. *Journal of Mental Science*, 105, 295–312.

Shooter, Mike (2007). Foreword to Rachel Freeth. *Humanising Psychiatry and Mental Health Care. The Challenge of the Person-Centred Approach.* Oxford: Radcliffe Publishing.

Siegel, Sidney (1956). *Nonparametric Statistics.* International student edition. Tokyo: McGraw-Hill Kogakusha.

Singh, Avinash C. and Bilsbury, Christopher D. (1989). Measuring levels of experiential states in clinical applications by Discan: A discretized analog method. *Behavioural Psychotherapy*, 17, 27–41.

Smail, David (2001). *The Nature of Unhappiness.* London: Constable.

Smith, Darrell and Kraft, William A. (1983). DSM-III. Do psychologists really want an alternative? *American Psychologist*, July, 777–785.

Spearman, Charles Edward (1927). *The Abilities of Man: Their Nature and Measurement.* London: Macmillan.

Steiner, John (2008). A personal review of Rosenfeld's contribution to clinical psychoanalysis. In: John Steiner (ed.). *Rosenfeld in Retrospect: Essays on his Clinical Influence.* Hove, East Sussex: Routledge.

Streiner, David L. and Norman, Geoffrey R. (1989). *Health measurement scales: A practical guide to their development and use.* Oxford: Oxford University Press.

Stulz, Niklaus, Lutz, Wolfgang, Leach, Chris, Lucock, Mike and Barkham, Michael (2007). Shapes of early change in psychotherapy under routine out-patient conditions. *Journal of Consulting and Clinical Psychology*, 75, 864–874.

Taylor, Michael Alan and Vaidya, Nutan Atre (2009). *Descriptive Psychopathology. The Signs and Symptoms of Behavioral Disorders.* Cambridge, Cambridgeshire: Cambridge University Press.

Thorne, Brian. (2007). Foreword to Rachel Freeth. *Humanising Psychiatry and Mental Health Care. The Challenge of the Person-Centred Approach.* Oxford: Radcliffe Publishing.

Watts, Fraser N. (1980). Clinical judgement and clinical training. *British Journal of Clinical Psychology*, 53, 95–108.

Wilkins, Paul (2010). *Person-Centred Therapy. 100 Key Points.* Hove, East Sussex: Routledge.

Wilson, G. Terence and Clark, David M. (1999). Introduction. In: D.M. Clark and G.T. Wilson (eds). *Cognitive Behaviour Therapy: Evolution and Prospects. A Festschrift in Honour of Dr S. Rachman. Behaviour Research and Therapy*, 37, Supplement 1 July 1999.

Wing, John K., Cooper, John E. and Sartorius, Norman. (1974). *Measurement and Classification of Psychiatric Symptoms: An Instruction Manual.* London: Cambridge University Press.

Wolpe, Joseph (1991). *The Practice of Behavior Therapy.* Fourth edition. New York: Pergamon Press.

Woolfe, Ray, Strawbridge, Sheelagh, Douglas, Barbara and Dryden, Windy (eds) (2010). *Handbook of Counselling Psychology.* Third edition. London: Sage.

Worsley, Richard (2007). Setting up practice and the therapeutic framework. In: Mick Cooper, Maureen O'Hara, Peter F. Scmid and Gill Wyatt (eds). *The Handbook of Person-Centred Psychotherapy and Counselling.* Basingstoke, Hampshire: Palgrave Macmillan.

Worsley, Richard (2009). *Process Work in Person-Centred Therapy.* Second edition. Basingstoke, Hampshire: Palgrave Macmillan.

Wright, James G. and Feinstein, Alvan R. (1992). A comparative contrast of clinimetric and psychometric methods for constructing indexes and rating scales. *Journal of Clinical Epidemiology*, 45, 1201–1218.

Wright, K.J.T. (1970). Exploring the uniqueness of common complaints. *British Journal of Medical Psychology*, 43, 221–232.

Yalom, Irving (2002). *The Gift of Therapy.* London: Piatkus.

Zajonc, Arthur (2009). *Meditation as Contemplative Enquiry. When Knowing Becomes Love.* Great Barrington, Massachusetts: Lindisfarne Books.

Index

Note: Locators followed by n denote footnotes.

Printed and bound by CPI Group (UK) Ltd, Croydon, CR0 4YY